CHARLES PARISH

YORK COUNTY, VIRGINIA

HISTORY AND REGISTERS

BIRTHS
1648—1789

DEATHS
1665—1787

By LANDON C. BELL

Please Direct All Correspondence and Book Orders to:

Southern Historical Press, Inc.
PO Box 1267
375 West Broad Street
Greenville, SC 29602-1267
----
southernhistoricalpress@gmail.com

ISBN #0-89308-865-X

Table of Contents

Introductory Note

Each clerk of a vestry of the established church of the Colony of Virginia kept two record books. In one, the vestry book, he recorded the transactions of the vestry at its various meetings, and in the other, the register, listed the births and deaths that occurred in the parish. The majority of these books have in course of time been lost, but those that remain—nearly half a hundred—are of very great value. To the historian the vestry books are the more important of the two kinds of record books, but to the genealogist the registers yield a greater amount of prized information.

The present volume is the Register of Charles Parish, York County, containing earlier entries than does any other Virginia church record book that has been preserved. It is on that account of unusual interest, and it is further of unusual interest and value because of the length of the period covered, 1648-1789.

The register is not printed as originally written, but, for the sake of easy reference, in two alphabetical lists, one for the births and the other for the deaths.

The immense labor of making these two alphabetical lists from originals frequently very hard to decipher has been carried through by Landon C. Bell, of Columbus, Ohio, who has also prepared introductory chapters giving the history of the parish, biographies of the rectors, and a description and history of the original book.

Mr. Bell was born in Lunenburg County, Virginia, and is a devoted Virginian. Though he now lives away from his native State, nothing delights him more than to delve into Virginia records, to make these, by printing, accessible to students everywhere, and to interpret them. He already has to his credit, in addition to several addresses and pamphlets, "The Old Free State," a two-volume history of Lunenburg County; "Cumberland Parish," containing the vestry book of the parish that was co-extensive with Lunenburg County when that county was first erected and decreased with it as successive counties were cut off from Lunenburg and successive parishes from itself—with appropriate historical and genealogical chapters; and "Sunlight on the Southside," which consists of lists of tithables (or tithes) in Lunenburg County in the period 1748-1783, furnished with a suitable introduction.

The present volume adds substantially to Mr. Bell's achievements. No one can look at the original book on photostat reproductions of which he worked without being astonished at his patience and at the same time being thankful for it.

It is sincerely to be hoped that he will have the time—his inclination is taken for granted—to prepare another church record book (whether a vestry book or a register) for printing, and that the appropriations of the Virginia State Library will be sufficient to pay for its publication.

After the present volume comes from the press, a second volume edited by Dr. Churchill Gibson Chamberlayne, a companion volume to his "Vestry Book of Stratton Major Parish, King and Queen County, Virginia, 1729-1783," will be published by the Library Board. It will be a great piece of good fortune if publication of this class of material may be kept up indefinitely till all the books have been made accessible to the public.

H. R. McILWAINE,
State Librarian.

Richmond, August 10, 1932.

Preface

The oldest volume of records of the Established Church in Colonial Virginia has never, until now, been printed. The principal records of the church establishment were the registers,—of births and christenings, of marriages, of deaths,—and the vestry books, or records of the proceedings of the vestries. The registers were required by law,—by a series of laws varying from time to time,—to be kept as public records. The proceedings of the vestries were kept currently as a matter of convenience and necessity. The fate of these records is a sad one; most of them have been lost or destroyed. And only a few of those that have survived have been published.

The earliest of these records now known to be in existence is the Parish Register of Births of Charles Parish (or its predecessor parish), York County, Virginia, the entries in which begin October 6, 1648.

The contents of this register and of the register of deaths for the same parish, beginning in 1665, are printed for the first time in the present volume.

In connection with these registers, it has seemed appropriate to attempt some historical account of the parish. This has been done in a few brief chapters, presenting such facts as are available respecting the history of the parish, its ministers, etc. The treatment is not very satisfactory, due, in part at least, to the paucity of material from which to draw, after this long lapse of time.

The registers are not printed verbatim as they appear in the original book entries; instead, the entries have been carefully rearranged so as to present the names of persons born and those who died, in alphabetical order in the nature of a self-indexing arrangement. Names so arranged do not appear in the index. All others are fully indexed in the usual way. This subject is more fully explained in the appropriate chapters, hereinafter.

Mary daughter of William Lane by Sarah his wife was born the 23d day of August.... 1679

Samuel son of George Pickett by Mary his wife was born August the 31st.... 1679

Martha daughter of John Maverie by Christyan his wife was born August 5th.... 1679

Elizabith Vanson daughter of Arthur by Mary his wife was born October the 3d.... 1679

Elinor daughter of Willm Jill by Ann his wife born the 9th day.... of October.... 1679
Ann his daughter born the same day and year....

Thomas son of Matthew Hubbard by Mary his wife was born November the 25th.... 1679

Sarah Hunt daughter of John by Elizabith his wife was born December the 5th.... 1679

Thomas Morgan son of Thomas by Elinor his wife was born January the 1st.... 1679

John Perkins son of Henry by Elizabith his wife was baptized Aprill 11th.... 1680

William son of Saml Johnson by Sarah his wife was born Aprill the 27th.... 1680

Charles Lawson son of Roger by Ann his wife was born May the 8th.... 1680

Sarah Ambros daughter of John by Rachell his wife was born In the Year.... 1680

Faccimiles of parts of pages of the original: pp. 9 and 12 of the Register of Births and p. 16 of the Register of Deaths.
H. R. McIlwaine,
State Librarian

John son of John Clark by Elizabeth his wife was born July the 17th 1675

Thomas son of Thomas Ragdell by Elinor his wife was born October the 2d 1675

Leonard son Evan Evans by Sarah his wife baptized October the 31th 1675

Henry Freeman son of Henry by Martha his wife born the twentieth of November .. 1675

Jane Fewlet daughter of Stephen by Agnes his wife was born November the 23d 1675

Elizabeth Davis daughter of Owen Davis was born December the 9th 1675

Mary daughter of Edward Bridges by Mary his wife was born January the 12th .. 1675

Margarett daughter of Robert Ross by Margarett his wife was born January the 25th .. 1675

Thomas son Gerald Conner by Mary his wife was born March the 22d 1675

John Penrie was born May 17th 1676

Erercel daughter of John Maurice by Christjana his wife was born Aprill 10th 1676

Thomas son of George Sallet by Catherine his wife was born Aprill 19th 1676

Anna daughter of Robert Sexton by Dorithy his wife was born May the 15th 1676

Elizabeth daughter of Henry Hayward by Dianah his wife was born May 25th 1676

John son of Richard Joans by Dorithy his wife was born May the 28th day 1676

Died In the Year 1711

Mary Avery Widow	January the 10th
Thomas Barber	January the 10th
Charles Son of Henry Frumary	January the 23d
Charles Wise	January the 24th

Died In the Year 1712

Dianah daughr of Edward Tabb	April the 13t
Daniel Taylor	September the 7th
Elizabeth daughr of Anthony Robinson	September the 16th
Anthony Son of Hastrange Calthorp	October the 2
Elizabeth wife of Joseph Potten	November the 7th
Charles son of William Morgan	November the 15th
Silas Pool	January the 26th
Samuel Johnson	March the 4th
Matthew Jones	March the 1st

Died In the Year 1713

John Wood	April the 1st
Michael Bartlett	June the 19th
John Skenloving	August the 22d
John son of William Tabb	August the 25th
John Hayward	August the 18th
James Bennett Junr	September the 14th
Sarah Lamb daughr of Daniel	September the 10th
Martha daughr of John Muckinsree	September the 15th
John Cox	October the 14th
Martha daughr of Matthw Barnes	October the 18th
Elizabeth daughr of James Burton	October the 24th
Samuel son of Charles Wood	November the 4th
Dorothy daughr of Robert Hay	March the 1st

Charles Parish, York County, Virginia, History and Registers

CHAPTER I

CHARLES PARISH

The early history of the parish whose registers are here presented is involved in a twilight of uncertainty. But it is certain that the registers are of a parish or of parishes of York County, Virginia.

The area of the parish (or parishes) for which we have these registers, is of the section of York County, Virginia, lying on Chesapeake Bay and York River, between Elizabeth City County and Yorktown, but, it seems, not embracing all that water frontage. Perhaps we can endeavor to be a little more definite, and be approximately correct. The parish, then, it seems, embraced the region "between Back Creek and Poquoson River."[1] This description would embrace the Bay frontage of the sections now known as Crab Neck and Fish Neck, and presumably the regions westward as far as the line between York and Warwick Counties. Whether the parish included any territory lying northward of Back Creek or any southward of Poquoson River may not be entirely clear. The boundaries were not, probably, defined with definiteness, and if so that information has not survived.

So this much can be safely affirmed of these registers, that they present the record of births and deaths for the periods indicated of persons who were born or who died

---

[1] *William and Mary College Quarterly,* XXII, 76. This description was given as of 1657.

within the general section indicated, whether the precise limits of the parish be or be not now capable of exact establishment. Furthermore, it seems certain that, whether always embraced in the same parish or not, the area in question was, during the years embraced in the registers, approximately that generally described above.

The only uncertainty, really, that arises is as to whether the area was always, during the periods covered by the registers, known as Charles Parish, or whether for a time it was embraced in an older parish, and was at some time, not definitely ascertained, in whole or in part, erected into Charles Parish, and, thereafter, the registers, without interruption, or indication of the time of transition, continued as the registers of Charles Parish. The point is historically interesting, but, really, not of great practical importance, at least to the genealogist.

"In 1634 the country [was] divided into 8 shires, which are to be governed as the shires in England."[1a] One of these shires or counties was Charles River; but the act dividing up the colony and creating the shires or counties is not now known to exist.

In March, 1642/3 (18th Charles 1st),[2] a law was passed which changed the names of Charles River County to the County of York.

While the general location of Charles River, later York County, is easily established, the original area and boundaries of this county are not definitely known. Nor is it known into what parish or parishes the county was originally laid out. The parish history of this section, in the early years of the colony, is especially obscure. The difficulty of tracing the history of the parishes is suggested by the following statement of Bishop Meade: ". . . it may be well to observe that at an early period there may

---

[1a] *Hening* I, 224.
[2] *Hening* I, 249.

be found the names of a number of parishes which once existed in that part of Virginia lying between Warwick and Charles City, below and above Jamestown and round about Williamsburg; as, for instance, Southwark, Chiskiack, Middletown, Harop, Nutmeg and Denbigh, Wilmington, Marston, which were soon merged into James City, York-Hampton, Bruton, and Westover parish. Soon after the settlement of the country, when the Indians abounded and it was dangerous to go far to worship, every little plantation or settlement in that region was made a parish. There is one parish, by the name of Westminster, which as yet I have been unable to locate, and which made a report to the Bishop of London in 1724. Its communicants only numbered sixteen. I incline to think it was somewhere on the Chickahominy. Its minister was the Rev. Mr. Cox."[3]

In his article on York-Hampton Parish, Bishop Meade says: "This was originally called Charles River parish, as the county of York was at first called Charles River county or shire, from the river whose early name was Charles, afterwards York River. The name of Charles River County was changed to that of York in 1642. Of the earliest history of this parish but little is known as there is no vestry-book to be found."[4] It will be observed that he gives no information as to when it was "originally called Charles River Parish." The language is unclear as to whether he means that the parish was called Charles River Parish when the county was called Charles River County, or whether it was "originally called Charles River Parish," when the name of the county was changed to York. If the latter, the name of the parish while the county was Charles River County is not suggested.

---

[3] *Old Churches, Ministers, etc.*, I, 239-40. The Mr. Cox referred to was the Rev. James Cox.
[4] *Old Churches, Ministers*, etc., I, 202.

In fact, little justification can be found for calling the parish "Charles *River* Parish,"—though it is well established that for a long time it was known as Charles Parish. Nor do we find any basis for the surmise which Bishop Meade indulges that Charles Parish (or Charles River Parish, as he calls it) was cut off from York-Hampton Parish.

In his account of Charles, or Charles River Parish, York County, Virginia, he says:

"This was separated from York-Hampton parish before the year 1754, but how long we have been unable as yet to ascertain. The Rev. Thomas Warrington was ordained in 1747 and was its minister in 1754, and until he went to Hampton in 1756. As I do not see his name as belonging to any other parish, it is probable that he entered at once on the ministry in this parish.

"The Rev. Joseph Davenport was the minister in 1773, 1774, and also in 1785. In the last year he appears in the convention with Mr. Robert Shield as lay delegate. This is all we can learn as to the parish of Charles,—so called because on York River, which was once called Charles River, and because York County was once called Charles River County."[5]

The Bishop, we must remember, was writing at a time when we did not have the same ready access to some sources of information which are now available. It is now easy to fix Charles Parish as in existence a good many years before 1754, and, furthermore, it is believed that the assertion that it was separated from York-Hampton Parish is erroneous. Let us examine the last question first.

By an act of September, 1696,[6] small parishes, not able to support a minister, might by action of their respective vestries apply to the governor to be allowed to unite and

[5] *Old Churches, Ministers and Families of Virginia*, I, 239.
[6] *Hening*, III, 151-153.

consolidate. Pursuant to this act, the vestries of the "Parishes of York & Hampton" on February 5, 1707 [1706/7], petitioned the Governor and Council to order that "the said parishes may be united and consolidated into one parish to be called and known by the name of Yorkhampton."[7]

The petition was held reasonable, and the Clerk of the Council was ordered to prepare the necessary instrument "for consolidating ye said Parishes according to ye prayer of the said petition."

This was the beginning of Yorkhampton Parish.

Charles Parish existed before this time, for it is mentioned as one of the parishes in York County, on July 8, 1702, in a list of parishes, ministers, tithables, clergy, etc. reported to the British Board of Trade, and preserved in the Board of Trade Papers, Volume 9, and reprinted in the *Virginia Historical Magazine*.[8]

But a list of parishes in Virginia, June 30, 1680, does not mention Charles Parish. Such a list is found in State Papers, Colonial-Virginia[9] and it is reprinted in the *Virginia Historical Magazine*.[10]

The parishes in York County as given in this list are:

A part of Brewton, Hampton, York and New Towson.

Mr. Rowland Jones was the minister of Brewton and Hampton parishes, Mr. Edw'd Foliott of York Parish and Mr. John Wright of New Towson. New Towson is a parish which seems to have been overlooked by Dr. Goodwin in his valuable volume *The Colonial Church in Virginia,* as well as by Bishop Meade in his *Old Churches, Ministers and Families of Virginia.*

There is an authentic record that in 1645 there was a parish in York County named New Poquoson. A record

[7] *Executive Journals, Council of Colonial Virginia,* III, 140.
[8] Vol. I, 373-377.
[9] Vol. 60, No. 410.
[10] Vol. I, 242-244.

book of York County, 1645 to 1648, contains this entry, under date of December 20, 1645:

"Whereas Thomas Waldoe was by the churchwardens of the New Poquoson presented for an abuse of the church and minister and for not receiving the sacrament, the Court doth therefore order him the said Waldoe to bring certificate under the hand of Mr. Charles Grundy minister of the said p'ish of his reformation of the said abuses to ye next court, otherwise to be censured by the court for the same."[11]

The legislative history of the parishes of York County has been but meagrely preserved. According to Dr. Goodwin's volume *The Colonial Church in Virginia,* the county had as many as five parishes: Chiskiack [the Chescake of *Hening's Statutes*] Parish, or Hampton Parish, 1639-40, Marston, or York Parish, 1654, New Pocoson Parish, Ext. 1692, Charles Parish, 1692, and Yorkhampton Parish.[12]

The extent of Marston Parish is briefly indicated in *Hening* as follows:

"From the head of the north side of Queen's Creeke as high as to the head of Scimino Creeke is made a distinct parish named Marston ordered by this Grand Assembly."[13] No statutory description of any of the other parishes named has been discovered.

A writer in *William and Mary Quarterly*[14] gives a list of the parishes of York County as they existed in 1657. Says this writer:[15]

"In 1657 the parishes in York County were (beginning on the West) *Marion,* between Queen's Creek and York River;

---

[11] *William and Mary Quarterly,* XXII, 79.
[12] Page 340.
[13] *Hening* I, 388.
[14] Vol. XXII, 76.
[15] The distinguished historian and scholar Dr. Lyon G. Tyler was the editor of the magazine at the time this article appeared. It is probably from his pen.

Middle plantation, comprising the settlement of that name on the north of Queen's Creek; *Chiskiack* or *Hampton* between Queen's Creek and Townsend Creek (afterwards Yorktown Creek); *York,* between Yorktown Creek and Back Creek; *New Poquoson,* afterwards *Charles River Parish* [*Charles Parish*], between Back Creek and Poquoson River."

This article, it will be observed, states that New Poquoson parish was later Charles River Parish.

Dr. Goodwin identifies, doubtless correctly, New Towson parish with Pocoson [New Pocoson?] parish in his brief mention of Rev. John Wright. He was, says Dr. Goodwin, "Minister of 'New Towson' (Pocoson) Parish, York County, in 1680," and that he "complained to the governor and council that Mr. Jonathan Davis, though not a qualified minister, had taken his pulpit."[16]

The Council minute dealing with the case speaks of the petition as that of "Mr. Jno. Wright Minister of Pocoton Parish," the date of the entry being June 23, 1680.[17]

As Charles River County was changed to York County in 1642/3 and as we find an authentic record of New Poquoson Parish in 1643, it is a safe assumption that the parish had borne that name at least from the time the name of the county was changed to York. How long New Poquoson Parish existed we do not know, but there is some basis for an opinion that its name was changed in 1680, for we find a minute of the Council of June 23, 1680, referring to Mr. John Wright as "Minister of Pocoton Parish."[18] And we find in the State Papers list of parishes as of June 30, 1680, Mr. John Wright given as the minister of New Towson Parish, Yorke County, Virginia, and we fail to

[16] *The Colonial Church in Virginia,* 317.
[17] *Executive Journals, Council of Colonial Virginia,* I, 3.
[18] *Executive Journals, Council of Colonial Virginia,* I, 3.

find new Poquoson Parish listed as a parish at all on this list.[19]

By 1702 we no longer find either the name of New Pocoson or New Towson on the list of Parishes for York County, and upon the official list for this year we do find Charles Parish, as one of the parishes of York County, but we are really without information as to how long, theretofore, the parish had existed under that name.

We thus see the names of New Poquoson, New Towson and of Charles Parish associated in such a way as to justify the tentative conclusion, at least, that in 1642/3 one of the parishes of York County was New Poquoson parish; that about 1680 the name was changed to New Towson parish; and that prior to July 8, 1702, the name was changed to Charles Parish and so remained to the end of the time covered by the registers herewith presented.

Charles Parish had a bitter and long-drawn-out controversy over the election of a vestry. The division of the sentiment of the parishioners as reflected by the vestry came to an issue over the question of repairing or building a church. But, it seems, the controversy involved a question more basic and important than that. The vestry records are not extant, so the full details of the matter cannot now be known.

There is ground for the belief that the controversy finally came to be one between those who supported and those who opposed Rev. James Sclater, the parish minister; and that the question of the power and authority of the colonial officials to keep a minister in the office of rector of a parish, against the will and wishes of the vestry, and to tax the inhabitants for his support, whether they wished his services or not, was involved in the case.

---

[19] *Virginia Hist. Mag.,* I, 242-244, where the list is reprinted from State Papers, Colonial-Virginia, Vol. 60, No. 410.

Beginning with the session of March 18, 1707 [1707/8], this controversy in one phase or another required the attention of the Council of State on many occasions. On the date above mentioned a proceeding was brought before the Council, which, in effect, challenged the right of certain vestrymen to vote upon questions coming before the vestry of Charles Parish. This brought in issue the tenure by which the vestrymen held their offices. The Court held the vestry was not legally constituted and ordered an election to legally elect twelve vestrymen. The proceedings on this occasion were as follows:

"On reading this day in Council the Complaint of Henry Hayward, Sen'., John Doswell and other Vestrymen of Charles Parish in York County against Thomas Nutting and others Vestrymen of the said Parish for opposing Mr. Thomas Cheesmans and Mr. Robert Shields voting in the said Vestry at the meeting appointed for advising of the repairing or building a Church. And upon hearing the allegations of both the said partys in Council this Board are of opinion that the present Constitution of the said Vestry is irregular and illegal. And for removing all differences that have or may arise in the said Parish by continuing the said Vestry It is ordered that a new vestry be fairly and legally elected and chosen by the Freehc¹ders and householders of the said Parish or the major part of them, who are hereby appointed to meet for that purpose at the Church of the said parish on Easter Monday next And to the end all persons concerned may have due notice of the time and place of the said Election It is ordered that Mr. James Slater Minister of the said parish make or cause to be made open publication hereof in the said parish Church immediately after Divine Service each Sunday between the date hereof and the date of Election: And for the more regular proceeding on the said Election It is ordered that Wm. Barbar Gent Sheriff of York County attend and take the poll, And the persons thereupon Elected are hereby enjoined before they enter upon their office respectively to take the Oaths directed by Law and to Subscribe to be conformable to the Doctrine and Discipline of the Church of England which Vestry being so chosen and qualify'd are together with the Minister to be thereafter deemed and accounted the vestry of the said parish."[20]

The Council on April 28, 1708, had before it a petition of the "new elected Vestry of Charles Parish and the counter petition of Thomas Roberts and others," which was "referred to the consideration of the next Council after the General Court, when it is ordered that the Clerk of the Council give notice to two of each party to attend and make out the allegations of their said petitions."[21] At its June 4, 1708, meeting, the Council "on the motion of several members of the old and new Elected Vestrys of Charles parish" ordered "that the Sherif of York County be impowered and required to summon all such persons as either party shal nominate to him to appear as Evidence for them before the honorable the President and Council on the 10ᵗʰ instant."[22]

The next proceedings recorded on the subject indicate that the inhabitants of Charles Parish were not dwelling together in peace, harmony and Christian concord, for upon the trial of the case on June 10, 1708, the following was the decree of the Council:

"Whereas upon reading at this Board the petition of severall persons lately elected Vestrymen of Charles Parish, praying that a *Dedimus* may issue for administering to them the oaths appointed by Law for qualifying them to act in that Station together with the Counter petitions of severall of the inhabitants of the said parish Complaining

---

[20] *Executive Journals, Council of Colonial Virginia*, III, 168.
[21] *Executive Journals, Council of Colonial Virginia*, III, 179.
[22] *Ibid.*, p. 183.

of the irregularity of the said Election. And upon hearing the Testimonys of the severall Witnesses brought by each party with the arguments of the Council thereupon, It hath been made appear to this Board that there were diverse indirect practices and irregular proceedings in the said Election tending rather to the widening the differences that had arisen in that parish than any way to unite the minds of the inhabitants there as was the true intention of and accordingly recommended by this Board: It is therefore the opinion of the Council that the said Election made on Easter Tuesday last be and it is hereby declared to be null and void And ordered that the Freeholders and householders of the said parish paying Scott and Lott[23] therein meet at the parish Church on Tuesday the 29th of this present moneth and there Elect and choose twelve of the most able and discreet men of the said parish to be of the vestry for the same And for the more regular proceeding in the said Election It is ordered that the Sheriff of York County attend and take the poll in such manner as he shal be directed by this Board and to the end all persons concerned may have due notice of the time and place of Election, It is ordered that the Minister of the said parish make publication here of in the said parish Church immediately after divine Service on each Sunday between this and the day of Election.

"Whereas the Sheriff of the County of York is directed to attend the Election of the Vestry of Charles parish on Tuesday the 29th of this present moneth and to take the poll at the same for his better guidance and direction therein and for avoiding all tumults and Confusion which usually happens on such occasions It is ordered that every Free-

---

[23] Scot and lot, "a customary duty in Great Britain formerly laid on all of a parish, according to their ability to pay; also, figuratively, obligations of every kind." "Scot and lot voters, voters in certain boroughs entitled to the franchise by paying scot and lot." *New Standard Dictionary.*

holder and householder paying Scott and Lott in the said parish and none other have vote at the said Election, And for clearing any doubts that may happen as to any person being a freeholder or householder the Sherif is impowered to administer to such person an Oath if required in the same manner as is directed by Law in the Election of Burgesses. The said Sherif shall seperately demand and accordingly take in writing from every person haveing vote in the said Election, the names of twelve men whom such person thinks most fitt to be vestry men in the said parish, and haveing so sett down in writeing such particular Election List or Number of twelve men he shal then examine all the said Lists and shall declare those twelve men to be the vestry whom (upon Security) he shall find to have most votes. And ordered that the said Sheriff make Return of his proceedings together with the severall Lists aforesaid to the Council office."[24]

The order to the sheriff of York County to hold this election, dated June 10, 1708, is preserved in *Calendar of Virginia State Papers*.[25]

The election held under this order did not settle the bitter controversy between rival factions in the parish.

The Council met on July 29, 1708; this was a little too soon after the election for the litigants to present a new controversy over the election of June 29; but when the Council next met, September 20, 1708, a new suit over the election of a vestry was laid before them, and the Council ordered:

"The severall petitions of the new Elected Vestry of Charles parish and of Henry Howard and others are referred till the 7th day of the General Court and ordered

---

[24] *Executive Journals, Council of Colonial Virginia*, III, 185-186.
[25] Vol. I, p. 122.

that the respective partys have notice to attend on the aforesaid day."[26]

The case came on to be heard before the Council on October 22, 1708. The facts developed indicate not only the great importance attached to the result of the election of a vestry, but also evidence an almost unbelievable amount of interest and strife engendered by the contest over the control of the parish.

The petition by Henry Howard, Edward Tabb, and others complained of an "undue and irregular election of a vestry for Charles parish on the 29th of June last past," because "votes of the parishioners were taken at their own houses twelve days before the day of the said Election and two days before publication of the order," and because of "diverse other irregularitys."

Upon the hearing the Council rendered its opinion "that the aforesaid Election of a Vestry for Charles parish was not made pursuant to the order of the Council and therefore the same is declared null and void."

It further decreed that in order that "a Vestry for the said parish may be fairly, freely, and impartially elected and Chosen," that "all the Freeholders and householders paying Scott and Lott within the said parish" should meet on the second of November, 1708, at the Church of the parish and "make choice of twelve of the most able and discreet men of the said parish to be the vestry for the same."

Capt. Lawrence Smith, Sheriff of York County was ordered to attend at the time and place indicated to take the poll.

The directions to him were substantially the same, as to the manner of holding the election, as those given for the election of June 29th, preceding. Additional directions were that if he was not able to conclude the poll on the

[26] *Executive Journals, Council of Colonial Virginia*, III, 192.

day named he might adjourn the same until "the next day and so from day to day if occasion require till the poll be finished." There was a provision also "that no person who has once given his Vote as aforesaid shall be permitted afterwards to alter the same."

The order of the Council concluded as follows:

"And forasmuch as this Board are informed that in the former Elections in the said parish diverse indirect practices have been used and some persons endeavored to carry the Election in a tumultous manner the said Sherif is hereby required to return the names of all such persons as he shall observe at this Election to be guilty in stiring up tumults as well as of such as shal appear to be Actors therein to the end they may be exemplarly punished And it is further ordered that the said sheriff return to the Council office a List of the persons so elected with the particular List of the Electors and likewise a List of all such persons haveing right of Election within the said parish that shall absent themselves from the same. And ordered that publication thereof be made in the Church of Charles parish each Sunday between this and the day of Election by the Minister imediately after divine service."[27]

The election held pursuant to this order was the occasion of another suit.

At a meeting held February 10, 1708 [1708/9], the Council:

"On reading the petition of the new elected vestry of Charles parish and a Counter petition of diverse Inhabitants of the said parish, . . . ordered that the said petitioners have notice to attend the next Council to make out the allegations of their respective petitions and that the Sherif of York County be also required to attend at the same

---

[27] *Executive Journals, Council of Colonial Virginia*, III, 197-98.

time to answer any objections that may be made against the late election of Vestrymen in the said parish."[28]

The Council on February 18, 1708, took the case under consideration, and found "that the said election [of November 2, 1708] was fairly and regularly made according to Law and the directions of this Board, and that it doth appear by the Return that Eleven of the said Vestrymen were chosen by a great Majority of the Inhabitants and it appearing also that there are two others returned who had an equal number of votes, It is the opinion of the Council that the Sherif amend his return by strikeing out one of them to make the number of the Vestry twelve and the return being amended accordingly.

It was ordered that Henry Howard, Thomas Nutting, Thomas Chisman, Thomas Roberts, Robert Curtis, Henry Howard junior, John Drewry, John Doswell, Jon. Doswell junior, Simon Stacy, Edward Tabb, and Anthony Robinson being duly Elected as aforesaid be sworn of a Vestry and that a *Dedimus* issue for that purpose directed to Robert Read and Wm Buckner Gent or any one of them to administer to the said Vestrymen the Oaths and Test prescribed by Law for qualifying them for the said Offices."[29]

It would seem that this should have definitely ended this long-drawn-out effort to get a vestry legally installed in Charles Parish. But not so, for on April 26, 1709, seven members of the newly elected vestry, who had qualified, were back advising the Council "that the other five persons" chosen had refused to take the oaths or to act as Vestrymen. The seven asked the advice of the Council whether they, the seven, could "act as a Vestry and proceed to Chose others in the room of those who have refused to qualify themselves."

[28] *Executive Journals, Council of Colonial Virginia,* III, 205.
[29] *Ibid.,* 207-208.

The Council gave its opinion "that the five persons that have refused be again desired to qualify themselves and in case they shall refuse then the petitioners may Choose five others of the most able and discreet freeholders to Compleat the number of the said Vestry."[30]

Still another echo of the controversy was heard before the Council, when on June 2, 1709, Lawrence Smith, William Barber and William Robertson presented a petition complaining of the vestry of Charles Parish because the vestry had "refused to make them any satisfaction for their trouble in the several orders for settling that Vestry."

It was ordered that "in case the said Vestry do not pay the petitioners for their services before the next Council that then the Churchwardens be summoned to attend this Board to show cause why they refuse the Same."[31]

It is presumed that the vestry paid them; for we find no further mention of the matter in the Council minutes.

The vestry as finally and legally constituted were evidently of the group which had opposed the minister of the parish, Reverend James Sclater, for they seem to have taken immediately steps to put an end to his functioning as the minister of that parish. They shut the church doors against him, and as the General Court afterwards found, measures were resorted to "endangering the public peace." This case illustrates the tenacity with which, in those days, ministers held on to their jobs and their salaries which were fixed by law, and collected by the sheriff; and the difficulty, even impossibility, of parishioners getting rid of a minister not to their liking.

Evidently the minister complained to the Governor, and the Governor communicated with the vestry and received their reply. The precise contents of these several communications we do not know. But at this point, in a let-

---

[30] *Executive Journals, Council of Colonial Virginia*, III, 216.
[31] *Ibid.*, 218.

ter from the Governor to the vestry under date of September 3, 1709, we do have a bit of authentic information. The letter is as follows:

"Gents: I have yours of the 31st past, and am sorry to find by it, there is so little appearance of your Reconcilement to your Minister. I can't tell how you may apprehend the consequences of such a proceeding, as you seem to have undertaken, but for my part, think it of so extraordinary a nature, both in respect to the whole Country and the Clergy in general, (for whom I shal always have a just and equal regard,) that I intend to have the advice of the Council thereon, at their first meeting, after which you shal have a further answer: In the mean time, I expect and require it of you, that you will give Mr. Sclater no interruption in the Exercise of his Ministry in your Parish, but that he may be permitted to discharge it as heretofore. I think it fitt also to satisfy you, that I can't agree in opinion with you as to removing ministers, that have so long officiated in a parish as Mr. Sclater has in yours without a legal hearing before proper Judges. I have some interest in your parish, and have a regard for its Inhabitants, and notwithstanding the just respect I have for the Clergy, you may depend on equal Justice and favour, and I shal be extremely Concerned, if you force me to begin the Execution of that Right, her Majesty hath been pleased to intrust me with, in such a manner as may not be gratefull to you. You seem to hint, I had received informations from Mr. Sclater. I can assure you Mr. Sclater has never given me any informations, that have prevailed with me, so much as my own observations, and the accounts of persons altogether disinterested, whom I had no reason to disbelieve, who have told me of your proceedings with astonishment at your rashness and inconsideration."[32]

---

[32] *Calendar of Virginia State Papers*, I, 133. This letter was from President Edmund Jenings.

The Governor, as he said he would, on September 12, 1709, called upon the Council to consider "the Dissentions and Controversys between the Vestry of Charles parish and Mr. James Slater their Minister." It ordered "that both partys attend this Board on the seventh day of the next General Court in order to a full hearing of the said disputes."[33]

The controversy came on for preliminary hearing on October 22, 1709, at the conclusion of which the court entered the following order:

"On hearing this day in Council the disputes between the Vestry of Charles parish in York County and Mr. James Slater their Minister. It appearing to this Board that the said Vestry have at Sundry times shutt the Church door against the said Minister to the great disturbance of the parish and endangering the public peace. It is ordered that the Churchwardens and Vestry of the said parish do not presume to shutt the Church doors or to hinder Mr. Slater from performing divine Service and preaching in the said Church as he formerly used to do and for the more decent Celebration of the publick Worship that the said Churchwardens and Vestry cause the books and ornaments of the Church to be putt up every Sunday as usual untill the differences between them and their Minister be legally determined."[34]

The vestry proved recalcitrant and refused to obey the order of the General Court, and were adjudged in contempt and the Attorney General of the Colony was ordered to prosecute the offending individuals as the following extract from the Council minutes of December 8, 1709, show:

The court recited its order of October 22, last, and then said: "it appearing by the orders and other proceedings of the said Vestry that they have since shutt the Church

[33] *Executive Journals, Council of Colonial Virginia*, III, 222.
[34] *Ibid.*, 225.

Doors and lockt up the reading Desk, and by other un-
warrantable means riotously hindered the said Mr. Slater
from the exercise of his Ministry to the Disturbance of the
peace and the Contempt of the aforesaid Order. It is therefore Ordered that Mr. Attorney General do consider of
the proceedings of the said Vestry and thereupon prosecute
according to Law such as have been guilty of the breach
of the Peace and Disturbance of the divine Service in the
said parish."[35]

The Vestry had certainly shown a remarkable firmness
or stubbornness, depending upon the point of view. But
they finally lost, for Reverend James Sclater continued as
minister of the parish for fourteen more years, until his
death in 1723. He doubtless felt that justice and right
had triumphed, while those who did not want him bitterly
resented having him saddled upon the parish, residing in a
house provided at public expense, collecting fees for marriages and baptisms, willy nilly, and receiving regularly his
salary of sixteen thousand pounds of tobacco.

The controversy between him and the vestry, the interruption of the churchly ordinances in the parish, was at its
height at a particularly unfortunate time, for it was a period
when the inhabitants needed all the supports and consola-
tion that the church and religion could provide. It was a
time when sickness and disease were rampant. On the
same day when the Council found that the church doors
were shut and the reading desk locked against Mr. Sclater,
and the Attorney General was ordered to prosecute those
responsible therefor, the Council also entered this order:

"Whereas it hath pleased God to afflict divers parts of
this Country with a rageing Distemper. It is ordered that
Wednesday the 11th of January be set apart as a day of
publick fasting and humiliation to deprecate the wrath of
Almighty God and to implore his mercy in removeing this

---

[35] *Executive Journals, Council of Colonial Virginia*, III, 229.

grevious Calamity and ordered that a Proclamation issue accordingly."[36]

The record shows that there were approximately three times as many deaths in the parish in 1709 as there were in 1708.

---

[36] *Executive Journals, Council of Colonial Virginia*, III, 229. The order entered on Dec. 8, 1709, for the service of fasting and humiliation on Jan. 11, 1709, set the date one month and three days from the date of the order. In other words, as the year then began March 25, January *followed* December, in any given year.

CHAPTER II

The Ministers of Charles Parish

The ministers, so far as the facts are now ascertained, of New Pocoson, New Towson and Charles Parish were: Charles Grundy, of New Pocoson, John Wright of New Towson, and Thomas Finney, James Sclater, James Falconer, Theodosius Staige, Thomas Warrington, Joseph Davenport, and Samuel Shield of Charles Parish.

Of Reverend Charles Grundy but little is known except the fact that he was Minister of "New Poquoson" Parish in 1645. The York County Court records preserve his name. On December 20, 1645, Thomas Waldoe was presented by the churchwardens "of the New Poquoson" for an abuse of the church and minister and for not receiving the sacrament. He was found guilty and ordered by the court to bring a certificate under the hand of Mr. Charles Grundy minister of the said parish of his reformation of the said abuses to the next court, otherwise to be censured by the Court for the same."[37]

Reverend John Wright is also assigned by Dr. Goodwin to New Pocoson Parish.[38] There is some slight confusion as to the parish which he served in 1680. In the list of parishes and ministers of Virginia, which bears date June 30, 1680,[39] he is given as the minister of New Towson Parish. But at a council meeting held at James City, June 23, 1683,[40] "Mr. Jnᵒ. Wright Minister presented his petition complaining that Mr. Jonathan Davis" who was not "a qualifyed Minister without leave given him assumed to

---

[37] *William and Mary Quarterly,* (1st Series), XXII, 79.
[38] *The Colonial Church in Virginia,* 340.
[39] State Papers, Colonial-Virginia, Vol. 60, No. 410; *Virginia Hist. Mag.,* I, 242-244.
[40] *Executive Journals of the Council of Colonial Virginia,* I, 3.

himself the Liberty of the pulpit which of right belonged to the said Mr. Jn°. Wright Minister of Pocoton Parish," etc. The Council ordered them both to appear before the Council on the 28th of June, 1680, but what disposition was made of the case does not appear, as there are no minutes of the Council for that date, and it seems not to have been referred to in any subsequent minutes.

There were two men of this name graduated from Oxford, one with a B. A., in 1673, the other with an M. A., in 1674/5.[41] Which one was this minister seems not certainly known.

Reverend Thomas Finney matriculated at New Inn Hall, Oxford, in 1650, and received his B. A. degree in 1655. He was Vicar of Perranzabuloe in 1661.[42] Almost nothing is known of his history in Virginia. The statement in *The Colonial Church in Virginia*[43] that he died in 1687 is an error, as the Register of Deaths of the parish contains the entry of his death in the year 1686, as follows:

"The Reverend Mr. Thomas Finney died December 8th and lyeth buried in the Chancell of New Poquoson Church."

Reverend James Sclater, who succeeded Reverend Thomas Finney as minister of Charles Parish in 1686, was a son of John Sclater of the City of Oxford. He matriculated at Oxford, November 14, 1673, at the age of sixteen, and secured the B. A. degree in 1677, and the M. A. degree in 1680. Just when he came to Virginia is not known, but, as stated, he became minister of Charles Parish in 1686,[44] and continued in the parish until his death November 19, 1723. The date of his death is erroneously given in both *The Colonial Church in Virginia*,[45] and in *William and Mary*

---

[41] *The Colonial Church in Virginia*, 317.
[42] *The Colonial Church in Virginia*, 268.
[43] p. 268, evidently based on *Colonial Churches*, 126.
[44] *William and Mary College Quarterly*, (1st Series), IV, 138.
[45] p. 304.

College Quarterly[46] as 1724. His death is entered in the Register of Deaths of the parish, as given above, November 19, 1723. He was one minister, at least, who maintained in fact the theory and claim of a life tenure in the parishes for the ministers. It seems that in addition to his services in Charles Parish he must have served also to some extent in Mulberry Island Parish, Warwick County, for in the list of ministers of 1714 he is shown as the minister of that parish. He ministered, too, a short time to Bruton Parish.

Considerable notice has already been taken of this minister in connection with his controversy with the vestry of Charles Parish over his right to the parish (in Chapter I hereof).

But his ministerial controversies were not the only litigations in which he engaged.

In 1688 he had a civil suit with Edward Thomas, a prominent Quaker. Thomas had denounced Sclater for speaking "in the course of his ministerial functions" what Thomas represented to be "blasphemous words." Sclater sued him for damages and recovered a judgment for fifty pounds sterling. Thomas was also "condemned to ask Slater's pardon on two successive Sundays in the church of Bruton Parish, in the face of the congregation; and also in the justices' presence at the next session of the County Court."[47]

Despite the fact that he had been for a short time minister of Bruton Parish in 1688[48] and on November 20, 1710, while Bruton Parish was temporarily without a minister, he was designated as one of seven ministers to be asked

---

[46] (1st Series), IV, 138.
[47] *Institutional Hist. of Va.*, (Bruce), I, 246. York County Records, Vol. 1687-91, p. 232, Va. St. Libr. The fact that the apology was directed to be made on two successive Sundays in Bruton Parish Church, would seem to indicate that Sclater was then minister of Bruton Parish. He is not so given by Dr. Goodwin in *The Colonial Church in Virginia.* See also: *Hist. of Bruton Parish* (Goodwin), 17, 26.
[48] *Hist. of Bruton Parish* (Goodwin), 17.

to preach once each for seven weeks, yet the vestry later rescinded that order by a new one as follows:

"Ordered—That whereas there was an order made the last Vestry for 7 ministers to preach on certain Sundays, wherein the Revd. James Sclater was one:—It is ordered by this meeting that the said Sclater be left out of the number, and that the Church Wardens give notice to the Rev. Arthur Tillyard to preach December 10th, and the rest in their order."[49]

Nor did this reverend gentleman confine his controversies to maintaining himself in his ministerial office and to suits for slander, but included also controversies over real estate.

On April 17, 1713, the General Court had before it the petition of "James Sclater Clerk" upon which it ordered "that the patent sued out by Henry Haward [Howard?] for land in York County be Stop'd until both parties be heard."[50]

On April 22, 1713, Henry Haward moved in the General Court "for a speedy determination of the Caveat entered by James Sclater Clerk against a patent prepared in his name for land in York County." It was accordingly ordered that notice be given Mr. Sclater, and "that both partys be heard in Council on Tuesday next."[51]

On April 30, 1713, the Council made the following order on the subject:

"On hearing this day in Council the petition of James Sclater Clerk for stopping a patent sued out by Henry Haward for fourty acres and a half of land lying in the County of York. It appearing to this Board that the said land hath always been reputed as Wast land, and so surveyed by the Father of the said Haward about twenty years ago. It is therefore Ordered that the patent already

---

[49] History of Bruton Parish (Goodwin), 27.
[50] Executive Journals, Council of Colonial Virginia, III, 335.
[51] Ibid., 337.

prepared be issued in the name of the said Henry Haward, Reserving to the said Mr. Sclater to dispute his Right at Law, in case the said land upon Tryal be found to be within the Bounds of his elder Patent."[52]

Whether Mr. Sclater further disputed at law, Mr. Haward's right to the land, we do not know.

Evidently Reverend James Sclater had many descendants. There are many entries of births of persons of this name in the Register of Births presented in this volume. *The William and Mary College Quarterly*[53] helps us in the analysis of the pedigree. The wife, according to this authority, which cites the will, proved August 17, 1724, of Rev. James Sclater was named Mary, (last name not known). His daughters were: Mary, wife of one Tabb; and Martha, the wife of John Brody. His will also mentions sons: James Sclater, and John Sclater, to each of whom he gave half his books.

The Register of Births does not always refer to James Sclater as Reverend James Sclater, but, according to this article, the following births to James and Mary Sclater were those of children of this minister:

1. Elizabeth Sclater, b. Nov. 10, 1688.
2. John Sclater, b. May 10, 1691.
3. Mary Sclater, b. April 2, 1692.
4. Sarah Schlater, b. Jan. 11, 1695.
5. James Sclater, b. Dec. 6, 1697.
6. Martha Sclater, b. July 22, 1700.
7. Mary Sclater, b. Oct. 16, 1702.

The son James Sclater married Elizabeth Sclater, daughter of Richard Sclater (d. Nov. 7, 1718); and Elizabeth sur-

---

[52] *Executive Journals, Council of Colonial Virginia*, III, 341.

[53] Vol. 4, 138, (1st Series): The note is presumably by the distinguished historian and genealogist, its editor at that time, Dr. Lyon G. Tyler.

viving him married, secondly, Daniel Moore, and died December 30, 1735.

Reverend James Falconer received the King's bounty for Virginia, July 20, 1709, having been ordained for Virginia, June 19, 1709.[54] He was, first, minister of Hungar's Parish, Northampton County, in 1719; and then of Elizabeth River Parish, Norfolk County, in 1720; and was minister of Elizabeth City Parish, Elizabeth City County, from 1720 to 1724. He became minister of Charles Parish, York County, Virginia, in 1725, and served the parish until his death in 1727. The parish register contains the entry of his death February 2, 1727. This seems to be the only entry in that name in the entire register. Considerable search discloses no further details of his life.

Reverend Theodosius Staige was the minister of Charles Parish from 1728 to 1747. The details of his education and preparation for the ministry seem not to have been preserved. He received the King's bounty for Virginia, on June 4, 1725. His first charge in Virginia seems to have been St. George's Parish, Spotsylvania County, which parish he served from 1726 to 1728.[55]

It is said that he married in Spotsylvania, but when and to whom we have not discovered.

Dr. R. A. Brock says that he came to Virginia with an unmarried sister; and that one of his sisters, Letitia Maria Ann Staige, married "in London Reverend James Marye, a native of Rouen, Normandy, France, the ancestor of the well known family of the name."[56]

The parish register of Charles Parish shows the births of the following children born to Reverend Theodosius Staige and Ann, his wife:

[54] *The Colonial Church in Virginia* (Goodwin), 268.
[55] *Old Churches, Families,* etc. (Meade), II, 69; *Hist. of St. George's Parish; The Colonial Church in Virginia* (Goodwin), 308.
[56] For a partial genealogy see "Huguenot Emigration to Virginia," in Vol. V, of the *Virginia Historical Collections.*

Ann Staige, b. March 26, 1731.
Gulielma Staige, b. Nov. 1, 1739.
Letitia Theodora Staige, b. Feb. 13, 1728/9.
Lucia Staige, b. Nov. 8, 1735.
Margareta Staige, b. July 25, 1732.
Willm. Staige, b. Sept. 21, 1733 (d. June 13, 1736).

The daughter Ann married Graham Frank. There is in Bruton Parish Church Yard a tomb with the inscription:

"Here Lyeth the Body of Ann
the Wife of Graham Frank
and Daughter of the Rev⁴. Mr.
Theod• Staige who died on
the Feast of S⁴ Andrew 1759
Aged 28 years."[57]

Graham Frank is mentioned by Bishop Meade[58] as a merchant of London and a correspondent of Reverend Samuel Shields and of the Nelsons.

Dr. Brock says that: "Another daughter of Mr. Staige married Samuel Thompson, Orange County, Virginia, and they had issue, among others possibly, a son, William Staige."[59]

"The name Staige," continues Dr. Brock, "is a favored Christian name in the Davis and other families of Virginia. A distinguished instance was the late Prof. John Staige Davis, M. D., of the University of Virginia."

The statement in Dr. Brock's note that Rev. Theodosius Staige "served also for a time in York-Hampton parish," is thought to be an error. He makes no mention of his long time service in Charles Parish. Dr. Goodwin does

[57] *Virginia Historical Collection*, XI, 69.
[58] *Old Churches and Families of Virginia*, I, 203.
[59] *Virginia Historical Collections*, XI, 69.

not mention him in connection with York-Hampton Parish.[60]

On November 2, 1736, the Governor and Council heard "the Petition and Complaint of the greater part of the Vestry and Inhabitants of Charles Parish against Mr. Theodosius Staige[61] their minister for not doing his duty in administering the Sacrament of Baptism and other misdemeanors." On consideration of the matter the Council held "that the differences which have arisen between the parties have proceeded from some groundless Scruples of the said Mr. Staige[62] and he having now upon the Governor's admonition promised to conforme to his duty for the future the said Complaint is thereupon dismiss'd."

In 1743 we again find the Reverend Mr. Staige in trouble with his vestry. On May 4, of that year the Governor and Council heard "the Complaint of the Vestry of Charles Parish in York County against the Reverend Mr. Theodosius Staige Minister of the said Parish for not Executing his Office in not Christening of Bastard Children and Opposing the Singing the New Version of Psalms, and praying that the said Mr. Staige may be removed from the said Parish." The Council were "Of opinion that Mr. Staige has been guilty of the several misdemeanors charged against him and order that he shall comply with the Vestry and endeavor to reconcil himself to the Parishioners, or that he be allowed Six Months to provide himselfe another Parish in Case they cannot agree."[63]

Apparently he and the Vestry came to an agreement, as he continued in the parish until his death there, December 26, 1747.

---

[60] *The Colonial Church in Virginia*, 308, 340.

[61] The name is rendered "Hoge" in the printing of *Executive Journals of the Council of Colonial Virginia*, IV, 384. This is purely an error of transcription.

[62] Here again rendered "Hoge," in the *Executive Journals*, IV, 384.

Reverend Thomas Warrington succeeded Rev. Mr. Staige as the minister of Charles Parish. He was licensed for Virginia, September 21, 1747, and received the King's Bounty on October 14, 1747. We have no details of his life before that time. He seems to have been minister of Charles Parish in 1749,[64] the parish probably having been vacant from the death of Mr. Staige in 1747 until that time. He remained in the parish until about 1756, when he became minister of Elizabeth City Parish, Elizabeth City County, which he served until his death in 1770. He was very active in opposition to the "Two-Penny Act."

The Parish Register of Charles Parish contains a record of the birth of a son and a daughter born to Rev. Thomas Warrington and Elizabeth, his wife. These were:

Francis Spencer Warrington, born January 20, 1749/50; and

Rachel Warrington, born January 20, 1753.

Commodore Louis Warrington was a grandson of the minister, Reverend Thomas Warrington.[65]

Reverend Joseph Davenport was born in Williamsburg, Virginia, Feb. 21, 1731/2, and was educated at William and Mary College. He was licensed for the ministry October 12, 1755, and received the King's Bounty, October 23, 1755. He was minister of Charles Parish from 1757 to 1785.[66]

He was loyal to the American cause in the Revolutionary War.[67]

The Reverend Joseph Davenport was Joseph, Junior. His parents were Joseph and Marg. Davenport.[68]

---

[63] *Virginia Hist. Mag.*, XVI, 27-28.
[64] *The Colonial Church in Virginia*, 314.
[65] *Old Churches, Ministers and Families of Virginia*, I, 232.
[66] *The Colonial Church in Virginia*, 262, 340.
[67] *Ibid.*
[68] *William and Mary College Quarterly*, V, 271.

Their children were as follows:

> Eliz*. and Mar*. Davenport, twins, born March 5, 1729/30.
> Jos. Davenport, Jun'. b. Feb. 21, 1731/2.
> Geo. Davenport, b. March 29, 1733.
> Mat. Davenport, b. Oct. 24, 1734.
> Jud. Davenport.
> Jas. Davenport.
> Peachy and Johan Shank Davenport, twins.
> Sarah Davenport.

There seems to have been another child not mentioned in this list, for Joseph Davenport's will, proved March 16, 1761, mentions among other children, Frances Anne Wright, "now in England."

The elder Joseph Davenport was named town clerk in the charter of Williamsburg in 1722. One of his sons, Matthew, was writing master at William and Mary College in 1766.

Joseph Davenport, Junior, went to England in 1755 to be ordained, carrying a strong letter of recommendation from President Thomas Dawson, of William and Mary College. He married Mary (last name not known), and died in Charles Parish. His will was proved in York County Court, May 1, 1788.[69]

A brief account of this minister in *William and Mary College Quarterly*[70] mentions a son William Davenport, b. December 10, 1763, and a daughter Eliza Hunter Davenport, who married William Hunter, son of William Hunter, printer of the Gazette.

The Reverend Samuel Shield was minister of Charles Parish in 1791 and 1792 and probably also in 1793, in which

---

[69] *William and Mary College Quarterly*, V, 272.
[70] V, 272.

year he died. He was a native of York County, Virginia, and was educated at William and Mary College, where he was medalist in 1769. He was licensed for the ministry in Virginia in 1774 and received the King's Bounty January 18, 1775.[71]

He was minister of Drysdale Parish, in King and Queen and Caroline counties in 1776. He was, probably, the first minister of St. Asaph's Parish, Caroline County, in 1785, upon its separation from Drysdale Parish. From 1786 to 1790 he was minister of York-Hampton Parish, and finally, as noted, of Charles Parish. He was President of the Convention of the Clergy in 1784 and wrote the petition of that year of the church to the Legislature. In 1786 and in 1790 he was supported by a minority for the office of Bishop.

He took the side of the Colonies in the Revolutionary struggle with the mother country.

---

[71] *The Colonial Church in Virginia*, 306.

CHAPTER III

The Registers of Charles Parish

The Register of Births of Charles Parish, the contents of which, arranged in alphabetical order, are here printed for the first time, with certain deficiencies presently to be pointed out, covers the span of years from 1648 to 1789,— a period of one hundred and forty-one years. In addition it has a single and final entry in 1800.

The Register of Deaths was kept in the same book, in the latter part of it, the book being reversed. The record of deaths, with certain omissions, extends from 1665 to 1787.

The manuscript volume comprising these registers is minus the title page, the loss of which is especially to be regretted, as, doubtless, it would have afforded some information regarding the parish in which the earliest entries were made.

As has already been noted, this parish register begins at a date (1648) earlier than any other known register or vestry book of the Colony of Virginia.

The Register of Births comprises one hundred and thirteen pages, exclusive of the index. The index occupied twenty-seven pages more; but the sheet containing the names which begin with the letter A is missing. Quite a number of the other index pages are partly gone, or mutilated so that many names cannot be deciphered at all, while others remain, or are legible, only in part. The damage to the index pages results from a variety of causes: the margins, edges, and corners are in many instances worn, frayed, and torn. Some are water-stained and blotted, and here and there holes are torn in the body of the sheets of paper so as totally to remove important parts of the writing thereon. The sheets carrying the names beginning with the letters S and T are torn about in half, the lower parts being the sections which are gone.

But despite these mutilations which the index has suffered, enough remains to enable us to know that we have all the pages of the register; and moreover to enable us in many instances to verify, here and there, a name which is indistinct in the register, and occasionally even to restore a name which has been wholly lost from the register.

The volume as it exists at the present time is in part a copy of an earlier volume, and in part consists of original entries first made in the existing volume.

It appears that the births from October 6, 1648, up to January 25, 1714, were recorded in a book which contained no space for more entries. On page 32 of the present volume, immediately after the entry of the last mentioned date, there appears the following:

"Memorandum: That the Old Register Book being full James Shelton then Clerk was ordered to gett a new one which he did and lost the same (to-wit) The Registerings from the date above-said [January 25, 1714] to the end of the year 1716.

"The under written names are of an enquiry made by Bernard Coudert who succeeded James Shelton; as clerk of the Parish Church and vestry."

Then follow the entries of births of eight persons occurring between March 9, 1715, and December 8, 1716, thus supplying the names, so far as could be done, for the period covered by the lost book.

The entry of the births occurring during the incumbency of Bernard Coudert, Clerk, are recorded in the present book, introduced by an entry evidently written by the person (Mr. Richard Hurst) who, in 1725, copied all the pre-existing entries. This entry occurs on page 32 of the existing volume, immediately following an entry dated March 2, 1715, and is as follows:

"Here Followeth the Registerings of the Births & Baptisms registered by Mr. Bernard Coudert Clerk Deceased, vizt."

On page 40 of the register, after the date December 10, 1725, there is the following entry:

"Registering Births Begun by me Rich⁴. Hurst Clk Vestry 1725."

The entry immediately preceding this entry was that of the birth of Frances Shield, dau. of Dunn Shield by Susanna, b. Nov. 24, 1725, bap. Dec. 10, 1725,—and the first entry by Rich⁴. Hurst, Clerk, after the notation of his assumption of the clerkship was as follows:

"Sarah Burcher daughter of Bartholomew by Dorithy his wife was born September the 13ᵗʰ, 1725, baptized 8ber the 24, 1725."

A companion entry on page 21, of the Register of Deaths at this time is fuller and very helpful. It is as follows:

"Registering of Deaths begun here by me R⁴. Hurst Clark of Charles Parish Church 1725 who also copied of this Book of Registers from the Old Regʳ. Book."

When Richard Hurst, in 1725, on page 40 of the Register of Births, made the entry showing when he began the registering of births he did not there state that the preceding entries down to that point had been copied by him. But such was the fact, as all the writing in the book from the beginning entry down to that point is in his handwriting; furthermore, the entry in the Register of Deaths above quoted affirms that he had copied "this Book of Registers" from the old book. The registers referred to were, of course, the Register of Births, and the Register of Deaths.

As we have seen, the book of registerings of births begun in 1648 was full in 1714. Who were the clerks who made the entries in that book we do not certainly know. There is an entry on December 18, 1705, of the death of

James Broster, clerk of the parish. But when his term began or ended, or how long he served, does not appear. Probably James Shelton made some of the entries, for he it was who was ordered to get a new book, the old book being full, and who lost the entries for a period of two years. How long James Shelton was clerk we do not know, but he seems to have been succeeded as clerk by Bernard Coudert in December, 1716, who probably continued to serve until 1723. The Register of Deaths has this entry of his death in the year 1723:

"Bernard Coudert Clerk of this parish—May the 30th"

Jones Irwin probably was the clerk who recorded the entries from 1722 to 1725 when Richard Hurst became clerk. In the margin of the Register of Births, opposite the entry of the birth of Samuel Drewry, February 28, 1722, is an entry which is not altogether distinct. It seems to be:

> "Jones
> Irwin
> Clerk begun
> here."

All of the entry is distinct except the "Jo"—in what is supposed to be Jones, and the "I" in what is supposed to be Irwin.

From the time Richard Hurst became clerk, in 1725, and copied the old registers, he probably continued to make the entries down to 1749; though the characteristics of the writing changed somewhat after 1736.

The entries from 1750 to 1752 are by a hand unidentified by this writer; but from 1752 or 1753 to 1778, Mr. Hine Russell was the clerk of the church. A record made on page 37 of the Register of Deaths, immediately following an entry dated Sept. 29, 1771, by the rector, Rev. Joseph Davenport, of an alleged dereliction of duty by Mr. Russell fixes his tenure as extending at least from 1757 to 1778. This record is as follows:

"Mr. Russell having declin'd the Clerkship of our Church early in the year 1778, He stil kept possession of the Register, til Feby. 1779, tho' often desir'd to send it to me. And as he had constantly kept it from the time I was receiv'd into the parish (Jan^ry 20, 1757) & was observ'd for several years of that Time, to be punctual in registering the Deaths, as well as the Births I was very easy, expecting to have found no Reason for Complaint. But when I receiv'd the Book, Feb^ry 16th 1779, I found the Register of Deaths brought down [no] lower than to 1772, & of that year but one register'd.

Jos: Davenport

Rector of Charles Parish

Feb^ry 16th 1779."

Another bit of evidence preserved in the Register of Births gives "Mr. Russell's" full name, and seems to fix him in the clerkship as early as 1753. This is a report to the clerk of certain births made by Thomas Chisman, the last of which was on November 13, 1753. It is addressed to Mr. Hine Russel.

In many instances scattered throughout the register, especially between 1668 and 1699, the entries contain matter descriptive of the parents, as for example:

"James son of John Brown of Denbigh parish by Hannah his wife" was born October 6, 1668.

and

"John son of James Price of York parish" was born April 6, 1669.

and

"James son of Alexander Moore of Old Poquoson," was born June 1, 1669.

and

"Mary daughter of Francis Bell by Ann his wife of Elizabeth City County."

In some cases the name of some parish or county is written in the margin opposite an entry.

The interpretation of this descriptive matter cannot always be made with certainty. In the main this seems to have been the case; that where the parents of the child were residents of some other parish, but the birth took place in the parish for which the register was kept, the fact of the birth there was noted, that being the parish in which the law directed the registering of the birth, and the descriptive matter was added in order to indicate the non-residence of the parents. Where the parents were residents of the parish for which the register was kept, nothing was added indicative of residence, it being assumed, presumably, that they were residents of that parish.

The Register of Births was, in the main, very well kept and though in places faded, dim and worn, yet all things considered it remains in a remarkable state of preservation, and while this is true, a few defects must be mentioned:

There is an entry where the scrivener wholly omitted the family name in making the entry. It is as follows:

"Margaret daughter of William by Diana his wife was born the 1ˢᵗ day of November 1667."

The entry of a birth in September, 1703, is missing. The entry is at the top of page twenty-seven. The margin of the page is so completely torn away that only a few unimportant words remain; all names are missing.

A somewhat similar situation occurs with reference to the first entry on page fifty-three. The family name and the name of the child are missing. A part of the entry remains. The brackets indicate the missing material, in the entry which, so far as it remains, is as follows:

"[   ] son of Adouston by [   ] his wife born March 21, 1737/8 baptized April 23, 17 [1738?]."

At the top of page 107 there is the entry of the birth of a child born December 24, 1781, baptized February 21, 1782, but the first line of the entry carrying all names is entirely gone.

And at the top of page 109 there was the entry of a birth, but so much of the page is missing that all names are missing. The date of birth April 19 remains, and by the context we know that the year was 1783. But that is all.

The Register of Deaths is entered upon forty numbered pages.

The first entry in the Register of Deaths was dated July 22, 1665, and the last entry was made on May 18, 1787.

The entries from July 22, 1665, to January 6, 1725, were made in an earlier book "the old Reg'. Book," copied by Richard Hurst in 1725. From 1725 to and including an entry on August 2, 1748, the entries in the Register of Deaths are probably all by the hand of Richard Hurst. And in this register, as is also true of the Register of Births, the entries from about 1750 to 1752 are by an unidentified person, possibly the Reverend Thomas Warrington. From 1753 to 1778 they are, it seems, by Mr. Hine Russell.

The entries from 1779 to 1787—the end—were quite certainly made by the Rev. Joseph Davenport. These entries are in his handwriting. We have an authentic specimen of his writing on page thirty-seven of the Register of Deaths, where he made the entry respecting "Mr. Russell" already noticed. The remainder of the entries are, evidently, in this hand. The Reverend Mr. Davenport is usually credited as minister of this parish from 1757 to 1785; but he made two entries of deaths in 1786 and one in 1787 which may indicate that he was still the incumbent of the parish in those years, or at least that it did not then have another.

The Register of Deaths as we have it at present is a volume of manuscript entries, those from 1725 to 1787 being the original entries, while those from 1665 to 1725 were copied from the original record, which is not now known to be in existence.

On the present original record, after an entry dated January 6, 1725, occurs this entry on page twenty-one of the Register of Deaths:

"Registerings of Deaths begun here by me R^d. Hurst Clark of Charles Parish Church 1725 who also copied of this Book of Registers from the Old Reg^{rs}. Book."

The General Assembly once complained that the registers of births and deaths were not kept up as was intended, that the requirement that the entries be made had fallen into "disuse." The register here under consideration contains evidence that the complaint was well founded. For example, the register contains no entry of a death in 1690; it is, of course, possible, but not likely, that none occurred that year. Again, on page fourteen of the register after an entry on October 5, 1714, there is an entry as follows:

"Two years Registerings of Deaths was lost by James Shelton then Clk of this Parish."

The next entry after that of October 5, 1714, was one on November 30, 1716.

As we have seen, there was a similar loss of the record of births for this period, some, at least, of which were supplied by the succeeding clerk of the parish.

Again, the registering of deaths was neglected from 1772 to 1779, as we learn from the entry referred to made by Reverend Joseph Davenport on February 16, 1779. It is a somewhat singular fact that while the registers of births and deaths were evidently kept in the same book, and should have been kept by the same person, yet during the period mentioned, from 1772 to 1779, the register of births was regularly kept, but the register of deaths was wholly neglected.

At the bottom of page seventy of the Register of Births after an entry of a birth on September 24, 1754, there is a notation: "So far sent to the Secretary's office;" in the margin of the record, just below the entry of a birth on August 10, 1755, is a memorandum: "ret^d. to the Secretary's office."

Similar entries are found in the Register of Deaths, as follows:

Opposite the entry of a death on December 19, 1754, occurs this:

"Ret^d to the Sect^y office."

Opposite an entry of July 2, 1755, was this:

"Ret^d. to the Secretary's office."

Below an entry dated November 21, 1755, was this notation:

"(Ret^d. to the Secret^s Office May 10th. 1756.)"

and below the entry of a death on March 17, 1756, was this entry:

"(Ret^d. to the Secet^s. office May 10th 1756)."

While it is clear from these entries that during most of the period covered by the registers the clerks did not make a habit of noting on the registers the dates when they made their returns, yet these few entries indicate that these lists were, at least a part of the time, returned to the office of the Secretary of the Colony as the law required should be done.

CHAPTER IV

The Register of Births of Charles Parish, 1648-1789

In order in fullest measure to make the contents of the Register available for ready reference, the names of all persons whose births are recorded therein have been arranged alphabetically, as in an index.

These Names Thus Arranged Do Not Appear in the Index, but the names of parents, and of all others except those whose names constitute the alphabetical list are indexed in the usual way.

This plan of publication, it will be readily perceived, presents the material of the register in a form most readily and easily consulted, and reduces the volume of the index by approximately one third; the material is thus not only presented in the most readily accessible arrangement, but in the briefest and most compact form as well.

A few pages in facsimile are presented as illustrations. An examination of these and of the entries therefrom as they are presented in the register as here printed in alphabetical arrangement will enable one to thoroughly understand the method here pursued. All of the material of the register is ca.efully preserved. No spelling or phraseology is changed, no name or date or other fact is omitted; only the order of the entries has been rearranged so as to permit the presentation of the list of births in alphabetical order.

Perhaps a word should be said at this point as to the old style and the new style of reckoning time, and changes in the calendar, since the registers of Charles Parish were in part kept under both systems.

When these registers began and for a long time thereafter the twenty-fifth of March was the beginning of the year. This was according to the Jewish computation which was observed in England until changed by statute in 1751. (24, George II,

Ch. 23, Sec. 1.). The first of the year was changed to the first of January.

This statutory change in England was made in order to adopt the reformed calendar of Pope Gregory XIII. The Gregorian calendar was known as the New Style. The calendar as adjusted by Julius Caesar, 45 B. C., was called the Julian Calendar, or Old Style.

Most European countries adopted the New Style long before England. For some time after its adoption by England, it was customary as to dates between January 1st and March 25th, to indicate both systems, giving the old date with the new annexed to it, thus: "January 1631/2," but the use of the old style was gradually dropped.

In September, 1752, eleven days were taken out of the calendar in order to make the civil year conform as nearly as possible to the solar year.

There is a good explanation of the whole subject in *Hening's Statutes at Large*, I, 393-395.

Before the alteration of the calendar in 1752, when March 25 was the beginning of the year, it was usual to write the months terminating in "er" thus: September, "7ber," or seventh month; October, "8ber;" November, "9ber," etc.

The entries in the Register of Births, arranged in alphabetical order, as above explained, are as follows:

A

Albeitton, Thomas, son of Ralph by Mary, b. Aug. 1, 1682.
    [Note: This name may be "Albritton"].
Albritton, Agnes, dau. of Thomas by Agnes, b. March 13, 1707.
Albritton, Benjamin, son of Ralph by Mary, b. July 22, 1700.
Albritton, Edward, son of Ralph by Mary, b. Dec. 17, 1686.
Albritton, James, son of Thomas by Agnes, b. September 17, 1705.
Albritton, John, son of Ralph by Mary, b. Sept. 2, 1688.
Albritton, Ralph, son of Ralph by Mary, b. July 10, 1696.

Albritton, Richard, son of Ralph by Mary, b. April 19, 1698.

Albritton, William, son of Ralph by Mary, b. July 7, 1691.

Aldridge, James, son of Henry by Sarah, b. Sept. 27, bap. Sept. 29, 1720.

Allen, Charles, son of William by Agnes, b. July 18, 1672.

Allen, Edmund, son of Richard and Ann, b. Nov. 13, 1751.

Allen, Henry, [twin with John], son of Henry and Sarah, b. Dec. 29, 1676, bap. March 13, 1768.

Allen, John, [twin with Henry], son of Henry and Sarah, b. Dec. 29, 1767, bap. March 13, 1768.

Allen, Mary, dau. of Thomas by Sarah, b. Feb. 14, 1719, bap. May 15, 1720.

Allen, William, son of William by Agnes, b. Jan. 1, 1673.

Allen, William, son of John and Frances, b. Dec. 1, 1766, bap. Jan. 11, 1767.

Allen, William, son of Richard and Ann, b. Oct. 24, bap. Dec. 24, 174[9].

Ambros, Sarah, dau. of John by Rachell, "was born in the year 1680."

Ambrose, John, son of John by Rachel, b. Oct. 1, 1682.

Anderson, John, son of Matthias by Hannah, b. July 5, 1706.

Anderson, Sarah, dau. of Matthias by Hannah, b. June 12, 170[8].

Applin, Richard, son of Richard by Margarett, b. Aug. 18, 1685.

Archer, Ann, dau. of Abraham by Amy, b. Feb. 3, bap. March 20, 1720.

Archer, John, son of Abraham by Amee, b. April 29, bap. June 3, 1723.

Armistead, Anne, dau. of Edward by Jane, b. Aug. — 1746, bap. Aug. — 17[46].

Armistead, Edward, son of Edward by Ja[ne], b. April 1, 1749, bap. April 30, [1749].

Armistead, Elizabeth Hawkins, dau. of William and Eliz*., b. July 27, 1800. (Back River).

Armisteàd, Francis Mennis, son of Samuel and Frankey, b. May 2, bap. June 2, 1782. (Eliz⁰. City).

Armistead, John Patrick, son of Robᵗ. and Hannah, b. April 7, bap. May 13, 1787.

Armistead, Judith, dau. of Wm. and Constance, b. July 29, bap. Aug. 8, 1762.

Armistead, Mary, dau. of Wm. and Constance, b. Dec. 22, 1765, bap. Jan. 26, 1766. (Eliz. City).

Armistead, Mary Manson, b. Nov. 6, 1789.

    [Note: Names of parents not given. The whole entry is: "Mary Manson Armistead born 6ᵗʰ Novʳ. 1789 & baptized by the Revᵈ. Mr. Shield."]

Armistead, Moss, son of Edward by Jane, b. May 4, bap. June 8, 1740.

Armistead, Rebecca, dau. of Edward and Martha, b. Jan. 22, 1761.

Armistead, Robert, son of Edward by Jane, b. Feb. 1737/8 bap. April 9, 1738.

Armistead, Robert, son of Wm and Constance, b. Sept. 30, bap. Oct. 30, 1768. ([ ]iz⁰ City).

Armistead, Samuel, son of Edward and Martha, b. Sept. 9, bap. Oct. 9, 1757.

Armistead, Samuel, son of Samˡ. and Frankey, b. June 6, bap. June 12, 1784. ([ ] City).

Armistead, William, son of Wm. and Constance, b. Aug. 16, bap. Nov. 17, 1771.

Armistead, William, son of Robert and Hannah, b. March 14, bap. May 1, 1785.

Ashbey, William, son of William by Sarah, b. Dec. 1, 1681.

Avory, Ann, dau. of James by Catherine, b. Feb. 15, 1691.

Avory, Catherine, dau. of James by Catherine, b. June 11, 17[04].

Avory, Elizabeth, dau. of Thomas by Sarah, b. July 30, bap. Aug. 31, 1722.

Avory, James, son of James by Catherine, b. April 9, 1700.

Avory, James, son of Thomas by Sarah, b. Dec. 11, bap. Jan. 24, 1724.

Avory, John, son of John by Edith, b. [March(?)] 23, 169[3].

Avory, John, son of James by Catherine, b. Dec. 24, 1694.

Avory, John, son of John by Ann, b. Sept. 9, bap. Oct. 28, 1722.

Avory, Mary, dau. of James by Catherine, b. March 29, 1689.

Avory, Thomas, son of James by Catherine, b. June 8, 1697.

Avory, Thomas, son of John by Ann, b. Dec. 11, bap. Dec. 13, 1719.

Avory, Thomas, son of Thomas by Sarah, b. Aug. 17, bap. Sept. 17, 1727.

B

Babor, Edward, son of Robert by Sarah, b. Oct. 12, 1686.

Badget, Mary, dau. of John by Marg'., b. April 24, 1749, bap. June 14, [ ].

Badgett, Ann, dau. of Thomas and Ann, b. Aug. 7, 1752.

Badgett, John, son of John and Margaret, b. Jan. 1, and bap. —, 1755.

Badgett, John, son of Thomas and Sarah, b. March 6, bap. April 4, 1756.

Badjett, Thomas, son of John and Margaret, b. Sept. 10, bap. Oct. 6, 1751.

Bains, Martha, dau. of John and Eliz'., b. Nov. 17, bap. Dec. 21, 1777.

Baker, Bartholomew, son of Saml. by Constant, b. Sept. 23, 1673.

Baker, Hannah, dau. of Samuel by Constant, b. Dec. 19, 1674.

Baker, Mary, dau. of Samuel by Constant, b. Jan. 17, 1678.

Baley, Sarah, dau. of Wm. and Anna, b. —, bap. Dec. 26, 1768. (Eliz'. City).

Baley, William, son of Wm. and Anna, b. Oct. 5, bap. Nov. 3, 1765.

Banks, Nancy, dau. of James Nicholas and Hannah, b. Aug. 16, bap. Sept. 20, 1783.

Baptis, Edward, son of Edward and Mary, b. April 28, bap. June 6, 1756.

Baptis, John, son of John and Sarah, b. Aug. 29, bap. Oct. 10, 1756.

Baptis, Mary, dau. of John and Sarah, b. May 18, bap. June 15, 1755.

Baptist, Diana, [twin with Lucy], dau. of Edward and Mary, b. Feb. 14, 1760.

Baptist, Edward, son of John and Sarah, b. Dec. 21, 1765, bap. Jan. 26, 1766.

Baptist, Frances, dau. of John and Sarah, b. March 23, bap. May 1, 1768.

Baptist, Lucy, [twin with Diana], dau. of Edward and Mary, b. Feb. 14, 1760.

Baptist, Martha, dau. of Edward and Mary, b. ——, bap. Dec. 8, 1751.

[Baptist], Nancy Gibbons, dau. of John and Sarah, b. [The entry of birth and baptism is gone, through wear of margin, as is the name of the family. The index indicates the name is Baptist. The entry before this is dated April 22, 1776, and the next following is May 12, 1776.]

Baptist, Rebecca, dau. of Edward and Mary, b. Jan. 10, bap. Feb. 10, 1754.

Baptist, Robert, son of John and Sarah, b. May 10, bap. June 13, 1762.

Baptist, Sarah, dau. of Edward and Mary, b. Aug. 19, bap. Sept. 21, 1757.

    [Note: On the margin opposite this name appears the following entry: "1820

$$\frac{1757}{63}."]$$

Baptist, Sarah, dau. of John and Sarah, b. June 18, 1760.

Barber, Leonard, son of Edward by Elizabeth, bap. Dec. 28, 1676.

Barber, Thomas, son of Thomas by Sarah, b. July 10, 1711.

Barham, Frances, dau. of Robert and Frances, b. July 9, bap. Aug. 8, 1773.*

Barham, John, son of Robert and Frances, b. Aug. 1, bap. Aug. 21, 1768.

Barker, Anabella, dau. of Mary, servant to Sam¹. Toplady, b. Aug. 20, 1691.

[The name may possibly be Arrabella Barker. It is difficult to decipher. It is certainly one or the other.]

Barnes, Aaron, son of Matthew by Mary, b. Oct. 20, bap. Nov. 21, 1725.

Barnes, Aaron, son of Aaron and Becca, b. Dec. 12, 1782, bap. March 23, 1783. (Warwick).

Barnes, Ann, dau. of Matthew by Annamaria, b. Dec. 1, 1700.

Barnes, Anne, dau. of John by Bridget, b. Nov. . . 1742, bap. Jan. 2, 1742.

Barnes, Bryan, son of Matthew by Mary, b. Jan. 16, 1712.

Barnes, Bryan, son of John by Bridget, b. May 28, bap. July 8, 1739.

Barnes, Christjan, dau. of Brian by Martha, b. March 21, 1676.

Barnes, Elizabeth, dau. of Matthew, by Anna Mariah, b. July 27, 1695.

Barnes, Elizabeth, dau. of John by Bridget, b. Oct. 18, bap. Oct. 24, 1741.

Barnes, Elizabeth, dau. of Aaron and Mary, b. Oct. 22, 1762.

Barnes, Frances, dau. of Matthew by Mary, b. Nov. 17, 1707.

Barnes, Frances, dau. of Mattw. by Mary, b. March 27, bap. May 3, 1729.

Barnes, Franky, dau. of Nathaniel and Diana, b. Feb. 13, bap. March 18, 1753.

Barnes, John, son of Matthew by Mary, b. May 31, 1710.

Barnes, John, son of Nathaniel and Elizabeth, b. Dec. 29, bap. Feb. 3, 1750.

Barnes, Johnny, son of Nathaniel and Dianah, b. July 8, bap. Aug. 12, 1755.

Barnes, Johnson, son of Nathaniel by Diana, b. May 25, bap. June 26, 1748.

Barnes, Martha, dau. of Matthew by Anna Maria, b. June 15, 1698.

Barnes, Martha, dau. of John by Bridget, b. Jan. 7, bap. Feb. 9, 1734.

Barnes, Mary, dau. of Matthew by Mary, b. Dec. 3, bap. Jan. 12, 1722.

Barnes, Mary, dau. of John by Bridget, b. Jan. 27, bap. Feb. 23, 1736.

Barnes, Mary, dau. of Bryant and Anne, b. June 25, bap. July 28, 1765. (of Warwick).

Barnes, Matthew, son of Matthew by Mary, b. Oct. 23, bap. Nov. 3, 1732.

Barnes, Matthew, son of Aaron and Mary, b. Jan. 7, bap. Feb. 10, 1765.

Barnes, Nathaniel, son of Matthew by Mary, b. Aug. 1, bap. Aug. 31, 1718.

Barnes, William, son of Aaron and Rebecca, b. Aug. 26, bap. Oct. 25, 1778. (Warwick).

Barnet, Joice, dau. of Wm. and Hannah, b. June 8, bap. Aug. 3, 1766.

Barns, Elizabeth, dau. of Brian, by Martha, b. July 17, 1673.

Bartlet, Dianah, dau. of Michael by Mary, b. July 18, 1657.

Bartlett, Alexander, son of Alexander, by Catherine, b. Nov. 21, bap. Dec. 2, 1720.

Bartlett, Michael, son of Michael by Mary, b. May 10, 1662.

Bartlett, Michael, son of John by Elinor, b. Sept. 13, 1674.

Bartlett, Samuel, son of Michael by Francis, b. June 26, 1684.

Batts, Anthony, son of Anthony by Mary, b. Nov. 22, 1686.

Bayley, Hannah, dau. of Thomas by Edith, bap. May 14, 1688.

Bayley, Thomas, son of Thomas by Edith, b. Nov. 1, 1672.

Bayley, William, son of Thomas "by Edith his wife of Elizabeth City," bap. Nov. 15, 1685.

Bean, Daniel, son of John by Ann, b. March 30, 1703.

Bean, Elizabeth, dau. of Wm. and Sarah, b. Feb. 3, bap. March 23, 1766, (Eliz*. City).

Bean, Lidwell, dau. of Lawflin by Elizabeth, b. Feb. 24, 1716, bap. June 16, 1717.

Bean, Martha, dau. of Wm. and Sarah, b. July 7, bap. Aug. 19, 1770.

Bearne, Mas.., son of Brian by Martha, b. Jan. 24, 1668.

Bell, Ann, dau. of Thomas by Priscilla, b. Feb. 8, 1690.

Bell, Mary, dau. of Francis by Ann, of Elizabeth City County, b. March 4, 1671.

Bell, Mary, dau. of Thomas by Mary, b. Nov. 2, bap. Dec. 1, 1723.

Bell, Robert, son of Thomas by Priscilla, b. Jan. 14, 16[99]. Of York Parish.

Bell, William, son of Thomas by Priscilla, b. Feb. 26, 1692.

Belven, Nancy, dau. of Wm. and Mary, b. Nov. 21, 1768, bap. Jan. 22, 1769.

Belvin, Mary, dau. of Wm. and Mary, b. Feb. 2, bap. March 23, 1766.

Belvin, William, son of William and Mary, b. Jan. 14, bap. Feb. 12, 1758.

Bennet, Catherine, dau. of James by Elizabeth, b. Feb. 19, 1700.

Bennet, Charles, son of James by Elizabeth, b. Nov. 1, 17[03].

Bennet, Charles, son of Charles decd. by Eliz*., b. June 20, 1736, bap. privately the same day.

Bennet, Elizabeth, dau. of James by Elizabeth, b. Dec. 28, 170[9].

Bennet, Elizabeth, dau. of Charles by Elizabeth, b. Dec. 5, bap. Dec. 25, 1729.

Bennet, Elizabeth, dau. of Charles by Elizabeth, b. Sept. 4, bap. Oct. 1, 1732.

Bennet, Frances, dau. of Charles by Elizabeth, b. July 29, bap. Aug. 27, 1727.

Bennet, James, son of James by Ann, b. May 8, 1691.

Bennet, James, son of James by Jane, b. Jan. 28, 1713.

Bennet, John, son of James by Jane, b. Dec. 1, bap. Dec. 24, 1716.

Bennet, Martin, son of James by Elizabeth, b. Oct. 25, 1706.

Bennet, Mary, dau. of James by Jane, b. July 16, bap. Aug. 16, 1719.

Bennet, Mary, dau. of Charles by Eliz*., b. Dec. 7, bap. Jan. 26, 1734.

Bennet, Sarah, dau. of James by Elizabeth, b. June 24, 1712.

Berrey, James, son of James by Mary, b. Oct. 2, bap. Dec. 6, 1719. Elizabeth City County.
    [The name is indexed Berry].

Berry, Charles, son of John by Elinor, b. Aug. 19, [1703].

Berry, Edward, son of Edward and Eliz*., b. Dec. 26, 1785, bap. March 12, 1786.
    [Note: In the margin under the word "Mulatto," opposite a previous entry is "Do"—for ditto. This seems to indicate that Edward Berry was a mulatto. However, above the word "Mulatto" in the margin appears the word "Warwick." It is a *possibility* that the "Do" was intended to "ditto" that word instead of the word "Mulatto"].

Berry, Frances, dau. of James and Mary, b. Sept. 5, bap. Dec. 21, 1777.

Berry, Giles, son of John by Elinor, b. March 4, 170[4].

Berry, James, son of James and Mary, b. May 14, bap. June 18, 1769.

Berry, James, son of Edward and Martha, b. June 5, bap. July 9, 1775.

Berry, John, son of John by Margarett, b. Oct. 27, 1691.

Berry, John, son of John by Mary, b. Feb. 22, [1699].

Berry, Joseph, son of John by Elinor, b. Nov. 11, 1710.

Berry, Martha, dau. of Edward and Martha, b. April 23, bap. June 14, 1778.

Berry, Mary, dau. of John by Elinor, b. April 12, 171[3]?

Berry, Sally, dau. of Edw⁴. and Eliz*., b. March 4, bap. May 18, 1783. ([ ]*, City).

Berry, William, son of John by Margarett, b. July 15, 1690.

Bevens, John, son of Thomas by Mary, bap. April 9, 1672.

Bevens, Mary, dau. of Thomas by Mary, b. March 2, 1673.

Bircher, Ann, dau. of Bartholomew by Elizabeth, b. July 29, 1707.

Bircher, Bartholomew, son of Bartholomew by Elizabeth, b. Feb. 11, 17[08].

Bircher, Dorithy, dau. of Bartholomew by Dorithy, b. Aug. 14, bap. Sept. 17, 1717.

Bircher, John, son of Bartholomew by Dorithy, b. Jan. 28, bap. March 6, 1719.

Bircher, Lewis[?], son of James and Elizabeth, b. July 7, bap. Aug. 5, 1750.

Bircher, Martha, dau. of Bartholomew by Dorithy, b. July 7, bap. Aug. 13, 1727.

Bircher, Mary, dau. of James by Martha, b. Dec. 26, bap. March 11, 1743.

Bircher, Sarah, dau. of James by Martha, b. Sept. 15, 1747, bap. Nov. 1, 174[7].

Bircher, William, son of Bartholomew by Dorithy, b. Jan. 19, bap. Feb. 18, 1721.

Birchir, John, son of Bartholomew by Elizabeth, b. November 1, 1705.

Birdsong, Agnes, dau. of James by Eliz*. b. July 9, bap. Sept. —, 1736.

Birdsong, Anne, dau. of John by Mary, b. April 24, bap. May 30, 1742.

Birdsong, Bennet, son of John by Mary, b. July 13, bap. Aug. 19, 1739.

Birdsong, Bennet, son of Charles by Frances, b. Nov. 14, 1746, bap. Jan. 6, 174[6].

Birdsong, Edmund, son of John by Mary, b. Feb. 12, 1737/8, bap. Feb. 18, 1737/8.

Birdsong, Enos, son of John by Sarah, b. Jan. 8, bap. Jan. 13, 1735.

Birdsong, Frances, dau. of John by Elizabeth, b. July 8, bap. Sept. 27, 1719.

Birdsong, James, son of John by Hannah, b. March 22, 1726, bap. May 7, 1727.

Birdsong, John, son of John by Sarah, b. Aug. 26, bap. Sept. 30, 1733.

Birdsong, John, son of Charles and Frances, b. Sept. 15, bap. Oct. 21, 1750.

Birdsong, Mary, dau. of John by Mary, b. — 1745, bap. Feb. 16, 1745.

Bivens, Thomas, son of Thomas by Mary, b. Feb. 10, 1670.

Blackstone, Alice, dau. of William by Elizabeth, bap. March 30, 1701.

Blackstone, James, son of William by Elizabeth, b. Dec. 18, [1698].

Blackstone, Sarah, dau. of William by Elizabeth, bap. March 20, 169[3].

Blackstone, William, son of William by Elizabeth, b. April 12, 1696.

Blake, John, son of Acy and Frances, b. Oct. 11, 1784, bap. April 17, 1785. (Hillsboro, N. Carolina).

Bland, Martha, dau. of Thos. and Eliz*. b. Feb. 9, bap. May 11, 1766.

Blith, Edith, dau. of Henry by Jane, b. Feb. 22, 1689.

Bond, Anne, dau. of John by Anne, b. Dec. 1, 1740, bap. Jan. 18, 1740/41.

Bond, Elizabeth, dau. of William by Ann, b. Feb. 20, 1692.

Bond, Elizabeth, dau. of John by Ann, b. Jan. 25, bap. Feb. 24, 1733.

Bond, Elizabeth, dau. of John by Sarah, b. July 30, bap. Aug. 21, 1743.

Bond, James, son of John by Ann, b. Oct. 28, bap. Nov. 26, 1732.

Bond, John, son of William by Ann, b. Oct. 1, 1696.

Bond, John, son of John by Ann, b. Jan. 5, bap. Feb. 19, 1720.

Bond, Mary, dau. of John by Ann, b. Feb. 22, bap. March 7, 1717.

Bond, Robert, son of John by Ann, b. July 9, bap. Aug. 4, 1728.

Bond, Sarah, dau. of John by Sarah, b. April 25, bap. June 3, 1747.

Bond, Thomas, son of John by Anne, b. June 29, bap. July 30, 1738.

Bond, William, son of William by Ann, b. July 5, 1689.

Bond, William, son of William by Jane, b. June 17, bap. Aug. 14, 1720.

Bond, William, son of John by Ann, b. Jan. 10, bap. Feb. 14, 1724.

Booker, Richard, son of George and Mary, b. Jan. 17, bap. March 5, 1779. (Eliz⁴. City).

Borradale, Henry, son of Henry by Elizabeth, b. April 3, [1708].

Borrodell, Ann, dau. of Henry by Elizabeth, b. Dec. 24, 1713.

Borrodell, Elizabeth, dau. of Henry by Elizabeth, b. Jan. 6, 1705.

Borrodell, Mary, dau. of Henry by Elizabeth, b. Jan. 10, 1710.

Borrodell, Sarah, dau. of Henry by Elizabeth, b. Jan. 6, 17[03].

Borrodell, Thomas, son of Henry by Judith, b. Oct. 1, bap. Dec. 14, 1720.

Borrowdell, John, son of Henry by Elizabeth, b. Oct. 20, 1701.

Boutwell, Elizabeth. dau. of Edwᵈ. and Frances, b. Nov. 9, bap. Dec. 24, 1780. ([Eliz⁴.] City).

[Boutwell], Martha, dau. of Edw. and Fra[ ], b. Oct. 1, bap. Dec. [1]?, 1782.

[Note: This entry is at the top of page 108, and is partly worn away. The name Boutwell does not appear, but is supplied from the index,—in this way: The name "Martha" is perfectly distinct,—and appears only once on page 108. A search of the index discloses: "Boutwell, Martha," on page 108.]

Boutwell, Roe, son of Edward and Frances, b. March 31, bap. April 25, 1779.

Bowen, Anne, dau. of Wm. and Sarah, b. Oct. 8, bap. Nov. 7, 1779.

Bowen, Diana, dau. of John and Lucy, b. Sept. 30, bap. Oct. 13, 1765. (Of York Hampton.)

Bowen, John, son of William and Mary, b. Dec. 29, 1775, bap. Feb. 4, 1776.

Bowin, Lucy, dau. of Wm. and Mary, b. Jan. 2, bap. Feb. 3, 1771.

Bowler, Sarah, dau. of James Bowler by Suzannah Townzen, b. April 13, 171[3].

Branton, Deborah, dau. of Thomas by Elizabeth, bap. April 22, 1683.

Brester [or Brister], John, son of John by Elizabeth, b. Nov. 6, 1689.

Bridges, Edward, son of Edward, by Mary, b. April 2, 1678.

Bridges, Mary, dau. of Edward by Mary, b. Jan. 12, 1675.

Brighting, Sarah, dau. of Samuel by Mary, b. Nov. 15, 1668.

Britton, Rebecca, dau. of Benj*. by Susann[ ], b. May 4, 1749, bap. May 6, 174[9].

Britton, Thomas, son of Thomas by Sarah, b. June 25, bap. July 16, 1722.

Britton, William, son of Benjam", by Susanna, b. Oct. 10, 1745, bap. Nov. — [—].

Brodie, Alexander, son of John by Martha, b. Feb. 4, bap. Feb. 6, 1726.

Broster, Elizabeth, dau. of John by Elizabeth, b. June 17, 1698.

Broster, James, son of John by Elizabeth, b. March 25, 1690.

Broster, John, son of John by Elizabeth, b. March 9, 1694.

Brown, Ann, dau. of William by Mary, b. Nov. 24, 1713.

Brown, Ann, dau. of Robt. by Mary, b. July 20, bap. Aug. 22, 1736.

Brown, Anne, dau. of William and Mary, b. Jan. 29, bap. June 10, 1781. ([Eli]z*. City).

Brown, Betsy, Dau. of William and Mary, b. May 29, bap. June 27, 1773.

Brown, Constant, dau. of Robert by Mary, b. Jan. 2, 1741/2, bap. March 1741[/2].

Brown, Dixon, son of Robert by Mary, b. Sept. 29, 1746, bap. Nov. 6, 1746.

Brown, James, son of John, of Denbigh Parish, by Hannah, "baptized here Nov*. 6th, 1668."

Brown, James, son of James by Eliz*. b. Feb. 22, "1748/9," bap. March 24, 1748.

Brown, Mary, dau. of Robert by Mary, b. Jan. 6, 1739/40, bap. Feb. 24, 1739/40.

Brown, Mary, dau. of James and Catherine, b. Nov. 27, bap. Dec. 31, 1752.

Brown, Mary, dau. of Wm. and Mary, b. Oct. 12, bap. Nov. 11, 1770.

Brown, Mary, dau. of Rich⁴. and Mary, b. June 14, bap. Nov. 2, 1783.

Brown, Phillip, son of Robert by Mary, b. Feb. 7, 1748/9, bap. Mar. 26, 1749.

Brown, Rachel, dau. of Robert and Mary, b. Oct. 18, bap. Nov. 16, 1755.

Brown, Robert, son of William by Ann, b. March 1, 1706. Denbeigh Parish.

Brown, Robert, son of Rob*. and Mary, b. April 2, bap. . . . ., 1752.

Brown, William, son of Robert by Mary, b. March 1, 1743, bap. April 1, 1744.

Bryan, Elizabeth, dau. of Timothy by Elizabeth, b. Oct. 27, bap. Nov. 9, 1717.

Bryan, John, son of Timothy by Elizabeth, b. Sept. 10, 1711.

Bryan, Sarah, dau. of Timothy by Elizabeth, b. Dec. 14, 1713.

Bryan, Thomas, son of Richard and Mary, b. March 29, bap. May 18, 1783.

Bryan, Timothy, son of Timothy by Sarah, b. April 14, bap. July 10, 1723.

Buck, Anne, dau. of John and Elizabeth, of "Eliz⁴. City." b. Feb. 3, bap. March 6, 1757.

Buck, "Anne, dau. of Fanny Buck, Born June 5ᵗʰ Bap. August 14ᵗʰ 1774."

Buck, James Lebe, "son of Fanny Buck born 8ᵗʰ March, Baptized 23ᵈ June 1771."

Bumpass, James, son of Robert and Uphan, b. March 17, bap. May 7, 1775. (Eliz⁴. City).

Bumpass, Mary, dau. of Robert and Uphan, b. March 1, bap. May 4, 1769. ([Elizabeth] City).

Bunoughs, Thomas, son of John by Eliz⁴. b. July 6, bap. Aug. 3, 1740.

Burcher, Lewis, son of Bartholomew by Dorithy, b. Jan. 7, bap. Feb. 21, 1723.

Burcher, Sarah, dau. of Bartholomew by Dorithy, b. Sept. 13, bap. 24, "8ber," 1725.

Burcher, William, son of James and Elizabeth, b. Oct. 16, bap. Nov. 16, 1755.

Burcher, William, son of James and Lucy, b. Feb. 22, bap. April 30, 1775.

Burgess, Thomas Powell, son of Wm. and Mary, b. March 15, bap. July 29, 1783. ([ ] City).

Burkhead, Elizabeth, dau. of Samuel by Sarah, b. Jan. 6, bap. Feb. 10, 1716.

Burkhead, Elizabeth, dau. of William by Elizabeth, b. March 6, 169[3].

Burkhead, Isabell, dau. of William by.Elizabeth, b. Aug. 10, 1696.

Burkhead, Jane, dau. of William by Elizabeth, b. Nov. 19, 1691.

Burkhead, Samuel, son of William by Elizabeth, bap. Feb. 5, 1686.

Burkhead, Sarah, dau. of Samuel by Sarah, b. April 20, bap. May 24, 1719.

Burkhead, William, son of William by Elizabeth, b. May 1, 1689.

Burnham, John, son of Thomas by Mary, b. Nov. 10, [1703].

Burnham, John, son of John and Patsey, b. Oct. 15, bap. Nov. 13, 1785. ([Wa]rwick).

Burnham, Lockey Miles Curtis, son of John and Patsey, b. Nov. 8, bap. Dec. 28, 1783. ([War]wick).

Burnham, Richard, son of Thomas by Sarah, b. July 18, 17[13].

Burnham, Sarah, dau. of Thomas by Sarah, b. June 24, 1705.

Burnham, Thomas, son of Thomas by Sarah, b. February 21, 17[09].

Burnham, William, son of Thomas by Sarah, b. Oct. 4, [1707].

Burt, John, son of Harwood and Margaret, b. May 21, bap. June 13, 1762.

Burton, Dianah, dau. of James by Elizabeth, b. March 2, 1715.

Burton, Elizabeth,
> The full entry is: "Elizabeth a legitimate daughter of Mary Burton [the name may possibly be Buxton. It is indistinct on the record] born December the 27th 1727 baptized March the 24th 1727."

Burton, James, son of James by Elizabeth, b. April 12, 1709.

Burton, John, son of James by Elizabeth, b. Dec. 27, 1712.

Burton, Martha, dau. of Lewis by Elizabeth, b. Aug. 4, bap. Sept. 7, 1717.

Burton, Mary, dau. of James by Elizabeth, b. Dec. 14, 1705.

Burton, Phillip, son of Lewis by Elizabeth, b. Aug. 16, 1712.

Button, Edward, son of Lewis by Ursella, b. Jan. 17, 1684.

Button, Elizabeth, dau. of James by Elizabeth, b. July 5, 1710.

Button, James, son of Lewis by Ursley, b. March 15, 1679.

Button, Lewis, son of Lewis by Ursella, "born baptized," May 2, 1687.

Button, Mary, dau. of Lewis by Ursley, b. July 31, 1682.

Butts, Mary, dau. of Anthony by Mary, b. Sept. 4, 1684.

Byby, Thomas, son of Ann Byby [No father named], b. Nov. 17, 1689.

C

Cable, Thomas, son of Edward by Sarah, bap. June 6, 1671.

Calbert, Alex^r. Johnson, son of Richard and Martha, b. Nov. 16, bap. Dec. 26, 1779.

Calbert, Hope, dau. of Richard and Martha, b. Feb. 10, bap. April 9, 1769.

Calbert, John, son of Richard and Martha, b. .., bap. March 16, 1766.

Calbert, Martha (twin with Mary), dau. of Rich^d. and Martha, b. March 5, bap. April 12, 1772.

Calbert, Mary (twin with Martha), dau. of Rich^d. and Martha, b. March 5, bap. April 12, 1772.

Callowhill, Ann, dau. of Francis by Ann Chapman, bap. Sept. 18, 1688.

Callowhill, Ann, dau. of James by Mary, b. Nov. 16, bap. Dec. 23, 1717.

Callowhill, Frances, dau. of Francis by Ann, b. Oct. 12, 1693.

Callowhill, Francis, "son of Francis by Ann Chapman widow," b. Aug. 13, 1686.

Callowhill, James, son of Francis by Ann, b. Nov. 5, 1691.

Callowhill, Nathaniel, son of Francis by Ann, b. Dec. 15, 1689.

Calthorp, Ann, dau. of James by Elizabeth, b. Feb. 15, 1672.

Calthorp, Anthony, son of Elistrange by Mary, b. Aug. 4, 1712.

Calthorp, Barbara, dau. of James by Elizabeth, b. May 23, 1683.

Calthorp, Butts, son of Charles by Elinor, b. Dec. .. bap. Feb. 6, 1731.

Calthorp, Charles, son of James by Elizabeth, b. Feb. 17, 1687.

Calthorp, Charles, son of Elistrange by Mary, b. Oct. 8, 17[09].

Calthorp, Christopher, son of James by Elizabeth, b. Feb. 20, 1672.

Calthorp, Elimelech [twin with Ruth], son of James and Elizabeth, b. Jan. 6, 1710.

Calthorp, Elistrange, son of James by Elizabeth, b. Sept. 4, 1680.

Calthorp, Elistrange, son of Charles by Amee, b. July 21, bap. same day, 1718.

Calthorp, Elizabeth, dau. of James by Elizabeth, b. Nov. 26, 1677.

Calthorp, Elizabeth, dau. of James by Elizabeth,
"No date when born" is the entry in the register. It occurs between one of Dec. 6, 1697, and another of Feb. 1, 1697.

Calthorp, Elizabeth, dau. of Elistrange by Ann, b. Dec. 21, bap. Jan. 24, 1722.

Calthorp, Frances, dau. of Elimelech by Mary, b. Sept. 19, bap. Oct. 30, 1729.

Calthorp, James, son of Elistrange by Mary, b. March 27, 1707.

Calthorp, James, son of Elimelech by Mary, b. June 2, bap. July 4, 1731.

Calthorp, John, son of Elimelech by Mary, b. Feb. 19, bap. Feb. 25, 1732.

Calthorp, Mary, dau. of Charles by Elinor, b. . ., bap. Feb. 10, 1733.

Calthorp, Ruth, [twin with Elimelech], dau. of James and Elizabeth, b. Jan. 6, 1710.

Calthorpe, Elizabeth, dau. of Charles by Elinor, b. . . . ., bap. Aug. 19, 1739.

Calthorpe, Frances, dau. of Charles by Elinor, b. Sept. 6, bap. Oct. 9, 1737.

Calthorpe, James, son of James, by Elizabeth, b. March 5, 1674.

Calthorpe, James, son of Charles by Elinor, b. Jan. 23, 1740/1, bap. April 5, 1741.

Calthorpe, Mary, dau. of Elimelech by Mary, b. Feb. 8, bap.
    March 10, 1733.

Calthorpe, Sarah, dau. of Charles by Elinor, b. March . ., bap.
    April 4, 1735.

Campbell, Charles, son of Charles by Sarah, b. Dec. 14, bap.
    Jan. 16, 1731.

Campbell, James, son of Charles by Sarah, b. March 22, 1732,
    bap. May 6, 1733.

Cantre, Ann, dau. of William by Ann, b. March 9, 1677.

Carnate, Mary, dau. of Cornelius by Ann, b. April 4, 1692.

Carter, Edward (twin with James), son of Jones and Mary,
    b. Sept. 29, bap. Oct. 10, 1776.

Carter, Hope, dau. of Thomas by Suzan, b. June 17, [1699].

Carter, James, (twin with Edward), son of Jones and Mary,
    b. Sept. 29, bap. Oct. 10, 1776.

Carter, Robert, son of Thomas by Susan, b. Nov. 10, 1695.

Cary, Anne, dau. of John and Sally, b. Nov. 7, 1767, bap.
    April 10, 1768. (Warwick).

Cary, Edward, son of John and Mary, b. Sept. 9, bap. Oct. 9,
    1757.

Cary, Gill Armistead, son of John and Susanna, b. March 18,
    bap. May 8, 1783. ([   ] City).

Cary, John, son of John and Mary, b. Oct. 16, bap. Dec. 5,
    1760.

Cary, Wilson Jefferson, son of Wilson and Jane Barbara, b.
    Feb. 6, bap. April 13, 1784. ([   ]ick).

Cattilla, Abraham, son of Matthew by Judith, b. March 18,
    1729/30, bap. May 3, 1730.

Cattilla, Angelica, dau. of William by Hannah, b. Dec. 10, bap.
    March 5, 1726.

Cattilla, Ann, dau. of "Mary Cattilla by Christopher Robinson,"
    b. March 31, 1710.

Cattilla, Ann, dau. of Abraham by Mary, b. March 26, bap.
    April 25, 1750.

Cattilla, Catherine, dau. of Mary, [other parent not named], b. Nov. 1, 17[03]. Elizabeth City County.

Cattilla, Edward, son of Matthew by Mary, b. Sept. 8, 1693.

Cattilla, Edward, son of Matthew by Judith, b. Dec. 11, bap. Jan. 11, 1724.

Cattilla, Elizabeth, dau. of Edward by Elizabeth, b. March 31, bap. May 23, 1725.

Cattilla, Frances, dau. of Matthew by Sarah, b. March 15, bap. March 2[7], 1740/1.

Cattilla, James, son of Mary, b. Sept. 16, 1693.
    [Father's name not mentioned].

Cattilla, John, son of Matthew by Sarah, b. Jan. 6, bap. March 12, 1737/8.

Cattilla, Judith, dau. of William by Ann, b. Dec. 20, 17[03].

Cattilla, Martha, dau. of Matthew by Sarah, b. Nov. 9, bap. Jan. 8, 1743.

Cattilla, Mary, dau. of Matthew by Sarah, b. Oct. 22, 1747, bap. Nov. 22, 17[47].

Cattilla, Matthew, son of Matthew by Mary, b. Sept. 2, 1697.

Cattilla, Matthew, son of Mary, bap. Dec. 12, 1700. [Father not named].

Cattilla, Matthew, son of Matthew by Judith, b. Sept. 20, "baptized private Novr. 5, 1732."

Cattilla, Rachel, dau. of Matthew by Judith, b. Jan. 18, bap. Feb. 16, 1734.

Cattilla, Sarah, dau. of Matthew by Judith, b. Sept. 20, bap. Oct. 29, 1727.

Cattilla, William, son of William by Ann, bap. April 12, 1702.

Cattilla, William, son of Matthew by Sarah, b. Sept. 14, bap. Sept. 21, 1746.

Cattillo, Matthew, son of Edward by Elizabeth, b. May 30, bap. June 26, 1720.

Cattillow, Anne, dau. of Edwd. and Anne, b. Aug. 4, 1770, bap. March 3, 1771.

Cattillow, Nancy, "bastard child of Martha Cattillow," b. Sept. ...., bap. Oct. 12, 1766.

Challice, Samuel, son of John and Dorothy, (of Warwick), b. Jan. 28, bap. May 5, 1765.

Challis, Lucy, dau. of John and Dorothy, b. Dec. 14, 1774, .bap. Feb. 19, 1775.

Challis, Mary, dau. of John and Dorothy, b. June 14, bap. Aug. 25, 1771.

Challis, Wm. Wager, son of John and Dorothy, (of "Warwᵏ.") b. March 14, bap. May 9, 1756.

> [Note: Following this entry is the notation: "Retᵃ. to the Secretary's office May 10, 1756."]

Chapman, Ann, dau. of John by Elizabeth, b. Oct. 8, [1698].

Chapman, Elizabeth, dau. of Walter by Ann, b. Feb. 11, 1678.

Chapman, Elizabeth, dau. of John by Elizabeth, b. Dec. 28, 170[9].

Chapman, John, son of Waller by Ann, b. Feb. 24, 1674.

Chapman, John, son of John by Elizabeth, b. Jan. 24, 1701.

Chapman, Walter, son of Walter by Ann, b. March 8, 1676.

Chapman, Walter, son of John by Elizabeth, b. Oct. 19, 1707.

Chapman, William, son of John by Elizabeth, b. Aug. 31, 1700.

Chapman, William, son of John by Elizabeth, b. Jan. 13, 170[4].

Chappel, Ann, dau. of Robert by Hannah, b. Jan. 2, 170[3].

Chappel, Joseph, son of Sacrid by ...... his wife, b. April 20, 170[8].

> [Blank space left for wife's name, in original].

Chappell, Alice, dau. of Robert by Hannah, b. Dec. 13, 1690.

Chappell, John, son of Sacra, by Elizabeth, bap. June 18, 1693.

Chappell, Richard, son of Robert by Hannah, bap. June 18, 1693.

Chappell, Robert, son of Zacharias of Denbeigh Parish, bap. Dec. 5, 1671.

Chisman, Ann, dau. of Thomas by Elizabeth, b. Dec. 20, 1692.

Chisman, Anna, dau. of John by Mary, b. March 15, 1730, bap. Apr. 4, 1731.

Chisman, Anna, dau. of John and Eliz⁵. b. Nov. 5, 1778, bap. Jan. 3, 1779.

Chisman, Anne, dau. of Thomas and Eliz⁵. b. Aug. 28, bap. Sept. 25, 1755.

Chisman, Anthony Robinson, son of Edmund and Mary, b. Oct. 6, bap. Dec. 9, 1779.

Chisman, Diana, dau. of Thos. and Diana, b. May 5, bap. June 9, 1765.

Chisman, Edmund, son of Tho⁵. and Elizabeth, b. May 2, bap. June 20, 1751.

Chisman, Edmund, b. May 20, 1751.

[Note: Marginal entry: "Died 13ᵗʰ April 84." This name and entry are on a sheet of paper signed "Thos. Chisman," posted in the register].

Chisman, Elinor, dau. of John by Elinor, b. Nov. 18, bap. Nov. 19, 1717.

Chisman, Elizabeth, dau. of Thomas by Elizabeth, b. Nov. 8, 1681.

Chisman, Elizabeth, dau. of John by Elinor, b. Dec. 15, 170[9].

Chisman, Elizabeth, dau. of John by Mary, b. July 26, 1737, bap. same day.

Chisman, George, son of Thomas by Elizabeth, b. Jan. 5, 1689.

Chisman, George, son of Thomas and Diana, b. April 26, bap. May 24, 1761.

Chisman, George, son of John and Elizabeth, b. . . . . . . , bap. Aug. 24, 1783.

Chisman, Henry, son of John by Elinor, b. Sept. 3, bap. Oct. 15, 1720.

Chisman, James, son of Thomas and Diana, b. April 24, bap. May 27, 1770.

Chisman, Jane, dau. of Thomas by Elizabeth, b. March 21, 1686.

Chisman, John, son of Edmund Jun., [Wife not mentioned], b. June 2, 1669.

Chisman, John, son of Thomas by Elizabeth, b. March 4, 1682.

Chisman, John, son of John by Elinor, b. June 25, 171[3].

Chisman, John, son of Thomas and Diana, b. April 11, 1763.

Chisman, John Buckner, son of John and Mary, b. April 2, bap. May 8, 1768.

Chisman, Katharine, dau. of John by Mary, b. July 3, bap. July 20, 1729.

Chisman, Mary, dau. of John by Elinor, b. Nov. 4, bap. Dec. 18, 1723.

Chisman, Mary, dau. of John and Mary, b. Oct. 2, bap. Nov. 3, 1765.

Chisman, Mildred, dau. of Thomas by Elizabeth, b. Feb. 19, 1675.

Chisman, Mildred, dau. of George by Mary, b. April 29, bap. June 3, 1739.

Chisman, Miles Cary, son of John and Elizabeth, b. Jan. 27, bap. April 8, 1781.

Chisman, Sarah, dau. of Thomas by Elizabeth, b. May 2, 1690.

Chisman, Thomas, b. Nov. 13, 1753.

> [Note: Marginal entry "Died a child." The name and entry are on a sheet of paper signed "Thos Chisman" and addressed to "Mr. Hine Russel," and posted in the register. It also has the entry of births of three negroes. It is posted on page 65 of the Register.]

Chisman, Thomas, son of Thoˢ. and Elizˢ. b. Nov. 13, bap. Nov. 26, 1753.

Chisman, Thomas, son of Thomas and Diana, b. July 3, bap. . . . ., 1759.

Chisman, Thomas, son of Edmund and Mary, b. May 13, bap. June 27, 1777.

Chisman, Thomas, son of George and Elizˢ. b. March 29, bap. June 16, 1784.

Clark, Ambrose, son of Henry by Frances, b. Oct. 13, bap. Nov. 25, 1721.

Clark, Elizabeth, dau. of Francis by Mary, b. Sept. 1, 1692.

Clark, Elizabeth, dau. of Francis by Mary, b. Feb. 22, 1696.

Clark, Frances, dau. of Henry by Frances, b. Aug. 17, 1710.

Clark, Frances, dau. of Francis by Mary, b. Sept. 13, 1706.

Clark, Henry, son of Francis by Frances, b. June 8, bap. Aug. 2, 1719.

Clark, John, son of John by Elizabeth, b. July 17, 1675.
        Note: ["mortus est."]

Clark, John, son of Francis Clarke, by Mary, b. July 22, 1698.

Clark, John, son of Henry by Frances, b. Aug. 25, 171[3].

Clark, Mary, dau. of Nicholas by Elizabeth, b. Nov. 8, 1690.

Clark, Mary, dau. of Francis by Mary, b. Jan. 13, 1701.

Clark, Mary, dau. of Henry by Frances, b. Dec. 3, 1705.

Clark, Mary, dau. of Henry by Frances, b. Dec. 17, 1707.

Clark, Nancy, dau. of James and Mary, b. Dec. 12, 1770, bap. Feb. 24, 1771.

Clark, Stephen, son of John [Wife not named], b. Feb. 14, 1670.

Clark, William, son of John by Mary, b. Dec. 23, 1668.

Clarke, Catherine, dau. of John by Elizabeth, b. Nov. 29, 1671.

Clarke, Catherine, dau. of John by Elizabeth, b. Dec. 1, 1672.

Clarke, Francis, son of John by Mary, b. Feb. 4, 1672.

Clarke, Henry, son of John by Elizabeth, b. Aug. 20, bap. Sept. 15, 1678.

Clarke, John, son of John by Mary, b. July 18, 1665.

Clarke, Mildred, an illegitimate daughter of Mary Clarke, b. March 7, bap. May 13, 1744.

Clausel, John Bollere[?], son of Clausel and Susanna, b. Sept. 10, bap. Nov. 13, 1768.

Clausel, Joseph Bannister, son of Clausel and Susanna, b. Sept. 29, bap. Nov. 25, 1770.

Cleefe, Elizabeth, dau. of Edward and Anne, b. Aug. 10, bap. Oct. 12, 1766.

Clevis, Sarah, dau. of Edward and Anne, b. Jan. 27, bap. April 23, 1769. ([Eli]z⁸. City).

Clifton, Barbara, dau. of Benjamin by Elinor, b. Aug. 13, [1699].

Clifton, Benjamin, son of Benjamin by Elinor, b. April 8, 1682.

Clifton, Benjamin, son of Benjamin by Sarah, b. Nov. 6, 1711.

Clifton, Benjamin, son of Benjamin by Dorothy, b. Sept. 20, bap. Oct. 26, 1740.

Clifton, Elinor, dau. of Benjamin by Elinor, b. 25th of . . . . 1692.

   [It was evidently 25th of Aug. 1692. But the month is not stated in the record.]

Clifton, Elinor, dau. of Benjamin by Sarah, b. March 13, 1713.

Clifton, Elinor, dau. of Richard by Mary, b. Sept. 16, bap. Sept. 24, 1718.

Clifton, Elizabeth, dau. of Benjamin by Elinor, b. Oct. 30, 1684.

Clifton, John, son of Benjamin by Elinor, b. May 1, 1690.

Clifton, John, son of Benjamin by Sarah, b. Sept. 30, 170[9].

Clifton, John, son of Benj^{s}. by Dorothy, b. . . . ., bap. Oct. 12, 1735.

Clifton, Mary, dau. of Thomas by Sarah, b. Mar. 5, 1738/9, bap. Apr. 15, 1739.

Clifton, Samuel, son of Benjamin by Elinor, b. Nov. 25, 1694.

Clifton, Sarah, dau. of Benj^{s}. by Dorothy, b. March 18, 1733, bap. May 26, 1734.

Clifton, Sarah, dau. of Thomas by Sarah, b. April 20, bap. May 17, 1741.

Clifton, Thomas, son of Benjamin by Sarah, b. Dec. 11, bap. Jan. 19, 1717.

Clifton, Thomas, son of Benj^{s}. by Dorothy, b. Sept. 8, bap. Oct. 16, 1737.

Cockerhill, Elizabeth, dau. of Samuel by Elizabeth, b. Jan. 25, 1709.

Cockerhill, Elizabeth, dau. of Samuel by Elizabeth, b. May 4, bap. May 31, 1719.

Cockerhill, Samuel, son of Samuel by Elizabeth, b. Nov. 27, bap. Jan. 29, 1721.

Colbert, Mary, dau. of William by Hope, b. Aug. 13, bap. Aug. 28, 1741.

Colbert, Richard, son of William by Hope, b. Sept. 14, bap.
    Oct. 22, 1738.
Colbert, Thomas, son of William by Hope, b. May 25, bap.
    June 24, 1744.
Cole, Abraham, son of John by Sarah, b. Nov. 8, 1702.
Cole, Celey, dau. of Ralph by Alice, b. March 8, 1690.
Cole, John, son of John by Sarah, b. Nov. 10, 170[4].
Cole, Mary, dau. of John by Sarah, b. March 16, 171[2].
Cole, William, son of John by . . . . . ., "his wife," b. Nov. 1,
    1710.
Coleson, Abigail, dau. of William by Dorithy, b. Aug. 16, 1702.
Coleson, Ann, dau. of William by Dorothy, b. April 7, 1698.
Coleson, William, son of William by Dorithy, b. May 2, 169[4].
Coleson, William, son of Issabella, (an illegitimate), b. March
    13, 1735, bap. Sept. 5, 1736.
Colison, Elizabeth, dau. of William by Dorithy, b. Feb. 4, 1690.
Collier, Diana, dau. of Lockey and Martha, b. April 14, bap.
    June 5, 1768.
Collier, Mary, dau. of Lockey and Margaret, b. March 28, bap.
    May 9, 1773.
Collier, Mary, dau. of Lockey and Margaret, b. June 8, bap.
    July 9, 1775. (Eliz*. City).
Colvert, Robert, son of William by Margarett, b. June 9, 1665.
Combs, Abraham (Mulatto), son of Edmund and Mary, b.
    March 8, bap. April 28, 1782.
Combs, Anne, dau. of Thomas and Anne, b. April 22, bap.
    June 25, 1769.
Combs, Anne, dau. of William and Mary, b. Dec. 14, 1778, bap.
    Feb. 14, 1779.
Combs, Edmunds, son of Thomas by Frances, b. Jan. 5, bap.
    March 10, 1747.
Combs, Elizabeth (Mulatto), dau. of William and Mary, b.
    Aug. 15, bap. Nov. 4, 1781.
Combs, Frances, dau. of Thomas and Anne, b. March 17, bap.
    April 14, 1776.

Combs, Frances, dau. of Edmund and Mary, b. July 25, 1777, bap. March 8, 1778.

Combs, Geo. Pickett (Mulatto), son of Edm⁴. and Mary, b. Dec. 5, 1786, bap. June 10, 1787.

Combs, Hebe (Mulatto), dau. of Thomas and Mary, b. March 2, bap. June 18, 1786.

Combs, James, son of Thomas by Frances, b. Nov. 19, bap. Dec. 18, 1745.

[Combs, Jane], Mulatto, dau. of Edm⁴. and Mary, b. Feb. 6, bap. May 2, 1784.

[Note: The name is missing at the top of page 110 where the margin is torn away. It is supplied from a study of the index.]

Combs, John, son of John by Sarah, b. "In the year 1707."

Combs, John, son of Thomas and Frances, b. ......, bap. Sept. 16, 1750.

Combs, John, son of Edm⁴. and Mary, b. Oct. 17, bap. Nov. 20, 1774.

Combs, John, son of William and Mary, b. Dec. 27, 1776, bap. Feb. 16, 1777.

Combs, Martha, dau. of Thomas and Anne, b. Feb. 17, bap. March 22, 1772.

Combs, Mary, dau. of William and Mary, b. July 11, bap. Sept. 14, 1783.

Combs, Sarah, dau. of John by Sarah, b. Jan. 10, 1712.

Combs, Thomas, son of Thomas by Frances, b. May 4, 1744.

Combs, William, son of Edmund and Mary, b. Feb. 14, bap. April 14, 1776.

Combs, William, son of John by Sarah, b. Nov. 13, 1706.

Combs, William, son of Thomas by Frances, b. Feb. 17, bap. March 20, 1742.

Combs, William, son of Edmund and Mary, b. Feb. 27, bap. April 16, 1780.

Combs, Willis, son of Thomas and Anne, b. May 4, bap. June 12, 1774.

Conner, Elizabeth, dau. of Gerrald by Mary, b. Aug. 26, 1672.

Conner, Richard, son of Gerrard by Mary, b. Oct. 27, 1673.

Conner, Thomas, son of Gerrald by Mary, b. March 22, 1675.

Conners, Elizabeth, [twin with June], dau. of Robert by Ann, bap. Sept. 20, 1685.

Conners, June, [twin with Elizabeth], dau. of Robert by Ann, bap. Sept. 20, 1685.

Connor, Hannah, dau. of Gerrald by Mary, b. June 30, 1686.

Connor, John, son of Gerrald by Mary, b. Feb. 17, 1683.

Connor, Sarah, dau. of Gerrald by Mary, b. Dec. 20, 1678.

Cook, Anne, dau. of John and Mary, b. May 26, bap. June 21, 1760.

Cook, Anne, dau. of Francis and Anne, b. Aug. 3, bap. Sept. 13, 1767.

Cook, Anne, dau. of John and Anne, b. June 4, bap. July 1, 1770.

Cook, Augustine, son of James and Mary, b. June 27, bap. July 30, 1769.

Cook, Benjamin, son of William and Anne, b. June 9, bap. July 13, 1760.

Cook, Bennett, son of Bennett and Rebecca, b. "Oct. 25, Priv. Bapt. Decr. 17th, 1775.   Received March 10th 1776." (York Hampton).

Cook, Catherine Parrot, dau. of James and Mary, b. March 15, bap. May 3, 1772.

Cook, Coleman, son of Bennet and Rebecca, b. March 3, bap. May 2, 1773.

Cook, Eliz*., dau. of James by Rebecca, b. Jan. 6, bap. Feb. 9, 1734.

Cook, Elizabeth, dau. of John and Mary, b. Sept. 10, bap. Oct. 8, 1753.

Cook, Elizabeth, dau. of Bennet and Eliz*. b. Jan. 2, bap. Feb. 11, 1770.

Cook, Frances, dau. of Francis and Rachel, b. Oct. 3, bap. Dec. 2, 1758.

Cook, Frances, dau. of Henry and Mary, b. April 14, bap. May 16, 1762.

Cook, Francis, son of William by Maryan, b. Feb. 25, 1694.

Cook, Francis, son of William by Maryan, b. Jan. 23, 17[03].

Cook, Francis, son of Francis by Mary, b. Oct. 27, bap. Dec. 27, 1729.

Cook, Francis, son of John and Mary, b. Nov. 1, bap. Nov. 30, 1755.

Cook, Francis, son of Francis and Anne, b. Sept. 16, bap. Nov. 15, 1772.

Cook, Hannah, [triplet with William and Patsy], dau. of John and Anne, b. Dec. 10, 1772, bap. March 28, 1773.

Cook, James, son of William by Mary, b. May 11, 17[08].

Cook, James, son of Francis and Anne, b. Jan. 25, bap. Feb. 23, 1766.

Cook, James, son of John and Anne, b. Dec. 8, 1775, bapt. Jan. 21, 1776.

Cook, John, son of William by Mary, b. Jan. 25, 1713.

Cook, John, son of William by Sarah, b. Jan. 25, 1714.

Cook, John, son of Francis by Mary, b. May 7, bap. June 4, 1727.

Cook, John, son of Henry and Mary, b. Oct. 13, bap. Nov. 9, 1760.

Cook, John, son of Francis and Anne, b. Jan. 2, bap. Feb. 19, 1775.

Cook, John Edwards, son of Francis and Rachel, b. Feb. 21, bap. March 23, 1760.

Cook, Lucy, dau. of Henry and Mary, b. Dec. 18, 1765, bap. Jan. 26, 1766.

Cook, Martha, dau. of William by Martha, b. July 16, bap. Aug. 13, 1727.

Cook, Mary, dau. of William by Arrabella, b. Aug. 20, 1671.

Cook, Mary, dau. of William by Maryan, b. [Dec.?] 18, [1698].

Cook, Mary, dau. of Francis, Junr. by Rachel, b. June 26, bap. June 29, 1757.

Cook, Mary, dau. of John and Mary, b. Oct. 13, bap. Nov. 6, 1757.

Cook, Mary, dau. of Francis and Anne, b. Sept. 9, bap. Oct. 29, 1770.

Cook, Mildred, dau. of Henry and Mary, b. Sept. 17, 1771, bap. April 12, 1772.

Cook, Miles, son of James and Mary, b. June 1, bap. July 17, 1774.

Cook, Patsy, [triplet with William and Hannah], dau. of John and Anne, b. Dec. 10, 1772, bap. March 28, 1773.

Cook, Rachel, dau. of Henry and Mary, b. March 17, bap. May 7, 1769.

Cook, Rebecca, dau. of John and Anne, b. Oct. 21, bap. Nov. 15, 1767.

Cook, Samuel, son of William by Margaret, b. April 13, 1696.

Cook, Samuel, son of Francis and Anne, b. Nov. 28, 1768, bap. Jan. 11, 1769.

Cook, Sarah, dau. of James and Mary, b. April 15, bap. May 31, 1767.

Cook, Thomas, son of Bennet and Rebecca, b. Dec. 21, 1767, bap. Jan. 31, 1768.

Cook, William, son of William by Maryan, b. July 28, [1699].

Cook, William, son of William and Anne, b. March 4, bap. April 3, 1757.

Cook, William, [triplet with Patsy and Hannah], son of John and Anne, b. Dec. 10, 1772, bap. March 28, 1773.

Cooke, Amey, dau. of Francis by Mary, b. . . . ., 1743, bap. July 17, 1743.

Cooke, Anabella, dau. of William by Arrabella, b. Sept. 21, 1665.

Cooke, Ann, dau. of William by Arrabella, b. March 24, 1668.

Cooke, Bennet, son of Francis by Mary [?], b. Feb. 26, 1740/1, bap. March 27, 1740/1.

Cooke, Elizabeth, dau. of William by Maryane, b. Sept. 25, 1687.

Cooke, Henry, son of Francis by Mary, b. Nov. 24, bap. Dec. 21, 1735.

Cooke, James, son of Francis by Mary, b. Oct. 14, bap. Oct. 21, 1732.

Cooke, James, son of Francis by Mary, b. Sept. 16, bap. Oct. 15, 1738.

Cooke, John, son of James by Rebecca, b. ...., bap. Feb. 6, 1736.

Cooke, Lazarus, [twin with Mary], son of Francis by Mary, b. Nov. 18, bap. Dec. 15, 1745.

Cooke, Martha, dau. of James by Rebecca, b. Aug. 22, bap. Oct. 18, 1741.

Cooke, Mary, dau. of James by Rebecca, b. Feb. 26, 1730, bap. April 25, 1731.

Cooke, Mary, [twin with Lazarus], dau. of Francis by Mary, b. Nov. 18, bap. Dec. 15, 1745.

Cooke, Rebecca, dau. of James by Rebecca, b. Nov. 27, bap. Jan. 26, 1745.

Cooke, Susanna, dau. of James by Rebecca, b. May 30, bap. June 24, 1733.

Cooke, William, son of William by Maryane, b. Oct. 12, 1689.

Cooke, Willm., son of Francis Cooke by Mary, b. Oct. 2, bap. Oct. 28, 1733.

Cooper, Samuel, son of Samuel by Ann, of York Parish, b. April 2, 1700.

Corlee, William, son of Edward by Ann, b. Feb. 28, 1730, bap. Apr. 4, 1731.

Cottillow, John Berry, son of Edwd. and Anne, b. Oct. 27, 1773, bap. Jan. 23, 1774.

Coudert, Ann, dau. of Bernard by M[ary?], b. July 26, bap. Aug. .., 1720.

Coudert, Frances, dau. of Bernard by Mary, b. March 17, 1721, bap. April 14, 1722.

Coudert, John, son of Bernard by Lidia, b. April 16, 1714.

Coudert, John, son of Wm. and Dianah, b. Aug. 10, bap. Sept. 7, 1755.

[Note: On the margin opposite this entry is this notation: "Ret⁴. to the Secretary's office."].

Coudert, Mary, dau. of Bernard by Lydia, b. Aug. .. [1708].

[This and the following entry are so mutilated, in part, that the year and day of month are illegible. The entries are preceded by one of June 12, 170[8] and followed by one of Aug. 25, 170[8].]

Coudert, William, son of Bernard, by Lidia, b. April 15, 1711.

Cowdert, Mary, dau. of Wm. and Dianah, b. Jan. 22, bap. Feb. 20, 1757.

Cox, Absalom, son of Thomas and Amy, b. Dec. 17, 1769, bap. Jan. 14, 1770.

Cox, Brittain, son of Thomas and Amy, b. March 12, bap. April 28, 1771.

Cox, Constant, dau. of David by Constant, b. Nov. .., 1741, bap. Dec. 20, 1741.

Cox, David, son of John by Elizabeth, b. Dec. 20, 1711.

Cox, Elizabeth, dau. of Thomas by Mary, b. Dec. 24, bap. Jan. 20, 1722.

Cox, Elizabeth, dau. of David by Constant, b. Feb. 5, 1739/40, bap. March 10, 1739/40.

Cox, Elizabeth, dau. of Joseph by Rachel, b. Oct. 2, bap. Oct. 31, 1742.

Cox, Elizabeth, dau. of Thoˢ. and Amy, b. April 23, bap. May 29, 1768.

Cox, James, son of Thos. and Amy, b. March 3, bap. April 26, 1778.

Cox, Jane, dau. of Thomas by Mary, b. Jan. 15, bap. Jan. 19, 1716.

Cox, Joel, son of Thomas and Amy, b. Jan. 7, bap. Feb. 5, 1775.

Cox, John, son of John by Elizabeth, b. March 27, 170[3].

Cox, John, son of David by Jane, b. Feb. 9, bap. March 23, 1734.

Cox, John, son of Joseph by Rachel, b. Oct. 5, bap. Nov. 23, 1740.

Cox, John, son of David by Dorcas, b. Dec. 15, bap. Jan. 16, 1744.

Cox, John, son of Thomas and Amy, b. Oct. 7, bap. (privately) Nov. 14, 1779.

Cox, Joseph, son of Thomas by Jane, b. Sept. 17, 1684.

Cox, Joseph, son of Thomas by Mary, b. Aug. 3, bap. Aug. 31, 1718.

Cox, Joshua, son of Thomas and Amy, b. Nov. 15, bap. Dec. 15, 1776.

Cox, Martha, dau. of Thomas by Mary, b. April 21, bap. May 21, 1721.

Cox, Mary, dau. of Thomas by Jane, b. May 10, 1687.

Cox, Mary, dau. of Thomas by Mary, b. Jan. 22, bap. Feb. 21, 1724.

Cox, Mary, dau. of Joseph by Rachel, b. Dec. 1, bap. Jan. 3, 1747.

Cox, Mary, dau. of Tho⁹. and Amy, b. July 11, 1766, bap. May 29, 1768.

Cox, Mildrid, dau. of John by Elizabeth, b. March 10, 1706.

Cox, Milley, dau. of David by Dorcas, b. Sept. 20, bap. Oct. 16, 1743.

Cox, Richard, son of David by Dorcas, b. Sept. 9, bap. Nov. 20, 1748.

Cox, Thomas, son of Thomas by Jane, b. April 23, 1690.

Cox, Thomas, son of Joseph by Rachel, b. June 8, bap. July 2, 1738.

Cox, Thomas, son of Thomas and Amy, b. July 25, bap. priv. Aug. 22, 1773.

Cox, Wealthy Britt, dau. of Thos. and Amy, b. Jan. 7, bap. June 10, 1781.

Craddock, John, son of Willᵐ. by Elizabeth, b. May 19, bap. June 18, 1738.

Craddock, William, son of William by Eliz⁺. b. July 19, bap. Aug. 23, 1741.

Crandal, Elizabeth, dau. of Thomas by Suzannah, b. Sept. 6, 1666.

Crandal, John, son of John and Eliz⁺. b. July —, bap. Aug. 30, 1778. (Warwick).

Crandall, Martha, dau. of Thomas by Elizabeth, b. May 30, 1707. Denbeigh Parish.

Crandall, Suzannah, dau. of Thomas by Suzannah, b. March 11, 1668.

Crandall, Thomas, son of Thomas by Suzannah, b. June 17, 1674.

Crandol, Elizabeth, dau. of John and Elizabeth, b. Jan. 29, bap. March 4, 1781. (Warwick).

Crandol, Elizabeth, [twin with Watkins], dau. of James and Martha, b. March 7, bap. March 9, 1781. (Warwick).

Crandol, Margaret, dau. of John and Eliz⁺. b. Oct. 8, bap. Nov. 14, 1784. (War^k.)

Crandol, Watkins, [twin with Elizabeth], son of James and Martha, b. March 7, bap. March 9, 1781. (Warwick).

Crawley, Peter, "Peter Crawley son of Wid⁰. Corley bound to John Davis born February 27ᵗʰ 1711."

Crisp, Margaritt, dau. of Francis by Ann, bap. Feb. .., 1671.

Croneher, William, son of Robert by Jane, b. Dec. 18, 1691.

Cross, Disey, dau. of Edwd. and Rebecca, b. Jan. 3, bap. Feb. 20, 1774.

Cross, Susanna, dau. of Wm. and Sarah, b. April 15, bap. June 1, 1766.

Croucher, Robert, son of Robert by Jane, b. Oct. 20, 1688.

Crussell, Christopher, son of Richard by Ann, b. Nov. 24, 1691.

Cunningham, Elizabeth, dau. of William and Mary, b. Nov. 15, 1772, bap. Jan. 17, 1773.

Cunningham, Frances, dau. of William and Mary, b. Oct. 15, bap. Dec. 8, 1776.

Cunningham, James, son of Wm. and Mary, b. Sept. 17, bap. Nov. 18, 1770.

Cunningham, Jane, dau. of George by Jane, b. July 7, 1696.

Cunningham, Mary, dau. of Wm. and Mary, b. Sept. 24, bap. Nov. 2, 1766.

Cunningham, Thomas, son of Wm. and Mary, b. Dec. 9, 1768, bap. Feb. 12, 1769.

Curtis, Ann, dau. of Edmund and Elizabeth, b. March 21, 1749, bap. April 19, 1750.

Curtis, Anna, dau. of Edmund and An[ ], b. Feb. 26, bap. May 6, 1781. (Warwick).

Curtis, Christopher, son of Edm^d. and Anne, b. Sept. 26, bap. Nov. 5, 1769.

Curtis, Damazinah, dau. of Thomas by Susannah, b. Jan. 26, bap. Feb. 25, 1721.

Curtis, Edmund, son of Edmund by Mary, b. Sept. 16, bap. Oct. 19, 1718.

Curtis, Edmund, son of Edmund and Anne, b. June 6, bap. July 7, 1754.

Curtis, Edmund, son of Edmund Junr. and Anne, b. Aug. 22, bap. Dec. 6, 1784. (War^k.).

Curtis, Elizabeth, dau. of Thomas by Susannah, b. Nov. 16, 1711.

Curtis, Elizabeth, dau. of Edmund by Mary, b. Aug. 21, 1712.

Curtis, Elizabeth, dau. of Edmund by Elizabeth, b. Sept. 9, bap. Nov. 20, 1748.

Curtis, Frances, dau. of Edmund by Mary, b. Dec. 26, 1706.

Curtis, Frances, dau. of Edmund by Elizab[eth], b. Nov. 19, 1746, bap. April 12, [1747].

Curtis, Henry, son of Edmund and Anne, b. March 20, bap. April 26, 1763.

Curtis, Lucey, dau. of Edmund by Elizabeth, b. Jan. 11, bap. Feb. 17, 1744.

Curtis, Mary, dau. of Edmund by Mary, b. March 14, 1710.

Curtis, Mary, dau. of Thomas by Suzannah, b. Dec. 24, bap.
Jan. 28, 1719.

Curtis, Mary, dau. of Edmund by Mary, b. Sept. 14, bap. Oct.
17, 1742.

Curtis, Mary, dau. of Edmund and Anne, b. Oct. 16, bap. Nov.
9, 1766.

Curtis, Robert, son of Edmund by Mary, b. Dec. 170[8].

Curtis, Robert, son of Edmund and Anne, b. Jan. 11, bap. Feb.
20, 1757.

Curtis, Sarah, dau. of Edmund by Elizth. b. Oct. 22, bap. Dec.
8, 1751.

Curtis, Sarah, dau. of Edmund and Anne, b. May 15, bap. June
1, 1760.

Curtis, ... "Sawney a boy belong^r. to Edmund Curtis
born June 20, 1754."

Curtis, Suzan, dau. of Thomas by Suzan, b. Oct. 9, bap. same
day, 1717.

Curtis, Thomas, son of Thomas by Susannah, b. Jan. 19, 1712.

Curtis, Thomas, son of Edm^d. and Anne, b. July 25, bap. Sept.
25, 1774.

Curtis, Thos. Cary, son of Edmund Junr. and Anne, b. Feb.
17, bap. March 9, 1786.   (Warwick).

D

Daniel, ..., son of John by Ann, b. Feb. 8, 1700.

Daniel, Elizabeth, dau. of John by Ann, b. Jan. 22, 1705.

Daniel, James, son of Darby of Denbeigh Parish, bap. April 6,
1669.

Daniel, John Reade, son of Cary Wills and Anne, b. Jan. 4,
bap. Feb. 27, 1780.   (Dinwiddie County).

Daniel, Mary, dau. of John by Ann, b. Aug. 14, 1702.

Dansterfield, Sarah, dau. of Samuel by Dorithy. "left blank
no age writt down."

  [This entry occurs between a birth entered as occurring
Aug. 30, 1692, and another of Dec. 20, 1692.]

Davenport, William, son of Joseph and Mary, b. Dec. 10, bap. Dec. 28, 1763.

Davies, Anthony, son of Richard by Ann, b. Sept. 4, 1676.

Davis, Ann, dau. of John by Eliz*. b. May 17, bap. June 16, 1734.

Davis, "Anne Daughter of Mary Davis Born January 22ᵈ Bap. Jany. 25ᵗʰ 1775."

Davis, Catherine, dau. of John by Elizabeth, b. Jan. 5, [1708].

Davis, Elizabeth, dau. of Elias by Mary . . . . . ., b. April 3, 1654.

Davis, Elizabeth, dau. of Owen, [Wife not mentioned], b. Dec. 9, 1675.

Davis, Jane, dau. of Edward by Patience, b. Sept. 17, 1707.

Davis, John, son of Andrew by Patience, b. May 18, 1682.

Davis, John, son of John by Elizabeth, b. Sept. 9, 1711.

Davis, Martha, dau. of John by Elizabeth, b. June 17, bap. Aug. 4, 17[28].

Davis, Mary, dau. of John by Mary, b. Jan. 1, 1713.

Davis, Mary, dau. of John by Elizabeth, b. Sept. 25, bap. Oct. 21, 1723.

Davis, Peter, son of John by Elizabeth, b. Dec. 1, bap. Dec. 30, 1725.

Davis, Sarah, dau. of Andrew by Patience, bap. July 27, 1679.

Davis, Sarah, dau. of John by Elizabeth, b. June 12, bap. July 8, 1721.

Davis, William, son of John by Elizabeth, b. Feb. 27, 1745, bap. May 11, 1746.

Dedman, Elinor, dau. of Samuel and Elinor, b. March 26, bap. May 28, 1775.

Dedman, Henry Howard, son of Samuel and Eleanor, b. Aug. 5, bap. privately Sept. 21 1772, bap. pub. May 30, 1773.

Dedman, John, son of Samuel and Elinor, b. Nov. 5, bap. Dec. 29, 1776.

Dedman, Samuel, son of Samuel and Eleanor, b. Aug. 28, bap. Oct. 17, 1773.

Delaney, Elizabeth, dau. of Thomas by Elizabeth, b. Nov. 19, bap. Dec. 16, 1715.

Delaney, John, son of Thomas by Susan b. . . . . . . [1721].

> [This name may be spelled D'laney. The part of the index carrying this name is torn away. The entry itself in the Register is the last on page 35, and is partly worn or torn away, the month day and year being wholly gone. The preceding entry is of Nov. 25, 1721, and the following is of Dec. 23, 1721.]

Delaney, Mary, dau. of Thomas by Susanna, b. Oct. 5, bap. March 21, 1730.

Delany, Elizabeth, dau. of Thomas by Elizabeth b. Nov. 19, bap. March 2, 1717.

D'enos [or D'enor], Constantia Noble, dau. of Augustina Rou[da?]lin, and Mary, b. July 7, bap. Sept. 7, 1783.

Dewberry, ..., ... of John and Mary, b. . . . ., bap. Dec. 1, 1751.

> [Note: The entire entry here is ". . . . . . Dewberry . . . . . . of John & Mary Dewberry born . . . . . . bapt. Dec. 1, 1751"]

Dewberry, Elizabeth, dau. of John and Mary, b. Sept. 13, bap. Oct. 28, 1764.

Dewberry, Giles, son of John and Mary, b. Feb. 20, 1770.

Dewberry, John, son of John and Mary, (of "Eliz⁸. City"), b. Feb. 20, bap. March 21, 1756.

Dewberry, Judith, dau. of John and Mary, b. Sept. 11, bap. Oct. 11, 1772. (Bruton).

Dewberry, Mary, dau. of John and Mary, b. March 19, bap. April 25, 1762.

Dewberry, Samuel, son of John and Mary, b. Jan. 5, bap. Feb. 3, 1754.

Dewberry, Sarah, dau. of John and Mary, b. Oct. 15, bap. Nov. 13, 1751.

Dewberry, William, son of John and Mary, b. Oct. 2, bap. Oct. 30, 1759.

Dickason, Charles, son of Richard, by Elizabeth, b. January 8, 1658.

Dicken, Elizabeth, dau. of John by Mary, b. Oct. 9, bap. Dec. 31, 1732.

Dicken, William, son of John by Mary, b. Aug. 9, bap. Sept. 14, 1735.

Dicken, William, son of William by Anne, b. Feb. 18, bap. March 24, 1744.

Digason, Elizabeth, dau. of Richard by Elizabeth, b. Nov. 27, 1671.

Digason, Jane, dau. of Richard by Elizabeth, b. Sept. 17, 1669.

Dixon, Ann, dau. of Richard by Damazinah, b. Dec. 11, 1700.

Dixon, Ann, dau. of James by Martha, b. March 8, 1732.

Dixon, Anne, dau. of James and Elizabeth, b. Dec. 6, 1757.

Dixon, Daniel, son of James by Martha, b. Sept. 1, bap. Oct. 16, 1737.

Dixon, Daniel Moore, [twin with Robert Sheild], son of Daniel and Sarah, b. Dec. 22, 1767, bap. Feb. 5, 1768.

Dixon, Diana, dau. of James and Eliz*., b. .., bap. March 16, 1766.

Dixon, Elizabeth, dau. of James and Eliz*. b. Dec. 28, 1754, bap. Feb. 6, 1755.

Dixon, Frances, dau. of James and Eliz*. b. Jan. 20, bap. March 18, 1768.

Dixon, James, son of James by Martha, b. Dec. 3, bap. Dec. 27, 1724.

Dixon, James, son of James and Elizabeth, b. Dec. 24, bap. .., 1763.

Dixon, Martha, dau. of James by Martha, b. July 26, bap. Aug. 25, 1722.

Dixon, Martha, dau. of James and Elizabeth, b. Aug. 19, bap. Sept. 25, 1752.
    [Note: On the margin is a notation as follows: "Married to Willis Wilson"].

Dixon, Mary, dau. of James and Elizabeth, b. Nov. 1, 1759.

Dixon, Merrit, son of James by Martha, b. May 31, bap. Aug. 4, 1734.

Dixon, Richard, son of James by Martha, b. Oct. 24, bap. Oct. 29, 1727.

Dixon, Robert Sheild, [twin with Daniel Moore], son of Daniel and Sarah, b. Dec. 22, 1767, bap. Feb. 5, 1768.

Dixon, Rosa, dau. of James and Eliz⁺. b. July 1, bap. Sept. 27, 1770.

Dixon, Thomas, son of James by Martha, b. Oct. 26, bap. Dec. 6, 1730.

Dixon, William, son of James by Martha, b. Nov. 10, bap. Feb. 7, 1719.

Dixon, William, son of James and Elizabeth, b. July 7, 1750, bap. Aug. 19, 1750.

> [Note: A marginal entry opposite this name says: "Died 1768."]

Dixon, Wm. Moore, son of James and Eliz⁺., b. Sept. 26, bap. Nov. 15, 1772.

Doswell, Catherine, dau. of John by Elizabeth, b. Oct. 23, 17[04].

Doswell, Edward, son of John by Elizabeth, b. Dec. 18, 1706.

Doswell, Elizabeth, dau. of John by Elizabeth, b. Dec. 23, 17[09].

Doswell, John, son of John Jun⁺. by Elizabeth, b. June 15, 1714.

Doswell, Mary, dau. of John by Elizabeth, b. Jan. 19, 1711.

Doswell, Nutting, son of John by Elizabeth, b. Sept. 3, 170[3].

Doswell, Richard, son of John by Elizabeth, b. Oct. 12, 170[8].

> [There is a marginal memorandum opposite this name, partly illegible. So far as I can read it, it is as follows: "..together male children born ......ometime."].

Doswell, Thomas, son of John Jun⁺. by Elizabeth, b. Nov. 29, bap. Dec. 16, 1717.

Dowry[?], Edward, son of John by Deborah, b. Aug. 2, 1686.

Draper, Hannah, dau. of John by Mary, b. April 17, 1687.

Draper, John, son of John by Mary, b. Oct. 16, 1689.

Draper, Josiah, son of John by Mary, b. Aug. 21, 1685.

Draper, Robert, son of John by Mary, bap. June 10, 1683.

Draper, Susanna, dau. of John by Mary, b. Jan. 30, 1680.

Draper, Susannah, dau. of John by Mary, b. Dec. 26, 1684.

Drewry, Anna, dau. of William and Anne, b. Nov. 20, [1781], bap. March 24, 1782.

Drewry, Anne, [twin with Elizabeth], dau. of William and Anne, b. May 8, bap. June 10, 1781. (Warwick).

Drewry, Beckey, dau. of John and Mary, b. April 2, bap. April 30, 1753.

Drewry, Benjamin, son of James and Catherine, b. Jan. 7, bap. Feb. 5, 1758.

Drewry, Betsy, dau. of Wm. and Jane, b. July 31, bap. Oct. 14, 1770.

Drewry, Catherine, dau. of John by Mary, b. May 14, 170[9].

Drewry, Daniel, son of Samuel by Mary, b. Sept. 30, bap. Dec. 23, 1739.

Drewry, Darling Hyde, son of Dan¹. and Milly, b. May 30, bap. Oct. 29, 1769.

Drewry, Deborah, dau. of Robert by Elinor, b. Dec. 19, bap. Jan. 23, 1731.

Drewry, Diana, dau. of James and Catherine, b. Jan. 25, 1762.

Drewry, Diana, dau. of Samuel Junr., and Mary, b. March 20, bap. April 15, 1764.

Drewry, Diana, dau. of William and Anne, b. April 9, bap. May 11, 1777.

Drewry, Dolphins, son of J[   ], and El[   ], b. April 2[?], bap. June 20, 1779. (Eliz⁺. City)

Drewry, Eliz⁺., dau. of Sam¹. by Mary, b. Dec. 31, bap. Jan. 27, 1733.

Drewry, Elizabeth, dau. of John by Deborah, b. July 17, 1677.

Drewry, Elizabeth, dau. of John by Mary, b. Oct. 23, 17[03].

Drewry, Elizabeth, dau. of Robert by Elizabeth, b. March 20, 1706.

Drewry, Elizabeth, dau. of Edward by Jane, b. Oct. 1, bap. Dec. 21, 1718.

Drewry, Elizabeth, dau. of John by Sarah, b. Jan. 6, bap. Feb. 7, 1719.

Drewry, Elizabeth, dau. of Robert by Elinor, b. June 30, bap. Aug. 1, 1725.

Drewry, Elizabeth, dau. of Samuel by Mar[   ], b. March 15, 1741/2, bap. April 25, 1[742].

Drewry, Elizabeth, [twin with Anne], dau. of William and Anne, b. May 8, bap. June 10, 1781. (Warwick).

Drewry, Esther Morrow, dau. of William and Anne, b. Jan. 12, bap. March 11, 1787.

Drewry, Frances, dau. of John by Mary, b. Feb. 10, 1739/40, bap. March 9, 1739/40.

Drewry, Hannah, dau. of Thomas by Mary, b. Oct. 28, bap. Nov. 27, 1720.

Drewry, Henry, son of Robert by Ann, b. Sept. 28, 17[03].

Drewry, Henry, son of Henry and Elizabeth, b. Nov. 28, 1780, bap. Feb. 11, 1781.

Drewry, Hope, dau. of Robert by Agnis, b. Aug. 5, 1714.

Drewry, Humphry, son of Thomas by Mary, b. Sept. 20, bap. Oct. 25, 1730.

Drewry, James, son of John by Deborah, b. Dec. 28, 1693.

Drewry, James, son of Robert by Agnis, b. June 12, bap. July 9, 1721.

Drewry, James, son of Samuel by Mary, b. Nov. 17, bap. Dec. 22, 1728.

Drewry, James, son of James and Catherine, b. April 29, bap. May 25, 1760.

Drewry, James, son of James and Catherine, b. April 29, 1760.

Drewry, James, son of Richard and Sarah, b. June 18, 1760.

Drewry, John, son of John by Deborah, b. July 24, 1673.

Drewry, John, son of John by Mary, b. March 1, 1695.

Drewry, John, son of John Jun'. by Sarah, b. Jan. 6, bap. Feb. 4, 1721.

Drewry, John, son of John by Sarah, b. Aug. 30, bap. Sept. 22, 1728.

Drewry, John, son of Samuel by Mary, b. Dec. 18, bap. Jan. 22, 1737.

Drewry, John, son·of John by Mary, b. Sept. 20, bap. Oct. 20, 1745.

Drewry, John, son of John and Mary, b. April 4, bap. May 12, 1751.

Drewry, John, son of Wm. and Rachel, b. Nov. 13, bap. . . . ., 1752.

Drewry, John, son of William and Martha, b. July 15, bap. Aug. 15, 1753.

Drewry, John, son of John and Eliz*. b. Dec. . . ., 1777, bap. May 3, 1778.

Drewry, John, son of William and Anne, b. Oct. 15, bap. Dec. 12, 1779.

Drewry, John, son of James and Mary, b. Dec. 29, 1783, bap. April 4, 1784.

Drewry, Margaret, dau. of Sam¹. by Mary, b. Dec. 15, bap. Jan. 18, 1735.

Drewry, Mary, dau. of John by Deborah, b. Oct. 14, 1688.

Drewry, Mary, dau. of John by Mary, b. Feb. 17, 1700.

Drewry, Mary, dau. of Robert by Agnes, b. Oct. 26, 1710.

Drewry, Mary, dau. of Thomas by Mary, b. June 5, bap. July 6, 1718.

Drewry, Mary, dau. of John Junr. by Sarah, b. May 6, bap. May 22, 1725.

Drewry, Mary, dau. of Robt. by Elinor, b. Dec. 9, 1733.

Drewry, Mary, dau. of Samuel by Mary, b. July 23, bap. Aug. 26, 1744.

Drewry, Mary, dau. of John by Mary, b. Jan. 21, bap. March 13, 1747.

Drewry, Mary, dau. of James and Catherine, b. Oct. 2, 1754.

Drewry, Mary, dau. of Morgan and Mary, b. Jan. 7, 1755.

Drewry, Mary, dau. of William and Anne, b. July 3, bap. Aug. 27, 1775.

Drewry, Mary, dau. of Henry and Elizabeth, b. Jan. 21, bap. March 16, 1782.

Drewry, Matthew, son of John by Mary, b. Aug. 7, bap. Sept. 5, 1742.

Drewry, Morgan, son of Robert by Elinor, b. July 1, bap. Aug. 10, 1729.

Drewry, Peter, son of Samuel by Mary, b. Dec. 25, bap. Jan. 23, 1731.

Drewry, Peter, son of William and Anne, b. Aug. 10, bap. Oct. 10, 1773.

Drewry, Peter, son of Henry and Dorothy, b. Jan. 27, bap. March 3, 1776.

Drewry, Rachell, dau. of Thomas by Mary, b. Jan. 26, 1713.

Drewry, Rachell, dau. of John by Rachell, b. April 7, bap. May 5, 172[8].

Drewry, Rachell, dau. of Thomas by Mary, b. June 3, bap. July 21, 1728.

Drewry, Richard, son of John by Rachell, b. Sept. 30, bap. Nov. 14, 1725.

Drewry, Richard, son of William and Martha, b. April 16, bap. May 18, 1755.

Drewry, Richard, son of John and Elizabeth, b. Feb. 15, bap. May 14, 1786. (Warw*.)

Drewry, Robert, son of John by Deborah, b. Oct. 22, 1679.

Drewry, Robert, son of Robert by Jane, bap. Nov. 18, 1683.

Drewry, Robert, son of Robt. by Agnes, b. Sept. 1, bap. Oct. 6, 1723.

Drewry, Samuel, son of John by Deborah, b. Feb. 28, 1690.

Drewry, Samuel, son of Thomas by Mary, b. Feb. 28, 1722, bap. March 30, 1723.

Drewry, Samuel, son of Samuel by Mary, b. May 9, bap. June 7, 1730.

Drewry, Samuel, son of James and Catherine, b. Jan. 22, bap. Feb. 22, 1756.

Drewry, Samuel, son of Samuel and Mary, b. Feb. 8, bap. May 11, 1766.

Drewry, Sarah, dau. of John by Mary, b. Feb. 23, 1705.

Drewry, Sarah, dau. of John by Sarah, b. July 21, bap. Aug. 10, 1723.

Drewry, Sarah, dau. of John by Sarah, b. July 21, bap. Sept. 8, 1723.

Drewry, Sarah, dau. of Robert by Elinor, b. Dec. 13, bap. Feb. 12, 1737.

Drewry, Sarah, dau. of Henry and Dorothy, b. Sept. 17, bap. Nov. 8, 1778.

Drewry, Thomas, son of John by Deborah, b. Sept. 12, 1684.

Drewry, Thomas, son of John by Mary, b. Sept. 18, [1698] [Page torn.]

Drewry, Thomas, son of Thomas by Mary, b. Sept. 17, bap. Oct. 12, 1725.

Drewry, Thomas, son of Johnson and Mary, b. Nov. 7, bap. Dec. 12, 1784. (Warw^k.)

Drewry, Whitaker, son of Thomas by Elizabeth, b. Aug. 30, bap. Sept. 24, 1727.

Drewry, William, son of John by Deborah, b. June 12, 1675.

Drewry, William, son of John by Rachell, b. Nov. 14, bap. Dec. 14, 1721.

Drewry, William, son of Robert by Elinor, b. April 7, bap. May 15, 1727.

Drewry, William, son of Samuel by Mary, b. .... 4, 1747, bap. May 3, 1747.

Drewry, William, son of John and Mary, b. Jan. 16, bap. Feb. 22, 1756.

Drewry, William, son of William and Martha, b. July 28, bap. Sept. 20, 1761.

Drewry, William Fuller, son of John and Eliz^a. b. Dec. 1, 1781, bap. Feb. 10, 1782.

Drewry, William, son of William and Anne, b. May 9, bap. Aug. 8, 1784.

Driskel, Ann, dau. of *Florence* by "Elizabeth his wife," b. July 17, 1710.

Drummond, Ellis, son of Thomas by Ann, b. March 21, 1717, bap. Apr. 20, 1718.

Drummond, Griffin, son of Thomas by Ann, b. Oct. 19, 1720.

Dunford, Arrabella, dau. of Phillip by Ann, bap. Oct. 2, 1692.

Dunn, Elizabeth, dau. of John and Elizabeth, b. Jan. 1, bap. April 13, 1766. (Warwick).

Dunn, John, son of Charles by Temperance, b. Oct. 12, 1673.

Dunn, John, son of [*illegible,*] b. July 19, bap. July 25, 1737.

Dunn, Mary, dau. of Charles by Temperance, b. June 10, 1671.

Dunn, Samuel, son of Samuel and Hannah, b. Feb. 4, bap. April 13, 1766. (Warwick).

Dunn, William, son of Willm. by Ann, b. Dec. 20, bap. Feb. 1, 1735.

Dunning, Mary, dau. of Thomas by Mary, b. March 3, 1667.

Dunston, Thomas, son of Thomas by Elizabeth, b. March 8, 1691.

Dunsterfield, Sarah, dau. of Samuel by Dorithy, b. April 23, 1690.

E

Ellet, Sarah, dau. of William by Suzan, b. Jan. 22, bap. March 2, 1718.
 [This name is indexed Ellett].

Elliott, Henry Mingham, son of John and Chives, b. Jan. 17, bap. April 27, 1777. ([Nor]thampton).

Elliott, Martha, dau. of John and Chevears, b. Jan. 24, bap. April 18, 1762.

Elliott, Nancy, dau. of John and Chivers, b. Jan. 14, bap. Feb. 28, 1768.

Elliott, Robert, son of John and Chivers, b. Oct. 12, 1765, bap. Feb. 2, 1766. (York Hampton).

Elliott, Seaton, son of Bernard and Anna, b. Jan. 15, bap. Feb. 18, 1781. (York Hampton).

Elliott, Thomas Townshend Mingham, son of John and Chives, b. Oct. 15, 1780, bap. June 17, 1781. (York Hampton).

Elliott, Wm. Howard, son of John and Chives, b. May 11, bap. July 1, 1770.

English, Edward, son of Thomas by Margarett, b. June 27, 1692.

Ennals, Suzannah, dau. of Bartholomew by Mary, b. Feb. 15, 1665.

Ennals, William, son of Bartholomew by Mary, b. May 5, 1668.

Ennols, Bartholomew, son of Bartholomew by Mary, b. April 11, 1667.

Evans, Francis, son of Mary, [other parent not named], b. March 18, 1688.

Evans, Leonard, son of Evan by Sarah, bap. Oct. 31, 1675.

Evans, Mary, dau. of Thomas, Sen., by Mary, b. Feb. 15, 1667.

Everitt, James, son of John by Mary, b. Oct. 8, 1667.

Everitt, Rebekah, dau. of Robert by Mary, bap. Dec. 6, 1670.

Everitt, Thomas, son of John by Mary, b. March 21, 1669.

F

Faison, Ann, dau. of Henry by Ann, b. March 29, 1692.

Faison, Elias, son of James by Frances, b. Oct. 15, bap. Nov. 10, 1742.

Faison, Elizabeth, dau. of Henry by Ann, bap. June 17, 1683.

Faison, Elizabeth, dau. of James by Mary, b. March 4, 170[4].

Faison, Elizabeth, dau. of Henry by Eliz*. b. Dec. 4, bap. Dec. 28, 1740.

Faison, Henry, son of Henry by Eliz*. b. March 3, bap. Apr. 29, 1739.

Faison, Henry, son of James by Frances, b. Oct. 28, bap. Dec. 16, 1744.

Faison, James, son of Henry by Ann, b. Dec. 2, 1680.

Faison, Rebekah, dau. of Henry by Ann, b. Jan. 6, 1688.

Farmer, Thomas, son of Thomas by Ann, bap. July 18, 1681.

Fason, Diana, dau. of Henry by Elizabeth, b. July 21, bap. Sept. 12, 1731.

Fason, Dixon, son of James by Frances, b. Dec. 5, 1729, bap. Jan. 4, 1729/30.

Fason, Elias, son of James, by Mary, b. Jan. 20, 170[9]. Denbeigh Parish.

Fason, Elizabeth, dau. of Henry Fason Van D . . . . by Rebekah, b. February 18, 1652.

Fason, Elizabeth, dau. of James by Elizabeth, b. Feb. 9, 1721, bap. March 25, 1722.

Fason, Henry, son of Henry Fason Van Doverag(?), by Rebekah, b. February 14, 1656.

Fason, Henry, son of Henry by Ānn, b. April 26, 1695.

Fason, James, son of James by Mary, b. Aug. 30, 1706.

Fason, James, son of James by Frances, b. Oct. 6, bap. Nov. 5, 1727.

Fason, Mary, dau. of Henry by Elizabeth, b. Dec. 10, bap. Feb. 5, 1726.

Fason, Sarah, dau. of James by Mary, b. March 15, 1718, bap. April 19, 1719.

Fason, Thomas, son of Henry by Elizabeth, b. March 2, bap. April 13, 1728/9.

Fenn, John Deadenford, son of Wm. and Elizabeth, b. Nov. 2, bap. Dec. 16, 1764.

Ferguson, Ann, dau. of William by Hope, b. Jan. 19, bap. March 14, 1735.

Ferguson, Elizabeth, dau. of William by Hope, b. Jan. 25, 1726, bap. April 3, 1727.

Ferguson, John, son of William by Hope, b. Sept. . ., bap. March 21, 1730.

Ferguson, Mary, dau. of Robert by Mary, b. March 16, 1666.

Ferguson, Mary, dau. of William by Eliz*. b. Feb. 26, bap. March 24, 1748.

Ferguson, Robert, son of William by Hope, b. March 30, bap. May 6, 1733.

Ferguson, William, son of John by Elizabeth, b. Jan. 10, 1700.

Ferguson, William, son of William by Hope, b. June 19, bap. July 24, 1724.

Figg, Ann, dau. of John by Izabel, b. Sept. 1, 1665.

Figg, Elizabeth, dau. of John by Elizabeth, b. Jan. 1, [1698].

Figg, Frances, dau. of John by Elizabeth, b. Nov. 9, 1691.

Figg, Issabel, dau. of John by Elizabeth, b. Sept. 25, 1696.

Figg, John, son of John by Izabel, b. March 12, 1666.

Figg, Matthew, son of John by Elizabeth, b. Nov. 6, 1693.

Fisher, Elizabeth, dau. of John by Elizabeth, b. .... 170[7].

Fisher, Sarah, dau. of Elizabeth, bap. Aug. 16, 1714.   [Father not mentioned].

Fleming, John, son of John by Mary, b. April 14, 1683.

Flemming, Lidia, dau. of John by Mercy, bap. Oct. 30, 1679.

Floyd, Henry, son of Thomas by Mary, bap. Jan. 5, 1677.

Floyd, Mary, dau. of James by Rebekah, b. Oct. 25, 1706.

Floyd, Thomas, son of Lawrence by Honour, b. Feb. 4, [1703].

Foreman, Hannah, dau. of Thomas by Ann, b. Aug. 4, 1679.

Foresith, Agnes, dau. of James by Grace, b. March 6, 1668.

Foresyth, Elizabeth, dau. of James by Grace, b. July 17, 1666.

Forgason, Davis, son of John by Elizabeth, b. Nov. 9, 1697.
    [This name is indexed Ferguson].

Forgason, Rose, dau. of Robt. by Mary, b. Dec. 9, 1677.

Forguson, Anne, dau. of William and Elizabeth, b. Sept. 21, bap. Oct. 26, 1755.

Forguson, Edward, son of William and Eliz*. b. May 28, bap. June 27, 1762.

Forguson, Elizabeth, dau. of Wm. and Eliz*. b. March 14, bap. May 8, 1768.

Forguson, John, son of Robert by Mary, b. Aug. 16, 1670.

Forguson, John, son of John by Mary, b. Sept. 23, 1706.

Forguson, Mary, dau. of John by Elizabeth, b. Feb. 20, [1703].

Forsyth, Elinor, dau. of James by Grace, b. April 5, 1675.

Forsyth, Mary, dau. of James by Grace, b. August 7, 1664.

Fraizer, Jonathan Graar, son of John and Rachel, b. March 20, bap. April 17, 1774.

Francis, Abraham, son of Abram and Mary, b. May 30, bap. June 25, 1769.

Francis, Betty, dau. of Thomas and Mary, b. Sept. . . . ., bap. Nov. 15, 1767.

Francis, Elizabeth, dau. of John by Susanna, b. Sept. 15, 1750.

Francis, Elizabeth, dau. of Abraham and Mary, b. May 26, bap. June 7, 1761.

Francis, John, son of Abraham and Mary, b. Feb. 20, bap. March 23, 1766.

Francis, Mary, "Mary, Daughter of Mary Francis (Bastard) born Jany. 20ᵗʰ, Baptiz'd March 23ᵈ. 1783."

Francis, Molly (bastard), "Molly, daughter of Mary Francis, born Novʳ. 15ᵗʰ 1785, Baptiz'd April 30, 1786."
  [Note: On the margin opposite this entry is written: "Bastard."]

Francis, Sarah, "Sarah, Bastard daughter of Mary Francis, born Octʳ. 28ᵗʰ, 1780, Pr. Baptiz'd Febry. 25ᵗʰ 1781."

Francis, Sukey, dau. of Betty Francis, b. Feb. . ., bap. April 10, 1768.

Francis, Wilson, "Wilson son of Abraham Francis & Elvy Mundel (Bastᵈ.), b. Dec. 1, 1779, bap. April 16, 1780.

Franklin, Anthony, son of Anthony by Elinor his wife, b. October 6, 1648.

Franklin, Anthony, son of Anthony by Mary, b. Oct. 5, 1683.

Franklin, Elinor, dau. of Anthony by Mary, b. July 5, 1680.

Franklin, Hannah, dau. of Anthony by Elinor, b. February 16, 1654.

Franklin, John, son of Anthony by Mary, b. Jan. 5, 1688.

Franklin, John, son of John by Sarah, b. Oct. 9, bap. Nov. 9, 1717.

Franklin, Mary, dau. of Anthony by Mary, b. March 23, 1691.

Franklin, Mary, dau. of William by Mary, b. April 19, bap. May 23, 1742.

Franklin, Phebe, dau. of Anthony by Elinor, b. January 10, 1650.

Franklin, William, son of John by Sarah, b. March 9, 1714, bap. April 9, 1715.

Franklyn, John, son of Willm. by Mary, b. Nov. 14, bap. Dec. 18, 1737.

Franklyn, Sarah, dau. of Willm. by Mary, b. April 22, bap. May 20, 1739.

Frazer, Elizabeth, dau. of John and Rachel, b. Jan. 8, bap. April 18, 1779. (Eliz^a. City).

Frazer, John, son of John and Rachel, b. Feb. 22, bap. March 29, 1776.

Frazer, Mary, dau. of John and Rachel, b. Feb. 24, bap. April 21, 1771.

Freeman, Ann, dau. of Henry by Elizabeth, b. Sept. 17, bap. Oct. 13, 1724.

Freeman, Anna Maria, dau. of Henry by Martha, b. April 30, 1673.

Freeman, Annamaria, dau. of Henry by Barbara, b. Oct. 22. 17[03].

Freeman, Betty, dau. of John Wilson and Ruth, b. Jan. 14, bap. March 20, 1774.

Freeman, Calthorp, son of Henry by Barbara, b. Sept. 4, 1706.

Freeman, Charles, [twin with Henry], son of Henry by Barbara, b. Nov. 24, 1711.

Freeman, Elinor, dau. of Henry by Elinor, b. Jan. 18, bap. Feb. 21, 1719.

Freeman, Elizabeth, dau. of John by Elizabeth, b. March 16, 1702.

Freeman, Elizabeth, dau. of Henry by Barbara, b. May 26, 1702.

Freeman, Elizabeth, dau. of Henry by Elizabeth, b. Feb. 15, bap. March 25, 1721.

Freeman, Elizabeth, dau. of Henry by Elizabeth, b. May 7, bap. June 15, 1729.

Freeman, Elizabeth, "Daughter of·Ruth Freeman Baptized 18ᵗʰ March 1770. 5 months old the last of this month."

Freeman, Frances, dau. of Henry by Elizabeth, b. Sept. 17, bap. Jan. 22, 1748.

Freeman, Frances, dau. of Jno. Moore and Martha, b. Jan. 8, bap. Feb. 5, 1769.

Freeman, Hannah, dau. of John by Elizabeth, b. Aug. 29, 1701.

Freeman, Henry, son of Henry by Martha, b. Nov. 20, 1675.

Freeman, Henry, son of John by Elizabeth, b. Feb. 24, 1697.

Freeman, Henry, [twin with Charles], son of Henry by Barbara, b. Nov. 24, 1711.

Freeman, Henry, son of Matthew by Martha, b. Feb. 24, 1739/40, bap. March 23, 1739/40.

Freeman, Henry, son of Matthew by Martha, b. Jan. 22, bap. March 1, 1746.

Freeman, Henry Curtis, son of John and Sarah, b. Nov. 17, 1778, bap. Jan. 3, 1779.

Freeman, James, son of Henry by Elizabeth, b. Oct. 14, bap. Nov. 17, 1731. York Hampton Parish.

Freeman, John, son of Henry by Martha, b. July 5, 1671.

Freeman, John, son of Henry by Barbara, b. March 18, 17[09].

Freeman, John, son of Henry by Elizabeth, b. Jan. 24, bap. March 5, 1726.

Freeman, John, son of Mattʷ. by Martha, b. May 6, 1749, bap. June 11, 174[9].

Freeman, Martha, dau. of John by Elizabeth, b. April 3, 1698.

Freeman, Martha, dau. of Henry by Elinor, b. Nov. [?] 21, 1713.

Freeman, Mary, dau. of John by Elizabeth, b. Nov. 26, 170[4].

Freeman, Mary, dau. of Matthew and Martha, b. Jan. 3, 1754.

Freeman, Naomi, dau. of John by Elizabeth, b. Sept. 29, 170[8].

Freeman, Nordan, son of Thomas by Mary, b. Oct. 1, 1710.

Freeman, Robert, son of John by Elizabeth, b. Feb. 9, [1699].

Freeman, Sarah, dau. of Henry by Elinor, b. Sept. 28, bap. Oct. 27, 1717.

Freeman, Sarah, dau. of Matthew by Martha, b. Feb. 5, 1741/2. bap. March 7, 17[41/2].

Fussell, Dorithy, dau. of William by Mary, b. April 20, 1697.

Fussell, Goshin, son of.Nicholas by Mary, b. Aug. 28ᵗʰ, 1673.

Fussell, John, son of Nicholas by Mary, bap. April 4, 1671.

Fussell, Thomas, son of Nicholas by Mary, b. Jan. 13, 1676.

Fussell, William, son of Nicholas by Mary, b. April 17, 1668.

Fussell, William, son of William and Mary, b. Feb. 26, 169[8].

G

Galden, John, son of John by Elizabeth, b. Oct. 30, bap. Nov. 27, 1720. Warwick County.

Gardener, Thomas, son of. Thomas by Ann, b. Nov. 11, 1672.

Garrett, Nancy, dau. of Richᵈ. and Mary, b. Aug. 8, bap. Nov. 19, 1780. (York Hampton).

Garrett, William, son of Richard and Mary, b. March 8, bap. May 4, 1783.

Garrow, Dinah, dau. of John by Martha, b. April 17, bap. May 27, 1739.

Garrow, John, son of John and Mary, b. Oct. 9, bap. Nov. 10, 1765. (York Hampton).

Garrow, Mary, dau. of John and Mary, b. Jan. 7, bap. Feb. 19, 1769. (York Hampton).

Gawen, John, son of William by Ann, bap. March 1, 1668.

Gemmell, William, son of John and Sarah, b. Jan. 12, bap. Feb. 13, 1757.

Gemmells, Fanny, dau. of John and Sarah, b. Feb. 19, bap. April 4, 1763.

Gemmells, William, son of John and Mary, b. March 7, bap. April 1, 1774.

Gemmels, David, son of James and Anne, b. Feb. 8, bap. March 12, 1758.

Gemmil, Elizabeth, dau. of James by Elizabeth, b. Feb. 4, bap. March 2, 1728/9.

Gemmil, Mary, dau. of John by Sarah, b. Nov. 1, 1747, bap. Nov. 29, 174[7].

Gemmil, Sarah, dau. of John and Sarah, b. Sept. 2, bap. Oct. 1, 174[9].

Gemmill, Ann, dau. of James by Eliz*. b. March 25, bap. April 8, 1733.

Gemmill, Dorothy, dau. of John and Sarah, b. June 22, bap. July 19, 1752.

Gemmill, Elizabeth, dau. of John and Sarah, b. Nov. 25, bap. Jan. 20, 1750.

Gemmill, James, son of James and Ann, b. Dec. 1, bap. Dec. 24, 1752.

Gemmill, James, son of John and Mary, b. Sept. 29, 1784, bap. Jan. 16, 1785.

Gemmill, Jane, dau. of James and Ann, b. Oct. 20, bap. Jan. 20, 1750.

Gemmill, John, son of James by Elizabeth, b. Dec. 18, bap. Jan. 6, 1725.

Gemmill, John, son of John and Sarah, b. Dec. 22, 1753.

Gemmill, Martha, dau. of John and Sarah, b. July 8, bap. Aug. 6, 1755.

Gemmill, Nathan, son of James and Anne, b. March 6, bap. March 30, 1755.

Gemmill, Samuel Broster, son of John and Mary, b. Oct. 7, Privately Bap. Oct. 20, 1781.

Gemmills, Anne, dau. of John and Sarah, b. Jan. 10, bap. Feb. 8, 1761.

Gemmills, Betsy, dau. of James and Elizabeth, b. June 22, bap. Aug. 11, 1782.

Gemmills, James, son of James and Elizabeth, b. May 26, bap. Aug. 15, 1784.

Gemmills, John, son of James and Eliz*., b. Nov. 10, 1786, bap. April 8, 1787.

Gemmills, John Broster, son of John and Mary, b. Nov. 27, bap. Dec. 28, 1782.

Gemmills, Mary, dau. of James, Junr. and Martha, b. Jan. 17, bap. March 5, 1780.

Gemmills, Mary, dau. of John and Mary, b. March 25, bap. Aug. 19, 1787.

Gemmills, Nancy, dau. of John and Mary, b. Sept. 18, bap. Nov. [3ᵈ], 1776.

Gemmills, Rachel, dau. of John and Mary, b. March 16, bap. April 18, 1779.

Gemmills, Sally, dau. of Nathan and Mary, b. April 17, bap. May 18, 1783.

Gemmills, Thomas, son of Nathan and Mary, b. July 17, bap. Aug. 26, 1781.

Gemmils, Mildred, dau. of John and Sarah, b. Aug. 11, bap. Sept. 8, 1765.

George, Elizabeth, dau. of Samuel by Elizabeth, b. June 27, bap. Sept. 6, 1724.   Denbeigh Parish.

George, James, "bastard son of Elizabeth George," b. Aug. 14, bap. Aug. 29, 1717.

George, Sarah, dau. of John by Elizabeth, b. Jan. 1, 1690.

Gibbons, Elizabeth, dau. of Thomas by Sarah, b. Sept. 13, 1699.

Gibbons, John, son of Thomas by Sarah, b. Nov. 22, 1701.

Gibbons, John, son of John by Rebecca, b. Aug. 8, bap. Sept. 17, 1738.

Gibbons, John, son of John by Rebecca, b. . . . . . . , 1740, bap. June 29, 1740.

Gibbons, Lawrence, son of John by Rebecca, b. June 7, bap. June 9, 1747.

Gibbons, Mary, dau. of John by Rebecca, b. October 10, bap. Nov. 6, 1748.

Gibbons, Rebecca, dau. of John by Rebecca, b. Oct. 5, bap. Nov. 11, 1744.

Gibbons, Thomas, son of Thomas by Jane, b. Feb. 6, 1696.

Gibbons, Thomas, son of Thomas by Sarah, b. June 31, [1704].

Gibbons, Thomas, son of John by Rebecca, b. Sept. 15, bap. Oct. 20, 1734.

Gibson, Priscilla, servant to Samuel Toplady, b. Sept. 3, 1676.

Gilbert, John, bastard son of Alice Gilbert, servant to Wm Wise, b. June 12, 1706.

Giles, Betsy, dau. of John and Mary, b. Feb. 14, bap. March 24, 1771.

Giles, Frances Patrick, dau. of John and Mary, b. Dec. 15, 1774, bap. Feb. 26, 1775.

Giles, Hugh, son of John and Mary, b. Nov. 28, 1776, bap. April 3, 1777.

Giles, John, son of John and Mary, b. March 28, bap. June 13, 1773.

Giles, Mary, b. May 10, bap. July 14, 1765.
    [Note: The names of her parents are not indicated. The whole entry is as follows: "Mary Giles born 10th May, Bap. 14th July 1765."]

Giles, Mary, dau. of John and Mary, b. Dec. 31, 1766, bap. Feb. 7, 1767.

Giles, Robert, son of John and Mary, b. March 28, bap. July 18, 1779.

Giles, Thomas, son of John and Mary, b. Oct. 15, bap. Nov. 27, 1768.

Gill, Edward, son of Edward "a servant to Edward Johnson," b. Dec. 27, 1682.

Golding, Elinor, dau. of John by Eliz^a. b. Jan. 10, bap. Feb. 2, 1734.

Goodwin, Anne, dau. of Peter by Mary, b. ...... 20, 1747, bap. ....

Goodwin, Elizabeth, dau. of John and Mary Allen, b. March 12, bap. April 17, 1766. (York Hampton).

Goodwin, Elizabeth, dau. of John and Rebekah, b. July 26, bap. Oct. 5, 1772. (York Hampton).

Goodwin, James, son of James and Margaret, b. March 6, bap. May 30, 1782. (Eliz^a. City).

Goodwin, John, son of Peter by Mary, b. Dec. 8, bap. Jan. 8, 1737.

Goodwin, Mary, dau. of Peter by Mary, b. April 12, bap. April 21, 1746.

Goodwin, Peter, son of Peter by Mary, b. July 4, bap. Aug. 5, 1739.

Goodwin, Peter, son of John and Mary Allen, b. Aug. 6, bap. Sept. 4, 1768.

Goodwin, Rachel, dau. of Peter by Mary, b. Feb. 24, 1741/2, bap. the same day.

Goodwin, Rachel, dau. of James and Margaret, b. March 9, bap. April 16, 1780. (Eliz*. City).

Goodwin, Rebecca, dau. of Peter by Mary, b. ...... 1740, bap. Jan. 18, 1740/41.

Gray, Elizabeth, dau. of Edward by Sarah, b. Oct. 12, [1699].

Grey, Ann, dau. of Edward by Sarah, b. Oct. 9, 1696.

Grey, Henry, son of Edward by Sarah, b. Nov. 4, 1688.

Grey, Sarah, dau. of Edward by Sarah, b. Jan. 13, 1693.

Grey, Sarah, dau. of John by Ann, b. Feb. 10, 1701.

Grey, William, son of John by Ann, b. Feb. 10, 1698.

Griggs, Elizabeth, dau. of John by Mary, b. Feb. 9, 1674.

Griggs, John, son of John by Margaree, b. April 8, 1652.

Grubb, Edward, son of Edward by Ann, b. Dec. 21, 1676.

H

Haines, Hannah, dau. of Richard by Suzannah, bap. Aug. 1, 1671.

> [Note: This name is indexed "Haines." It is not clear in the entry, but seems to be "Hunis."]

Hale, Thomas, son of John by Mary, b. Jan. 14, 1691.

Hall, John, son of John by Mary, b. Dec. 24, 1685.

Hall, John, son of John by Mary, b. Oct. 10, 1688.

Hall, Powell, son of Thomas and Polly, b. July 22, 1785, bap.
March 14, 1786. (Glocester).

[Note: The name Powell is partly torn away in the
register. The index makes certain what it is.]

Hall, Timothy, son of John by Mary, b. Aug. 27, 1695.

Halland, Sarah, dau. of Daniel by Mary, b. July 27, 1698.

Hallaway, David, son of James by ...... [Wife's name not
given], b. May 2, 1664.

Hallaway, George, [twin with David], son of George by Annah,
b. Aug. 18, 1690.

Halloway, Anne, dau. of James and Elizᵃ. b. Jan. 9, bap. April
4, 1760.

Halloway, Bennet, son of George by Elizᵃ. b. ......, bap. Oct.
22, 1738.

Halloway, Elizabeth, dau. of Peter and Elizabeth, b. Aug. 16,
bap. Oct. 27, 1771.

Halloway, James Russell, son of Peter and Elizᵃ. b. June 1,
bap. Aug. 7, 1768.

Halloway, Peter Vance, son of Robᵗ. and Diana, b. Dec. 6,
1785, bap. April, 1786.

Halloway, Sarah, dau. of James and Elizᵃ. b. May 5, 1764, bap.
March 31, 1765.

Halloway, William, son of James and Elizᵃ. b. Jan. 6, bap.
Feb. .., 1757.

Hankins, William, son of John by Eliza'th, b. May 5, bap.
June 10, 1733.

Hansford, Lewis, son of Thomas Junr. and Martha, b. Sept.
3, 1783, bap. March 7, 1784.

Hansford, Thomas, son of Thos. Junr. and Martha, b. Sept.
14, 1784, bap. June 26, 1785.

Hardgrove, James, son of James by Elizabeth, b. March 1,
1670.

Hardgrove, James, son of Daniel by Mary, b. Aug. 5, 1700.

Hardgrove, Mary, dau. of Daniel by Mary, b. Dec. 28, 1705.

Hardgrove, Mary, dau. of Daniel by Mary, b. . . . . . . [1708].
    [This and the next entry above it are illegible as to
    date. They are preceded by an entry of June 12, 170[8],
    and followed by one of Aug. 25, 170[8].]

Hardgrove, Robert, son of James, by Elizabeth, b. Sept. 28,
    1668.

Harris, Sarah, dau. of Thomas by Bytrus [?], b. March 6,
    [1698].

Harrison, John, son of William and Sarah, b. April 10, bap.
    May 11, 1777.

Harrison, Martha, dau. of Richard and Martha, b. March 23,
    bap. April 20, 1766.

Harrison, Mary Pate, dau. of Richard and Martha, b. March
    7, bap. April 1, 1764.

Hatchell, Elizabeth, dau. of William, [other parent not named],
    bap. Jan. 2, 17[03].

Haughton, Elizabeth, dau. of Willm. by Ann, b. March 11,
    1728/9, bap. April 13, 1728/9.

Haughton, Peter, son of William by Ann, b. Sept. 10, bap.
    Oct. 18, 1724.

Haughton, William, son of William by Ann, b. Oct. 30, bap.
    Nov. 25, 1721.

Hawkins, Amie[?], dau. of Edward by Elinor, b. June 8, 1682.

Hawkins, Ann, dau. of Samuel by Sarah, b. Dec. 4, bap. Jan.
    29, 1720.

Hawkins, Elizabeth, dau. of Thomas by Eliz^a. b. June 28, bap.
    July 30, 1732.

Hawkins, John, son of Samuel by Sarah, b. Jan. 22, bap. Feb.
    21, 1722.

Hawkins, John, son of Thomas by Elizabeth, b. June 27, bap.
    July 26, 1730.

Hawkins, Martha, dau. of Thomas by Elizabeth, b. Jan. 6,
    bap. Jan. 7, 1727.

Hawkins, Martha, dau. of Matthew by Sarah, b. Feb. 26, 1726,
    bap. April 9, 1727.

Hawkins, Pinkeman, son of Matthew by Sarah, b. Feb. 27, 1728/9, bap. March 30, 1729.

Hawkins, Rebecca, dau. of Matthew by Sarah, b. May 28, bap. June 25, 1732.

Hawkins, Samuel, son of Samuel by Sarah, b. Oct. 3, bap. Nov. 30, 1726.

Hawkins, Thomas, son of Matthew by Sarah, b. June 13, bap. July 23, 1725.

Hawkins, William, son of Matthew by Sarah, b. March 1, bap. Mar. 11, 1730.

Hay, Anthony, son of Nath'. by Anne, b. June 26, bap. July 24, 1737.

Hay, Dorithy, dau. of John by Mary, b. Jan. 14, 1670.

Hay, Dorithy, dau. of Robert by Hannah, b. Feb. 6, 1713.

Hay, Dorithy, dau. of Robert by Mary, b. Nov. 3, bap. Dec. 6, 1732.

Hay, Elizabeth, dau. of John by Mary, b. Dec. 17, 1666.

Hay, Elizabeth, dau. of Capt. William by Bridget, b. Nov. 4, 1667.

Hay, Elizabeth, dau. of Robert by Rachell, b. Jan. 17, 1697.

Hay, Elizabeth, dau. of John and Frances, b. Sept. 13, privately bap. Sept. 19, 1781.

Hay, James, son of Robert by Rachell, b. Feb. 23, 1700.

Hay, James, son of John by Mary, b. Aug. 23, bap. Oct. 11, 1729.

Hay, James, son of Nath'. by Ann, b. Sept. 13, bap. Oct. 15, 1738.

Hay, James, son of John and Frances, b. Oct. 17, bap. Dec. 12, 1783.

Hay, John, son of John by Mary, b. Nov. 15, 1673.

Hay, John, son of Robert by Rachel, b. April 7, 1692.

Hay, John, son of John by Mary, b. Jan. 30, bap. March 18, 1721.

Hay, John, son of Robert by Mary, b. March 4, 1730, bap. Apr. 11, 1731.

Hay, John, son of James and Mary, b. Nov. 8, bap. Dec. 18, 1757.

Hay, Mary, dau. of Robert by Mary, b. June 18, bap. July 16, 1738.

Hay, Rachel, dau. of Rob⁺. by Mary, b. Aug. 29, bap. Nov. 3, 1734.

Hay, Rachel, dau. of Robert by Mary, b. Dec. 7, bap. Dec. 8, 1740.

Hay, Rachel, dau. of Robert by Anne, b. Dec. 11, 1744.

Hay, Rachell, dau. of John by Mary, b. July 2, bap. July 29, 1720.

Hay, Robert, son of John by Mary, b. May 19, 1663.

Hay, Robert, son of Robert by Rachell, b. Aug. 31, 1694.

Hay, Rob⁺., son of Rob⁺. by Mary, b. May 20, bap. June 27, 1736.

Hay, William, son of Capt. William by Bridget, b. Oct. 3, 1666.

Hay, William, son of John by Mary, b. Jan. 24, 1668, [1669?]

Hay, William, son of Robert by Rachell, b. June . ., [1699].

Hays, Mary, dau. of Robert by Elizabeth, b. Dec. 15, 1690.

Hays, Mary, dau. of John by Mary, b. March 8, 1723, bap. April 8, 1724.

Hays, Robert, son of John by Mary, b. Aug. 19, bap. Oct. 16, 1726.

Hayward, Ann, dau. of Henry by Elizabeth, b. Jan. 4, 1710.

Hayward, Anne, dau. of John by Anne, b. March 23, 1736/7, bap. Apr. 24, 1737.

Hayward, Dianah, dau. of Henry by Dianah, b. Jan. 15, 1683.

Hayward, Dianah, dau. of William by Mary, b. May 12, 1700.

Hayward, Edward, son of Henry, Sr., by Elizabeth, b. Oct. 28, 17[09].

Hayward, Elinor, dau. of Henry by Dianah, b. July 25, 1690.

Hayward, Elinor, dau. of William by Mary, b. Dec. 22, 1710.

Hayward, Elinor, dau. of Francis by Diana, b. Sept. 23, bap. Oct. 28, 1739.

Hayward, Elizabeth, dau. of Henry by Dianah, b. May 25, 1676.

Hayward, Elizabeth, dau. of Henry by Elizabeth, b. June 1, [1704].

Hayward, Elizabeth, dau. of John by Ann, b. May 26, bap. June 24, 1733.

Hayward, Elizabeth, dau. of Fran°. J°. by Dinah, b. Dec. 3, bap. Jan. 8, 1737.

Hayward, Francis, son of Francis, Gent. by Martha, b. Feb. 24, 1732, bap. April 14, 1733.

Hayward, Francis, son of Henry by Dianah, b. Oct. 15, 1694.

Hayward, Francis, son of Henry by Dianah, b. Feb. 27, 1696.

Hayward, Francis, son of Henry by Elizabeth, b. May 15, 1700.

Hayward, Francis, son of William by Mary, b. Jan. 15, 1707.

Hayward, Francis, son of William by Sarah, b. Sept. 30, bap. Oct. 28, 1739.

Hayward, Groves, son of William by Mary, b. [November] 19, 1697.

Hayward, Henry, son of John by Margarett, b. October 16, 1651.

Hayward, Henry,—Robert son of a negro woman belonging to, —bap. April 5, 1670.

Hayward, Henry, son of Henry by Dianah, b. Sept. 1, 1679.

Hayward, Henry, son of William by Mary, b. Sept. 13, 170[4].

Hayward, Henry, son of Francis by Martha, b. Nov. 22, bap. Dec. 18, 1727.

Hayward, Henry, son of William by Elizabeth, b. June 9, bap. July 27, 1729.

Hayward, Henry, son of John and Ann, b. Feb. 15, bap. Feb. 26, 174[9].

Hayward, John, son of John by Bridget, b. Aug. 28, 1672.

Hayward, John, son of John by Bridget, b. April 5, 1675.

Hayward, John, son of Henry by Dianah, b. March 27, 1692.

Hayward, John, son of William by Mary, b. March 31, 1695.

Hayward, John, son of Henry by Elizabeth, b. March 16, 1707.

Hayward, John, son of John by Ann, b. May 14, bap. June 15, 1735.

Hayward, John, son of Henry and Frances, b. Dec. 19, bap. Dec. 30, 1750.

Hayward, Margarett, dau. of Henry by Dianah, b. Aug. 15, 1688.

Hayward, Margarett, dau. of William by Mary, b. Sept. 21, 1690.

Hayward, Martha, dau. of Fran*. by Martha, b. Dec. 27, bap. Jan. 7, 1737.

Hayward, Mary, dau. of William by Mary, b. Aug. 28, 1692.

Hayward, Mary, dau. of Henry by Dianah, b. Nov. 6, 1681.

Hayward, Mary, dau. of Francis by Martha, b. Sept. 10, 1722.

Hayward, Mary, dau. of Elinor (an illegitimate), b. . . . ., bap. Sept. 8, 1734.

Hayward, Sarah, dau. of John by Ann, b. July 15, bap. Sept. 12, 1731.

Hayward, William, son of John by Mary, b. February 2, 1658.

Hayward, William, son of Henry by Dianah, b. March 1, 1685.

Hayward, William, son of Henry by Elizabeth, b. March 26, 1702.

Hayward, William, son of William by Mary, b. June 13, 1702.

Hazelgrove, Daniel, son of James by Mary, b. Jan. 26, 1665.

Hazelgrove, Elizabeth, dau. of Daniel by Mary, b. Feb. 28, 1696.

Hazelton, Dunning, son of Thomas by Constant, b. July 22, 1693.

Hazelton, Elizabeth, dau. of Thomas by Constant, b. Feb. 15, 169[8?].

Hazelton, Mary, dau. of Thomas by Constant, b. Nov. 7, 1689.

Hellen, John, son of Nathaniel by Ann, b. Jan. 26, 1695.

Heritage, James, son of William by Elizabeth, bap. Dec. 12, [1703].

Hewitt, John, son of John by Martha, b. July 30, bap. Aug. 14, 1743.

Hewlet, Jane, dau. of Stephen by Agnes, b. Nov. 23, 1675.

Hewlet, Lilla [?], dau. of Stephen [?] by Agnes, b. Nov. 3, 1678.

Hewson, Charles, son of Wm. and Mary, b. Aug. 4, bap. Sept. 6, 1772.

Hewson, Mary, dau. of William and Mary, b. Feb. 14, bap. April 28, 1782. (Eliz⁴. City).

Hewson, Sarah, (Mulatto), dau. of William and Mary, b. July 10, bap. Aug. 22, 1784.

Hide, Ann, dau. of James by Mary, b. Oct. 3, 1693.

Hide, Dianah, dau. of James by Mary, b. Oct. 20, 1690.
     [This name is indexed Hyde].

Hill, Elizabeth, dau. of Samuel by Agnes, b. March 11, 1689.

Hill, Samuel, son of Samuel by Agnes, b. April 11, 1695.

Hill, Sarah, dau. of Samuel by Agnes, b. Feb. 23, 1692.

Hill, Thomas, son of Thomas by Sarah, b. Dec. 28, 1706.

Hilsman, Hinde, son of Bennet by Frances, b. Jan. 25, bap. March 17, 1744.

Hilsman, Mary, dau. of Bennet by Frances, b. Oct. 15, bap. Nov. 15, 1742.

Hilsman, William, son of Bennet by Frances, b. Dec. 20, bap. Jan. 25, 1740/41.

Hinde, Elizabeth, dau. of Thomas by Elizabeth, b. Feb. 27, 1700.

Hinde, Hannah, dau. of Thomas by Hannah, b. July 1, 1673.

Hinde, Hannah, dau. of Thomas by Elizabeth, b. Sept. 6, 1690.

Hinde, James, son of Thomas by Elizabeth, b. Feb. 13, 16[98].

Hinde, John, son of Thomas by Elizabeth, b. Feb. 25, 1695.

Hinde, Thomas, son of Thomas by Elizabeth, b. Oct. 1, 1693.

Hines, James, son of Robert by Mary, b. Aug. 2, 1694.

Hobday, Nancy Buckner, dau. of Isaac and Mary, b. March 30, bap. May 11, 1766. (York Hampton).

Hobson, Armager, son of Robert by Rachell, b. Aug. 13, 1696.

Hobson, Armager, son of Charles by Sarah, b. Dec. 19, 1712.

Hobson, Charles, son of Richard by Ann, b. Dec. 1, 1684.

Hobson, John, son of Richard by Ann, b. Jan. 28, 1693.

Hobson, John, son of Charles by Sarah, b. Aug. 16, bap. Nov. 4, 1723.

Hobson, John, son of Charles Jun'. and Sarah, b. Sept. 23, 1777, bap. Jan. 25, 1778.

Hobson, Marth[a], [twin with Mary], dau. of Charles, Junr., and Sarah, b. Nov. 4, 1779, bap. March 5, 1780.

Hobson, Mary, dau. of Ann of Elizabeth City Co., b. Aug. 9, 1688.

 [No husband mentioned].

Hobson, Mary, [twin with Martha], dau. of Charles Junr. and Sarah, b. Nov. 4, 1779, bap. March 5, 1780.

Hobson, William, son of Ann, a mullatto, "his age tore out of the Register."

 [This entry occurs between one dated Aug. 13, 1696, and another dated May 18, 1696.]

Hogens, Ruth, dau. of James by Marg". b. May 29, bap. July 8, 1739.

Hogg, Stephen, son of Charles and Sally, b. Dec. 5, 1786, bap. March 11, 1787.

Holland, Catherine, dau. of Daniel by Mary, b. Sept. 22, 1694.

Holland, Elizabeth, dau. of Daniel by Mary, b. Feb. 24, 1692.

Hollaway, Ann, dau. of David by Elizabeth, b. June 26, 1697.

Hollaway, David, [twin with George], son of George by Annah, b. Aug. 18, 1690.

Hollaway, Elizabeth, dau. of George by Elizabeth, b. Sept. 8, 1704.

Hollaway, George, [twin with David], son of George by Annah, b. Aug. 18, 1690.

Hollaway, George, son of David by Elizabeth, b. Feb. 20, 170[9].

Hollaway, James, son of James by Ann, b. June 1, 1667.

Hollaway, James, [twin with Rebekah], son of David by Elizabeth, b. Jan. 18, 1711.

Hollaway, John, son of David by Elizabeth, b. Dec. 7, 1701.

Hollaway, Mary, dau. of George by Anna, bap. June 4, 1693.

Hollaway, Mary, dau. of George by Anna, b. Dec. 13, 1695.

Hollaway, Matthas, dau. of David by Elizabeth, b. June .., [1699].

Hollaway, Rebekah, [twin with James], dau. of David by Elizabeth, b. Jan. 18, 1711.

Hollier, Mary, dau. of Simon and Mary, b. April .., bap. June 15, 1766.

Hollihawk, Elizabeth, dau. of Thomas by Margarett, b. Dec. 24, 1707.

Holloway, Anne, dau. of Peter and Eliz". b. Oct. 3, 1773, bap. March 13, 1774.

Holloway, Charles, son of George by Anna, b. April 15, 1688.

Holloway, David, son of David by Elizabeth, b. Jan. 27, 17[03].

Holloway, David, son of David by Frances, b. July 28, bap. Aug. 28, 1737.

Holloway, Dianah, dau. of George by Elizabeth, b. Dec. 4, 171—.

Holloway, Elizabeth, dau. of David by Elizabeth, b. Oct. 1, 1705.

Holloway, Elizabeth, [twin with John], dau. of David by Frances, b. April 6, bap. May 3, 1741.

Holloway, Elizabeth, dau. of James by Eliz"., b. March 25, 1742, bap. April 25, 17[42].

Holloway, Elizabeth, dau. of Thomas and Amy, b. Aug. 17, bap. Sept. 30, 1787.

Holloway, Hindes, son of James Jun. and Hannah, b. May 9, bap. June 2, 1754.

Holloway, James, son of George by Hannah, b. Jan. 16, 1685.

Holloway, James, son of James by Elizabeth, b. Feb. 26, 1744, bap. March 31, 1745.

Holloway, John, [twin with Elizabeth], son of David by Frances, b. April 6, bap. May 3, 1741.

Holloway, Lucy, dau. of James, Junr. and Eliz". b. July 18, bap. Aug. 22, 1762.

Holloway, Martha, dau. of James by Eliz". b. Jan. 10, 1739/40, bap. Feb. 17, 1739/40.

Holloway, Martha, dau. of Peter and Elizabeth, b. Dec. 10, 1776, bap. April 6, 1777.

Holloway, Mary, dau. of James by Mary, b. May . ., bap. May 30, 1736.

Holloway, Mary, dau. of James by Elizabeth, b. Jan. 30, bap. March 10, 1747.

Holloway, Peter, son of James by Elizabeth, b. Oct. 20, bap. Nov. 20, 1737.

Holloway, Peter, son of Peter and Eliz*. b. Dec. 13, 1769, bap. Jan. 28, 1770.

Holloway, Priscilla, dau. of David by Elizabeth, b. Oct. 30, 1705.

Holloway, Robert, son of Peter and Eliz*., b. Oct. 13, bap. Nov. 24, 1765.

Holloway, Robert Owen, son of James and Eliz*. b. June 2, bap. June 30, 1753.

Holloway, Sarah, dau. of George by Elizabeth, b. Dec. 2, 17[13].

Holloway, Sarah, dau. of David by Frances, b. Sept. 24, bap. Oct. 29, 1732.

Holloway, Thomas, son of James by Elizabeth, bap. Aug. 5, 1673.

Holloway, Thomas, son of James and Elizabeth, b. Sept. 23, bap. Oct. 21, 1750.

Holloway, William, son of George and Eliz*. b. Dec. 24, bap. Feb. 1, 1735.

Holloway, William, son of Peter and Elizabeth, b. Nov. 12, bap. (privately), Nov. 13, 1779. Rec*. Sept. 10, 1780.

Homes, Elizabeth, dau. of Richard by Jane, b. Oct. 31, 1722, bap. July 13, 1723.

Hope, Ann, dau. of John by Mary, "of Denbeigh," b. Dec. 5, 1691.

Hopkins, Benjamin, son of Joseph and Dorothy, b. June 23, bap. July 30, 1758.

Hopkins, Joseph, son of Benjamin by Ann, b. September 30, 1710.

Hopkins, Samuel, son of Benjamin by Ann, b. Oct. 15, 1702.

Hopson, Anne, dau. of Armoger and Mary, b. Nov. 14, 1785, bap. March 12, 1786.

[Note: In the margin under the word "mulatto" opposite a previous entry is "Do,"—for ditto. This seems to indicate that Anne Hopson was a mulatto. However above the word "mulatto" in the margin appears the word "Warwick." It is a *possibility* that the "Do" was intended to "ditto" that word instead of the word "mulatto."]

Hopson, Charles (Mulatto), son of Charles and Sally, b. Nov. 4, 1785, bap. March 12, 1786.

Hopson, Edward, son of Charles and Sarah, b. Nov. 20, 1783, bap. March 28, 1784.

Hopson, Frances, dau. of Charles by Sarah, b. Sept. 30, 1713.

Hopson, James, son of John and Mary, b. Aug. 1, bap. Sept. 14, 1783.

Hopson, Nancy, (Mulatto), dau. of John and Mary, b. March 27, bap. May 8, 1785.

Hopson, Polly, (Mulatto), dau. of John and Mary, b. April 10, bap. May 20, 1787.

Hopson, Sarah, dau. of Charles by Sarah, b. May 23, bap. July 26, 1719. Elizabeth City Co.

Horn, John, son of Henry by Hesther, they being servants to Henry Freeman, bap. Dec. 27, 1677.

Houghton, Frances, dau. of William by Ann, b. Feb. 26, 1730, bap. Apr. 4, 1731.

Houghton, John, son of William by Ann, b. Aug. 11, bap. Aug. 21, 1726.

Houghton, Nathaniel, son of William by Ann, b. Feb. 14, bap. March 16, 1722.

Houghton, Sarah, dau. of Wil^m. by Ann, b. Feb. 14, bap. April 1, 1732.

Houghton, William, son of William by Amee[?], b. Feb. 12, 1691.

Howard, Anne, dau. of Robert and Anne, b. Sept. 7, 1771.

Howard, Elinor, dau. of John and Anne, b. March 23, bap. April 20, 1753.

Howard, Elizabeth, dau. of Henry and Frances, b. Aug. 15, 1752.

Howard, Frances, dau. of John by Anne, b. May 18, bap. June 12, 1748.

Howard, Frances Calthorpe, dau. of Edwd. Calthorpe and Sarah, b. July 9, bap. Aug. 17, 1783.

Howard, Francis, son of John by Anne, b. April 29, bap. May 30, 1741.

Howard, Francis, son of Henry by Frances, b. Jan. 7, bap. Feb. 5, 1748.

Howard, Francis, son of William and Anne, b. . . . ., bap. Nov. 19, 1785.

Howard, Henry, son of Henry and Frances, b. July 1, bap. July 13, 1755.

Howard, Henry, son of Wm. and Anne, b. Aug. 30, bap. Oct. 1, 1780.

Howard, "James a boy belong^s to Henry Howard born . . . . & bap. 7th July 1754."

Howard, Lucy, dau. of Henry and Frances, b. Jan. 23, 1764.

Howard, Margarett, dau. of John by Anne, b. Dec. 31, 1738, bap. Jan. 28, 1738/9.

Howard, Martha, dau. of Henry and Frances, b. Oct. 4, 1761.

Howard, Mary, dau. of John by Anne, b. Sept. 18, bap. Oct. 30, 1743.

Howard, Mary, dau. of Henry by Frances, b. . . . . 1746, bap. . . . . .

Howard, Robert, son of John by Anne, b. Oct. . . . ., bap. Dec. 7, 1745.

Howard, Sally Miller, dau. of E. Calthorpe and Sarah, b. Dec. 5, 1784, bap. March 6, 1785.

Howard, William, son of Henry and Frances, b. Feb. 23, 1759.

Howell, Mary, "an illegitimate, Daughter of Elizabeth Howell," b. July 15, bap. Aug. 26, 1764.

Howell, William, "an illegitimate son of Mary Howell," b. June 26, bap. Sept. 2, 1764.

Howell, William: "William son of Elizabeth Howell born 2ᵈ September 1771. Baptized 1ˢᵗ March 1772."

Huason, Mary, dau. of Mary Huason, servant to Francis Callowhill, b. Feb. 27, 1696.

Hubard, Zacharias, son of Cuthbert and Mildred, b. March 28, bap. June 22, 1766.

Hubbard, John, son of Matthew by Mary, bap. Nov. 18, 1683.

Hubbard, Mary, dau. of Mary, [No father named], b. Dec. 5, 1689.

Hubbard, Mary, dau. of Thomas by Martha, b. July 31, 17[03].

Hubbard, Matthew, son of Matthew, by Mary, b. Feb. 16, 1681.

Hubbard, Thomas, son of Matthew by Mary, b. Nov. 25, 1679.

Hubbard, Thomas, son of Thomas by Martha, b. Dec. 25, 170[4].

Hues, Robert, son of Robert by Mary, b. March 22, 1695.

Hues, Thomas, son of Robert by Mary, b. Nov. 15, 1697.

Hughes, Thomas, son of Thomas by Bridget, b. May 22, bap. May 29, 1744.

Hull, Joseph, son of Joseph by Judith, b. Oct. 1, 1694.

Hunley, Ann, dau. of Charles by Ann, b. March 28, bap. "8ber 17," 1731.

Hunt, Ann, dau. of John, Junʳ. by Rebekah, b. Feb. 23, 1710.

Hunt, Curtis, son of Thomas and Elizabeth, b. Aug. 28, bap. Oct. 2, 1785.

Hunt, Diana, [twin with Mary], dau. of Thos. and Mary, b. May 28, bap. June 17, 1781.

Hunt, Dinah, dau. of John and Susannah, b. Nov. 15, bap. Dec. 12, 1736.

Hunt, Elizabeth, dau. of John by Elizabeth, b. Feb. 4, 1691.

Hunt, Elizabeth, dau. of John and Eliz·., b. June 4, bap. July 8, 1756.

Hunt, Frances, dau. of John by Elizabeth, b. April 4, 1689.

Hunt, Frances, dau. of Tho⁸. and Mary, b. Feb. 26, bap. April 10, 1774.

Hunt, James, son of George by Sarah, b. Sept. 26, 1674.

Hunt, John, son of John by Elizabeth, b. Oct. 17, 1681.

Hunt, John, son of John by Margarett, b. July 17, 1652.

Hunt, John, son of Richard by Elinor, b. Nov. 14, 1697.

Hunt, John, son of John by Susanna, b. Aug. 8, bap. Sept. 3, 1738.

Hunt, John Birdsong, son of John by Eliz. b. April 6, bap. May 14, 1758.

Hunt, John, son of Thomas and Mary, b. March 8, bap. April 17, 1778.

Hunt, Joseph, son of Richard by Elinor, b. Sept. 17, 1701.

Hunt, Mabel, dau. of John by Elizabeth, b. Aug. 4, 1684.

Hunt, Margarett, dau. of John by Margarett, b. April 5, 1654.

Hunt, Martha, dau. of Tho⁸. and Mary, b. Feb. 10, bap. April 12, 1772.

Hunt, Mary, dau. of John by Rebekah, b. Jan. ..., 1712.

Hunt, Mary, [twin with Diana], dau. of Thos. and Mary, b. May 28, bap. June 17, 1781.

Hunt, Ralph, son of John by Margarett, b. May 11, 1660.

Hunt, Ralph, son of Richard by Elinor, b. Sept. 18, 1693.

Hunt, Rebecca, dau. of John by Eliz⁸., b. Jan. 9, bap. Feb. 16, 1755.

Hunt, Richard, son of Ralph by Elinor, b. January 11, 1656.

Hunt, Richard, son of John by Margarett, b. January 12, 1656.

Hunt, Richard, son of John by Elizabeth, b. Dec. 12, 1686.

Hunt, Richard, son of Richard by Elinor, b. April 17, 1700.

Hunt, Sarah, dau. of John by Margarett, b. Feb. 4, 1666.

Hunt, Sarah, dau. of George by Sarah, b. Dec. 1, 1671.

Hunt, Sarah, dau. of John by Elizabeth, b. Dec. 5, 1679.

Hunt, Sarah, dau. of John by Elizabeth, b. June 25, 1695.

Hunt, Susanna, dau. of John by Susanna, b. May 29, bap. June 28, 1741.

Hunt, Thomas, son of John by Susanna, b. Jan. 30, bap. March 13, 1742.

Hunt, Thomas, son of Thomas and Mary, b. March 2, bap. April 14, 1776.

Hunt, William, son of John by Margarett, b. January 16, 1661.

Hunt, William, son of John and Elizabeth, b. June 2, bap. July 13, 1760.

Hunt, William, son of John Birdsong and Sally, b .Oct. 6, 1786, bap. Feb. 18, 1787.

Hunt, William, son of Thos. and Eliz*. b. Jan. 29, bap. priv. Feb. 3, 1784.

Hurst, Edward, son of Rich'd. by Eliz*. b. Sept. 23, bap. "8ber" 19, 1733.

Hurst, Sarah, dau. of Rich⁴. by Eliz*. b. April 15, bap. June 20, 1736.

Hurst, William, son of Richard by Elizabeth, b. Dec. 8, 1730, bap. Apr. 11, 1731.

Huson, Anne, dau. of Wm. and Mary, b. Jan. 17, bap. March 12, 1775.

Huson, Fanny, dau. of John and Mary, b. April 10, bap. July 22, 1770.   (Eliz*. City).

Huson, John, son of William and Mary, b. Aug. 22, 1777, bap. March 8, 1778.

Hyde, Mary, dau. of James by Elizabeth, b. Dec. 20, 17[08].

J

Jabbo[?], John, son of Abram by Sarah, b. Dec. 21, 1665.

Jackson, Thomas, son of Anthony by Amee [?], b. Feb. 28, 1685.

Jaggitts, John, son of John and Mary, b. Oct. 6, bap. Nov. 1, 1761.

James, Abner, son of John by Elizabeth, b. Oct. 7, bap. Nov. 6, 1726.

James, Ann, dau. of George by Elizabeth, b. Feb. 23, 17[08].

James, Anne, dau. of Thomas by Mary, b. ——, bap. ——.
  [Note: This entry occurs next after one of June 27,
  1743, and next before one of Feb. 6, 1743.]
James, Cary, son of William by Martha, b. Feb. 18, 1739/40,
  bap. April —, 1740.
James, Elizabeth, dau. of John by Elizabeth, b. April 28, 1705.
James, Elizabeth, dau. of Samuel by Ruth, b. Oct. 23, bap. Nov.
  19, 1732.
James, Elizabeth, dau. of Samuel by Ruth, b. July 30, bap.
  Aug. 31, 1740.
James, Elizabeth, dau. of Thomas by Mary, b. May 2, 1742,
  bap. June 6, 1743.
James, Enos, son of John by Elizabeth, b. July 23, bap. Aug.
  20, 1721.
James, George, son of George by Anne [?], b. Jan. 4, 1676.
James, George, son of George by Elizabeth, b. Oct. 19, 1706.
James, George, son of Tho⁰. and Mary, b. Nov. 25, bap. Jan.
  20, 1750.
James, James Calthorp, "an illegitimate son of Frances James,"
  b. Nov. 21, bap. Dec. —, 1762.
James, John, son of George by Anne [?], b. March 20, 1678.
James, John, son of John by Elizabeth, b. Feb. 18ᵗʰ, 1706.
James, John, son of George by Elizabeth, b. Nov. 20, 1711.
James, John, son of Samuel by Ruth, b. Dec. 15, bap. Jan. 14,
  1738/9.
James, John, son of Immanuel by Sarah, b. Aug. —, 1740, bap.
  Aug. 6, 1740.
James, John, son of Immanuel by Sarah, b. ——— 1741, bap.
  Sept. 20, 1741.
James, Martha, dau. of John by Eizabeth, b. March 5, 1716,
  bap. April 28, 1717.
James, Mary, dau. of George by Anne [?], bap. Sept. 4, 1681.
James, Mary, dau. of John by Temperance, b. Aug. 17, 1701.
James, Mary, dau. of George by Elizabeth, b. Jan. 17, bap. Feb.
  17, 1716.

James, Mary, dau. of John by Elizabeth, b. Aug. 25, bap. Sept. 27, 1719.

James, Mary, dau. of Sam¹. by Ruth, b. May 15, bap. June 16, 1734.

James, Mary, dau. of Thomas and Mary, b. June 10, bap. July 8, 1759.

James, Nathaniel, son of John by Elizabeth, b. Jan. 5, bap. Feb. 17, 1723.

James, Roberts, son of George by Elizabeth, b. May 29, 1714.

James, Roberts, son of Thomas and Mary, b. Nov. 14, bap. Dec. 14, 1755.

James, Samuel, son of John by Elizabeth, b. Sept. 22, 170[9].

James, Samuel, son of John by Elizabeth, b. Feb. 25, 1714, bap. March 25, 1715.

James, Sarah, dau. of John by Elizabeth, b. Oct. 11, 1712.

James, Thomas, son of George by Elizabeth, b. Oct. 11, bap. Nov. 23, 1718.

James, Ufan, dau. of Thomas and Mary, b. March 26, 1752, bap. —— 1752.

James, William, son of George by Elizabeth, b. May 12, 170[4].

James, William, son of William by Ann, b. Oct. 15, bap. Nov. 14, 1736.

James, William, son of William by Martha, b. Oct. 20, bap. Dec. 20, 1741.

James, William Marlow, son of Thomas by Mary, b. Jan. 13, bap. March 13, 1747.

Jarvis, Anne, dau. of George by Mary, b. Nov. — 1742, bap. —— 1742.

Jarvis, Chrismas, son of John by Elizabeth, b. March 6, 1709.

Jarvis, Elizabeth, dau. of George by Eliz*. b. Oct. 12, bap. Nov. 7, 1731.

Jarvis, Elizabeth, dau. of Christmas and Mary, b. April 19, bap. May 25, 1755.

Jarvis, Frances, dau. of George by Mary, b. Nov. 5, bap. Dec. 29, 1747.

Jarvis, Francis, son of John by Elizabeth, b. Aug. 19, 1707.

Jarvis, George, son of John by Mary, b. April 14, 1705.

Jarvis, George, son of George by Mary, b. Sept. 4, bap. Nov. 3, 1744.

Jarvis, James, son of John by Elizabeth, b. July 23, 1712.

Jarvis, James, son of George by Eliz*. b. Aug. 13, bap. Sept. 8, 1734.

Jarvis, John, son of John by Elizabeth, b. Oct. — [1699].

Jarvis, John, son of George by Elizabeth, b. May 5, bap. June 15, 1729.

Jarvis, John, son of Christmas and Mary, b. Jan. 8, bap. Feb. 5, 1753.

Jarvis, John, son of George and Margaret, b. Feb. 13, bap. April 21, 1771.

Jarvis, John, son of John and Unity, b. May 7, bap. June 17, 1781. (York Hampton).

Jarvis, Martha Tucker, dau. of George and Margaret, b. July 11, bap. Aug. 18, 1782. ([Eli]z*. City).

Jarvis, Mary, dau. of John by Elizabeth, b. Aug. 20, bap. Sept. 15, 1717.

Jarvis, Mary, dau. of George by Elizabeth, b. July 2, bap. Aug. 3, 1727.

Jarvis, Mary, dau. of George by Eliz*. b. ——, bap. March 20, 1736.

Jarvis, Mary, dau. of Christmas and Mary, b. May 6, 1763.

Jarvis, Mary Williams, dau. of George and Margaret, b. March 1, bap. April 9, 1780. (Eliz*. City).

Jarvis, Rebecca, dau. of George by Mary, b. March 5, 1748/9, bap. June 16, [ ].

Jarvis, Thomas, son of George by Mary, b. Dec. 16, bap. Feb. 22, 1740/41.

Jarvis, Wilkinson, son of George by Mary, b. March 3, 1738/9, "baptiz'd at York."

Jarvis, William, son of John and Unity, b. March 31, bap. May 18, 1783. ([   ]pton).

Jeggitts, Fanny, dau. of John and Mary, b. June 24, bap. July 15, 1764.

Jeggitts, Gerrard, son of Garden and Mary, b. June 26, bap. July 28, 1765.

Jeggitts, Joseph, son of Garden and Mary, b. Jan. 17, 1762.

Jeggitts, Martha, dau. of Garden and Mary, b. Oct. 28, bap. Dec. 11, 1768.

Jeggitts, Mary, dau. of John and Mary, b. Dec. 25, 1766, bap. Jan. 26, 1767.

Jeggitts, Thomas, son of John and Mary, b. Dec. 18, 1767, bap. Jan. 1, 1768.

Jenkins, John Bushell, [twin with William], son of Richard and Frances, b. Dec. 17, 1770, bap. Feb. 24, 1771.

Jenkins, William, [twin with John Bushell], son of Richard and Frances, b. Dec. 17, 1770, bap. Feb. 24, 1771.

Jewell, Patience, dau. of Mary Jewell, bap. March 7, 1696. [No father mentioned.]

Jill, Ann, dau. of William by Ann, b. Oct. 29, 1679. [twin to Elinor].

Jill, Elinor, dau. of William by Ann, b. Oct. 29, 1679. [twin to Ann].

Joans, John, son of Richard by Dorithy, b. May 28, 1676. [This is doubtless the same as Jones].

Joans, Mary, b. Sept. 18, 1679. [Parents not named].

John, Thomas, son of Wil by Catherine, b. June 25, bap. Aug. 13, 1727.

Johnson, Elizabeth, dau. of George by Mary, b. August 18, 1661.

Johnson, Elizabeth, dau. of John by Elizabeth, b. Sept. 19, 1686.

Johnson, Elizabeth, dau. of Andrew by Elizabeth, b. Oct. 8, 170[9].

Johnson, Elizabeth, dau. of Joseph by Elizabeth, b. April 26, bap. May 25, 1718.

Johnson, Elizabeth, dau. of John by Elizabeth, b. Feb. 20, bap. March 19, 1723.

Johnson, George, son of John by Mary, b. May 7, bap. June 16, 1715.

Johnson, John, son of George by Mary, b. June 2, 1664.

Johnson, John, son of John by Elizabeth, b. Oct. 11, 1688.

Johnson, John, son of Andrew by Elizabeth, b. March 2, 1706.

Johnson, John, son of John, Sen'. by Mary, b. Dec. 24, bap. Jan. 26, 1717.

Johnson, John, son of John by Mary, b. March 26, bap. May 2, 1731.

Johnson, Joseph, son of John by Elizabeth, b. Nov. 11, 1695.

Johnson, Martha, dau. of Joseph by Elizabeth, b. Oct. 29, bap. Nov. 25, 1721.

Johnson, Mary, dau. of John by Elizabeth, b. May 17, 1690.

Johnson, Mary, dau. of John by Sarah, b. Jan. 21, bap. Feb. 5, 1716.

Johnson, Mary, dau. of Joseph by Elizabeth, b. Dec. 16, bap. Feb. 7, 1719.

Johnson, Mary, dau. of James by Jane, b. Sept. 16, bap. Oct. 18, 1724.

Johnson, Rachel, dau. of Joseph by Elizabeth, b. Feb. 12, bap. March 18, 1723.

Johnson, Rachell, dau. of John by Mary, b. Jan. 31, bap. March 10, 1722.

Johnson, Samuel, son of Samuel by Sarah, bap. Aug. 1, 1687.

Johnson, Sarah, dau. of John by Elizabeth, b. Nov. 18, [1698].

Johnson Sarah, dau. of John by Elizabeth, b. Jan. 10 [?], bap. Feb. 21, 1719.

Johnson, William, son of Samuel by Sarah, b. April 27, 1680.

Johnson, William, son of John by Sarah, b. Aug. 23, 1713.

Johnson, William, son of John by Mary b. Oct. 17, bap. Dec. 6, 1719.

Jones, Elizabeth, dau. of Jonathan by Elizabeth, b. 1707. [No month or day noted].

Jones, Elizabeth, dau. of Job by Elizabeth, b. Oct. 8, 170[9].

Jones, Elizabeth, dau. of Job by Sarah, b. March 7, 1740/1, bap. May 31, 1741.

Jones, Elizabeth dau. of Jno. Riddlehouse and Mary, b. Oct. 12, bap. Dec. 4, 1768.

Jones, Elizabeth Riddlehurst, dau. of Thomas and Lucy, b. March 20, bap. May 12, 1782. (Warwick).

Jones, Esther, dau. of William by Patience, b. March 23, bap. Apr. 29, 1725.

Jones, Joanna, dau. of David and Levina, b. Feb. 24, bap. Oct. 19, 1783. ([ ]wk)

Jones, Job, son of Job by Elizabeth, b. March 27, 1710.

Jones, John, son of Job by Elizabeth, b. Sept. 25, bap. Nov. 1, 1719.

Jones, John Riddlehurst, son of John Riddlehurst and Mary, b. March 31, bap. June 8, 1783.

Jones, Mary, dau. of Job by Elizabeth,. b. Feb. 9, 170[3].

Jones, Mary, dau. of William by Patience, b. Jan. 4, bap. Feb. 1, 1718.

Jones, Mary, dau. of John Riddlehurst and Mary, b. Dec. 3, 1778, bap. Jan. 31, 1779. (Warwick).

Jones, Sarah, dau. of Job by Elizabeth, b. July 16, 1712.

Jones, Sarah, [twin with Susanna], dau. of John Riddlehurst and Mary, b. Jan. 5, bap. March 4, 1781. (Warwick).

Jones, Susanna, [twin with Sarah], dau. of John Riddlehurst and Mary, b. Jan. 5, bap. March 4, 1781. (Warwick).

Jones, William, son of William by Elizabeth, b. Sept. 29, 1692.

Jones, William, son of Job by Elizabeth, b. Jan. 29, 1705.

K

Kees, Edward, son of William by Sarah, b. July 22, 1693.

Kees, Elizabeth, dau. of William by Sarah, b. Dec. 9, 1689.

Kees, John, son of William by Sarah, b. Feb. 25, 1687.

Kees, William, son of William by Sarah, b. June 19, 1691.

Kelly, Mary, dau. of James by Suzan, b. May 8, 1711.   Elizabeth City.

Kerby, Anne, dau. of William and Margaret, b. Aug. 31, bap. Sept. 30, 1760.

Kerby, Arthur, son of Robert by Catherine, b. June 20, 1702.

Kerby, Bennet, son of Robert by Catherine, b. October 7, 1705.

Kerby, Bennet, [twin with James], son of Bennet by Frances, b. Jan. —, bap. Feb. —, 1729/30.

Kerby, Bennet, son of Bennet by Frances, b. Oct. 17, bap. Nov. 14, 1731.

Kerby, Bennett, son of William and Margaret, b. Dec. 11, 1775, bap. Jan. 21, 1776.

Kerby, Charles, son of Robert by Catherine, b. Aug. 19, 1707.

Kerby, Elizabeth, dau. of Robert by Catherine, b. Oct. [1]?, 1690.

Kerby, Elizabeth, dau. of Bennet by Frances, b. —— 1746, bap. August 3, [1746].

Kerby, Elizabeth, dau. of Wm. and Margaret, b. July 29, 1768, bap. Feb. 19, 1769.

Kerby, Frances, dau. of Thomas by Frances, b. Nov. 11, 170[9].

Kerby, Frances, dau. of Ben'. by Frances, b. May 13, bap. June 3, 1734.

Kerby, Frances, dau. of John by Mary, b. June 10, bap. July 8, 1748.

Kerby, Hannah, dau. of Robert by Catherine, b. Jan. 24, 170[8].

Kerby, Henry, son of Robert by Catherine, b. May 21, 1700.

Kerby, James, son of Robert by Catherine, b. June 11, 1703.

Kerby, James, [twin with Bennet], son of Bennet by Frances, b. Jan. —, bap. Feb. —, 1729/30.

Kerby, James, son of Wm. and Margaret, b. Oct. 19, bap. Nov. 9, 1766.

Kerby, John, son of Robert by Catherine, b. July 19, 1698.

Kerby, John, son of Thomas by Frances, b. July 21, bap. July 23, 1718.

Kerby, John, son of Robert by Elizabeth, b. Sept. 16, bap. Oct. 15, 1723.

Kerby, John, son of John by Mary, b. April 6, bap. May 14, 1744.

Kerby, John, son of Bennet and Frances, b. April 15, bap. [   ] [1751].

Kerby, Martha, dau. of Thomas by Frances, b. Jan. 9, 1713.

Kerby, Martha, dau. of Bennet by Frances, b. —— 1743, bap. June 27, 1743.

Kerby, Martha, dau. of Bennit and Frances, b. Nov. 21, 1753.

Kerby, Martha, dau. of Thos. and Margaret, b. Dec. 28, 1765, bap. Feb. 23, 1766. (Eliz⁴. City).

Kerby, Mary, dau. of William and Margaret, b. Sept. 30, bap. Oct. 14, 1764.

Kerby, Mary, dau. of Robert by Catherine, b. Sept. 1, 1692.

Kerby, Mary, dau. of Robert by Catherine, b. April 25, 1694.

Kerby, Mary, dau. of Bennet by Frances, b. Aug. 23, bap. Sept. 14, 1740.

Kerby, Mary, dau. of John and Mary, b. May 2, bap. June 17, 1750.

Kerby, Mary Sheild, dau. of John and Eliz⁴. b. April 6, bap. May 29, 1774.

Kerby, Patsey Moore, dau. of John and Elizabeth, b. July 17, bap. Sept. 21, 1776.

Kerby, Rachel, dau. of John and Mary, b. Sept. 24, bap. Oct. 22, 1754.

[Note: After this entry, which is the last one on page 70 of the Register, is this notation: "So far sent to the Secretary's office."].

Kerby, Rachel, dau. of John and Mary, b. Sept. 24, bap. Oct. 27, 1754.

Kerby, Rachell, dau. of Robert by Catherine, b. March 10, 1713.

Kerby, Robert, son of Thomas by Mary, b. May 1, 1662.

Kerby, Robert, son of Robert by Catherine, b. Aug. 23, 1696.

Kerby, Robert, son of Robert by Elizabeth, b. May 30, bap. June 14, 1721.

Kerby, Robert, son of John and Mary, b. July 12, bap. Aug. 16, 1752.

Kerby, Sally, dau. of Wm. and Margaret, b. Aug. 25, bap. Oct. 10, 1773.

Kerby, Sally Sclater, dau. of John and Eliz*. b. June 26, bap. Nov. 8, 1778.

Kerby, Sarah, dau. of Robert by Catherine, b. April 4, 1711.

Kerby, Sarah, dau. of John by Mary, b. May 1, bap. May 30, 1746.

Kerby, Suzanna, dau. of Robert Junr. by Elizabeth, b. Jan. 6, bap. Jan. 6, 1725.

Kerby, Thomas, son of Robert by Mary, b. June 20, 1686.

Kerby, Thomas, son of Bennet by Frances, b. ———— 1742, bap. privately ———— 1742.

Kerby, Thomas, son of John by Mary, b. Aug. 20, bap. Sept. 12, 1742.

Kerby, Thomas, son of Bennet by Frances, b. Oct. 25, bap. Nov. 27, 1748.

Kerby, William, son of Thomas by Frances, b. Aug. 5, 17[08].

Kerby, William, son of Bennet by Frances, b. July 16, bap. Aug. 29, 1736.

Kerby, William, son of Wm. and Margaret, b. March 27, bap. April 28, 1771.

Kerby, William, son of John and Mary, b. July 13, 1770, bap. April 28, 1771.

Kibble, Edward, son of Edward by Sarah, bap. March 2, 1668.

Kibble, Margarett, dau. of Thomas by Ann, b. Dec. 28, 1665.

Kibble, Thomas, son of Thomas by Ann, b. March 2, 1668.

King, Anne, dau. of Michael and Anne, b. Sept. 20, bap. Oct. 24, 1782. (Eliz*. City).

King, Elinor, dau. of John by Elinor, b. ———— 1705.

[The page is torn and the entry partly destroyed. It occurs at the top of page 28. The preceding entry is dated Nov. 4, 1705; the entry following is dated Nov. 29, 1705].

Knight, Ann, dau. of John by Bridget, b. Dec. 28, 1709.

Knight, Edmund, son of John by Bridget, b. April —, 1713.

Knyveton, Frances, dau. of Francis by Susannah, bap. April 9, 1672.

L

Lamb, Ann, dau. of Daniel by Abigail, b. Oct. 3, bap. Nov. 9, 1724.

Lamb, Anthony, [twin with William], son of Anthony by Hannah, b. Feb. 12, 1681.

Lamb, Anthony, son of John by Frances, b. Oct. 7, bap. Nov. 27, 1720.

Lamb, Anthony, son of Anthony by Sarah, b. Dec. 21, bap. Jan. 23, 1731.

Lamb, Anthony, son of Anthony by Rachel, b. Dec. 18, 1744, bap. March 31, 1745.

Lamb, Daniel, son of Anthony by Harriet, b. Feb. 12, 1692.

Lamb, Daniell, son of Anthony by Sarah, b. Sept. 2, bap. Oct. 6, 1728.

Lamb, Dan'. son of Dan'. by Abigal, b. Dec. 11, bap. Jan. 4, 1735.

Lamb, Elizabeth, dau. of Daniel by Abigal, b. Feb. 18, bap. March 19, 1726.

Lamb, Elizabeth, dau. of Anthony and Elizabeth, b. Jan. 25, bap. Feb. 27, 1757.

Lamb, Elizabeth, dau. of Thomas and Diana, b. Nov. 23, 1759, bap. Jan. 13, 1760.

Lamb, Hannah, dau. of Anthony by Hannah, b. Sept. 25, 1690.

Lamb, Hannah, dau. of John by Frances, b. July 30, bap. Sept. 28, 1723.

Lamb, Hannah, dau. of Daniel by Abigal, b. July 10, bap. Aug. 17, 1729.

Lamb, John, son of Anthony by Hannah, b. Aug. 22, 1679.

Lamb, John, son of Daniel by Abigail, b. June 11, bap. July 7, 1717.

Lamb, John, son of Anthony by Sarah, b. July 19, bap. Aug. 23, 1723.

Lamb, John, son of Anthony by Rachel, b. Nov. 8, bap. Dec. 26, 1742.

Lamb, John, son of John by Mary, b. Oct. 12, bap. Nov. 8, 1747.

Lamb, Martha, dau. of Anthony by Sarah, b. July 24, bap. Aug. 28, 1720.

Lamb, Mary, dau. of Anthony by Hannah, b. Feb. 5, 1686.

Lamb, Sarah, dau. of Daniel by Abigail, b. Sept. 5, 1713.

Lamb, Thomas, son of John by Mary, b. May 27, bap. June 22, 1746.

Lamb, Thomas, son of Thomas and Diana, b. March 7, bap. April 11, 1762.

Lamb, Ursella, dau. of Anthony by Hannah, b. March 11, 1683.

Lamb, William, [twin with Anthony], son of Anthony by Hannah, b. Feb. 12, 1681.

Lamb, William, son of Daniel by Abigail, b. March 26, bap. May 1, 1722.

Lamb, William, son of John by Mary, b. Jan. 1, bap. Feb. 12, 1743.

Lane, Mary, dau. of William by Sarah, b. Aug. 23, 1679.

Latimore, Mary, dau. of George and Mary, b. Oct. 9, bap. Nov. 11, 1770.

Latinger, Edward, son of George by Elizabeth, b. March 31, bap. April 8, 1729.

Lawson, Sarah, an illegitimate daughter of Sarah Lawson, b. Feb. 16, 1739/40, bap. in March 1745.

Lee, Samuel, son of Thomas by Jane, b. March 9, 1707.

Lee, Thomas, son of Thomas by Jane, bap. April 29, 1705. Elizabeth City.

Level, Rebekah, dau. of James and Jane, b. "about 11th August, Bap. Septr. 13th, 1764."

Lewellen, Lydia, dau. of James by Ágnes, b. Nov. 8, bap. Dec. 11, 1726.

Lewelling, Fanny, dau. of Alex^r. and Eliz^a. b. June 3, bap. Aug. 8, 1779. (Warwick).

Lewelling, James, [twin with John], son of Alex^r. and Elizabeth, b. Aug. 15, bap. Sept. 13, 1772.

Lewelling, John, [twin with James], son of Alex^r. and Elizabeth, b. Aug. 15, bap. Sept. 13, 1772.

Lewelling, Mary, dau. of Alex^r. and Eliz^a. b. March 26, bap. April 22, 1770.

Lewelling, Nancy, dau. of Alex^r. and Eliz^a. b. May 30, bap. June 26, 1768. ([ ]liz^a. City).

Lewelling, Simon, son of Alexander and Eliz^a. b. Dec. 10, 1776, bap. Feb. 16, 1777.

Lewis, Ann, dau. of Henry by Ann, b. Nov. 19, 1674.

Lewis, Ann, dau. of Roger by Ann, b. May 6, 1682.

Lewis, Charles, son of Roger by Ann, b. May 8, 1680.

Lewis, David, son of David [Mother not mentioned], b. October 21, 16[53?].

Lewis, David, son of David by Ann, b. Jan. 29, 1690.

Lewis, Elias, son of David by Ann, b. Nov. 24, 1700.

Lewis, Elinor, dau. of Roger by Ann, b. Oct. 15, 1688.

Lewis, Elizabeth, dau. of Henry by Ann, b. July 29, 1665.

Lewis, Elizabeth, dau. of Roger by Ann, b. Feb. 25, 1683.

Lewis, Henry, son of Henry by Ann, b. Oct. 1, 1669.

Lewis, John, son of David by Mary, b. June 19, 1663.

Lewis, John, son of John by Jane, b. March 1, 1688.

Lewis, John, son of David by Ann, b. Aug. 31, 1692.

Lewis, Roger, son of Roger by Ann, bap. Sept. 29, 1678.

Lewis, Sarah, dau. of David by Ann, b. Jan. 28, 1688.

Lewis, Sarah, dau. of Roger by Mary, b. Feb. 16, 1691.

Lewis, Sarah, dau. of Owen by Elizabeth, b. March 16, 17[08].

Lewis, Thomas, son of Henry by Ann, bap. June 6, 1671.

Lilbourn, John, son of John by Mary, b. April 2, bap. May 9, 1742.

Lilbourn, Reuben, son of John by Mary, b. April 30, bap. June
1, 1740.

Lilbourn, Reuben, son of Reuben and Eliz*. b. Sept. 7, bap.
Nov. 7, 1773.

Lilburn, Elizabeth, dau. of William by Amidian, b. Feb. 17,
1716, bap. April 7, 1717.

Lilburn, Henry, son of Thomas by Priscilla, b. May 13, 1677.

Lilburn, John, son of Thomas by Priscilla, b. Sept. 13, 1674.

Lilburn, Polly, dau. of Reuben and Betsy, b. Nov. 22, bap. Dec.
29, 1776.

Lilburn, Thomas, son of Thomas by Priscilla, b. Jan. 25, 1671.

Lilburn, William, son of Thomas by Priscilla, b. Dec. 16, 1680.

Lilburne, Elizabeth, dau. of Thomas by Priscilla, b. March 2,
1668.

Lilly, John, son of John, of Milford Haven, by D[orothy?],
bap. Aug. 3, 1669.

Lister, Elizabeth, dau. of John and Mary, b. July 26, bap. Sept.
6, 1772.

Lister, Mary, dau. of John and Mary, b. Nov. 16, 1770, bap.
Jan. 27, 1771.
    [Note: Marginal note: "Died 1789."].

Logwood, Lane, dau. of Thomas by Mary, b. Jan. 11, 1702.

Logwood, Mary, dau. of Thomas by Mary, b. Oct. 28, 1705.

Logwood, Sarah, dau. of Thomas by Mary, b. Sept. 16, 1700.

Loury, Thomas, son of John and M[   ], b. Feb. 15, bap.
May 7, 1769. ([Elizabeth] City).

Love, Betty, dau. of Elias by Elinor, b. —— 1744, bap. Nov.
4, 1744.

Love, Elias, son of Silas by Elizabeth, b. Dec. 4, 1672.

Love, Elias, son of Elias by Elizabeth, b. Oct. 18, bap. Nov.
17, 1717.

Love, Elias, son of Elias by Elinor, b. Sept. 2, bap. Sept. 29,
1747.

Love, Elias, son of Elias and Eleanor, b. Dec. 6, 1751, bap.
Feb. 26, 1752.

Love, Elizabeth, dau. of Silas by Sarah, b. Jan. 4, 1712.

Love, Elizabeth, dau. of Elias by Elizabeth, b. May 2, 1714.

Love, Elizabeth, dau. of Elias by Elinor, b. April 27, bap. May 22, 1743.

Love, Henry, son of Elias by Elinor, b. —————— 1741, bap. Nov. 8, 1741.

Love, Justinian, son of Elias by Elizabeth, bap. April 23, 1696.

Love, Justinian, son of Justinian by Elizabeth, b. Nov. 25, bap. Nov. 26, 1723.

Love, Justinian, son of Justinian by Elizabeth, b. Jan. 22, bap. Jan. 23, 1725.

Love, Mary, dau. of Silas by Elizabeth, b. Dec. 23, 1676.

Love, Mary, dau. of Silas by Sarah, bap. Oct. 20, 1681.

Love, Mary, dau. of Elias by Elizabeth, b. Oct. 2, [1698].

Love, Mary, dau. of Justinian by Elizabeth, b. Aug. 24, bap. Sept. 20, 1730.

Love, Sarah, dau. of Elias and Eleanor, b. Sept. 20, bapt. Oct. 18, 1750.

Love, Silas, son of "Silas by Silas," b. Dec. 22, 1683.

[Note: This should evidently be son of "Silas by Elizabeth" or son of "Silas by Sarah"—A person of this name had a wife by these names.]

Love, Silas, son of Silas by Sarah, b. April 27, 1710.

Love, Thomas, son of Justinian by Elizabeth, b. July 1, bap. July 21, 1728.

Love, Thomas, son of Elias by Elinor, b. Oct. 28, bap. Nov. 27, 1748.

Lovel, Benjamin, son of Benjamin by Susanna, b. Oct. 5, 1693.

Lovel, Hugh, son of Benjamin by Suzana, b. Jan. 28, 1697.

Lovett, Catherine, dau. of John by Elizabeth, b. Sept. 22, 1693.

Loyle, Bridget, dau. of John by Sarah, b. June 21, 1676.

Lucas, Ann, dau. of James by Elinor, b. Aug. 2, 1697.

Lucas, Edward, [twin with Richard], son of James by Elinor, b. Jan. 26, 1700.

Lucas, Elizabeth, [twin with John], dau. of James by Elinor, b. June 10, 1692.

Lucas, James, son of James by Elinor, b. April 17, 1689.

Lucas, John, [twin with Elizabeth], son of James by Elinor, b. June 10, 1692.

Lucas, Richard, [twin with Edward], son of James by Elinor, b. Jan. 26, 1700.

Lumley (Luamly), Martha, dau. of George by Elizabeth, b. Jan. 21, 171[3].

[The name in the text seems to be Luamly. It is indexed Lumley].

Lyell, Elizabeth, dau. of John by Ann, b. Dec. 23, 1711.

Lyell, Frances, dau. of John by Ann, b. May 30, 1716.

Lyell, Gerrard, son of John by Ann, b. Feb. 12, 1713.

Lyell, John, son of John, Jun'. by Hannah, b. Jan. 30, bap. March 19, 1719.

Lyell, William, son of John by Ann, b. March 23, 170[7].

M

Mackay, Elizabeth, dau. of Daniel by Elizabeth, b. Sept. 25, bap. Nov. 5, 1727. Denbeigh Parish.

Mackendree, James, son of John by Isabel, b. June 22, 1677.

Mackendree, John, son of John by Izabel, b. Dec. 27, 1666.

Mackendree, John, son of John by Martha, b. June 17, 1705.

Mackentosh, Jane, dau. of Enos by Elizabeth, b. July 12, 1669.

Mackentosh, Mary, dau. of Enos by Elizabeth, b. February 11, 1662.

Mackey, Daniel, [twin with Michael], son of Michael by Mary, b. Dec. 26, 1701.

Mackey, Mary, dau. of Michael by Mary, bap. Jan. 28, [1699].

Mackey, Michael, [twin with Daniel], son of Michael by Mary, b. Dec. 26, 1701.

Mackey, William, son of Michael by Mary, b. April 7, 169[8].

Mackintosh, Daniel, son of Enos by Elizabeth, b. April 2, 1672.

Mackintosh, Daniel, son of Daniel by Frances, b. March 26, 1697.

Mackintosh, Elizabeth, dau. of Enos by Elizabeth, b. March 23, 1666.

Mackintosh, Enos, son of Enos by Elizabeth, b. April 26, 1682.

Mackintosh, Francis, son of Daniel by Frances, b. June —, [1699].

Mackintosh, Samuel, son of Enos by Elizabeth, b. June 3, 1674.

Mackintosh, Simon, son of Enos by Elizabeth, b. Oct. 2[?], 1676.

Mackintosh, Susanna, dau. of Rich⁴. and Eliz⁴. b. Feb. 21, bap. May 11, 1766.

Maholland, Jenny, dau. of William and Mary, b. March 11, bap. April 26, 1778. (Eliz⁴. City).

Maholland, Mary, dau. of William and Mary, b. April 12, bap. May 12, 1776. (Eliz⁴. City).

Maholland, Nancy, dau. of Wm. and Mary, b. March 9, bap. April 3, 1774.

Maholland, William, son of William and Mary, b. Dec. 9, 1780, bap. Jan. 28, 1781. ([Eli]z⁴. City).

Mallicote, Frances, dau. of William by Frances, b. April 7, 170[9]. Denbeigh Parish.

Mallicote, Frankey, dau. of Philip and Eliz⁴. b. June 26, bap. July 29, 1781. (Warwick).

Mallicote, John, son of John by Susannah, b. Feb. 24, 1736/7, bap. Apr. 24, 1739.

Mallicote, Mary, dau. of William by Frances, b. March 12, 1706. Denbeigh Parish.

Mallicote, Mary, dau. of John by Susanna, b. ——— 28, bap. Sept. 1, 1734.

Mallicote, Philip, son of Philip and Eliz⁴. b. April 6, bap. May 18, 1783. ([ ]ick[?]).

Mallicote, Thomas, son of John by Susanna, b. ——— 1740, bap. May 11, 1740.

Mallicote, Thomas, son of John and Frances, (of Warwick), b. Feb. 6, bap. March 31, 1765.

Mallicote, William, son of John by Susanna, b. Dec. 8, bap. Jan. 7, 1732.

Mallicote, William Gibbs, son of [Ma]llory and J[ ], b. July 22, [1781], bap. April 7, [1782]. (Warwick).

[Note: The name Mallicote is not legible in the entry, but is supplied by the index.]

Mallory, Elizabeth Tabb, dau. of Edward and Rachel, b. Jan. 1, bap. April 30, 1769. ([Elizabeth] City).

Mallory, Mary, dau. of Wm. and Jane, b. Sept. 2, 176[ ]. ([Eliz]ᵃ. City).

[Note: Sister of William Stith Mallory].

Mallory, William Stith, son of Wm. and Jane, b. May 10, 177[ ]. ([Eliz]ᵃ. City).

[Note: Wm. and Jane Mallory were parents of Mary Mallory, b. Sept. 2, 176[ ], and of William Stith Mallory also.]

Maloe, Phebe, dau. of John by Phebe, b. Feb. 27, 1709.

Maney, Catharine, dau. of Wm. and Mary, b. Sept. 15, bap. Nov. 13, 1768.

Maney, John Walker, son of Robᵗ. and Sophia, b. Oct. 28, 1784, bap. April 24, 1785. ([ ] City).

Maney, William, son of Robert and J [?]————, b. Sept. 4, [1782], bap. March 2, 1783.

Manning, Elizabeth, dau. of Thos. and Sarah, b. Jan. 6, bap. Feb. 23, 1766. (Warwick).

Manson, Ann, dau. of Peter by Elizabeth, b. June 4, [1699].

Manson, Anna, dau. of Robᵗ. and Mary, b. Aug. 20, bap. 22ᵈ [Aug.], 1771.

Manson, Elizabeth, dau. of Peter by Elizabeth, b. April 3, 1701.

Manson, Frances, dau. of Peter by Elizabeth, b. July 28, 1707.

Manson, Hannah, dau. of Robert and Mary, b. Jan. 16, bap. Feb. 22, 1778.

Manson, Hannah, dau. of Robt. and Mary, b. Jan. 30, bap. March 9, 1786.

Manson, James, son of Peter by Elizabeth, b. Jan. 13, 170[4].

Manson, John, son of Peter by Elizabeth, b. Feb. 14, 1702.

Manson, John, son of Peter by Hannah, b. Sept. 5, bap. Sept. 22, 1728.

Manson, John, son of Robert and Mary, b. Oct. 21, bap. Nov. 21, 1773.

Manson, Mary, dau. of Peter by Hannah, b. Nov. 3, bap. Dec. 18, 1726.

Manson, Mary, dau. of Robert and Mary, b. Jan. 10, bap. Feb. 11, 1776.

Manson, Nathaniel, son of Peter by Elizabeth, b. April 10, 1710.

Manson, Otis, son of Peter by Tomazine[?], b. Nov. 1, 1690.

Manson, Peter, son of Peter by Tomazin, b. May 28, 1691.

Manson, Peter, son of Peter by Elizabeth, b. Aug. 25, 1697.

Manson, Polly, dau. of Robert and Mary, b. Jan. 12, bap. Feb. 20, 1780.

Manson, Robert Pescud, son of Robert and Mary, b. Jan. 23, bap. March 21, 1784.

Manson, Thomas Pescud, son of Robert and Mary, b. April 9, bap. May 12, 1782.

Manson, Waller, son of Peter by Elizabeth, b. Dec. 8, 1713.

Many, Isabella, dau. of Wm. and Mary, b. June 4, bap. July 7, 1771.

Marshall, John, son of William. "No date in the old Book."
    [The entire entry is as follows: "John son of William Marshall no date In the old Book." The entry occurs between one of Nov. 1st and another of Nov. 29, 1713].

Mason, Arrabella, dau. of Thomas by Grace, bap. Jan. 24, 1668.

Mason, Edward, son of Edward and Margaret, b. March 5, bap. April 30, 1758.

Mason, Grace, dau. of Thomas by Grace, b. November 10, 1666.

Mason, Mary Gerrard, dau. of Robert and Sarah Lewis, b. March 20, bap. April 17, 1772.

Matthews, Ann, dau. of William by Arrabella, b. March 6, 1676.

Matthews, Catherine Lee, dau. of William Peter and Margaret, b. May 4, bap. May 20, 1779. (Eliz". City).

Matthews, John, son of Wm. and Mary, b. Aug. 19, bap. Oct. 4, 1769.

Maurice, Ezerell, dau. of John by Christjana, b. Apr. 10, 1676.

Maurice, John, son of John by Christjan, b. March 8, 1681.

Maurice, William, son of Thomas by Ann, bap. Feb. 4, 1682.

Maurice, William, son of John by Goodlove, b. April 2, 1689.

Maver, John, son of Alex". by Mary, b. Feb. 3, bap. March 10, 1733.

Maver, Marg". [twin with Mary], dau. of Alex". by Mary, b. Aug. 25, Oct. 2, 1737.

Maver, Mary, [twin with Marg"], dau. of Alex". by Mary, b. Aug. 25, bap. Oct. 2, 1737.

Maver, Susana, dau. of Alex". by Mary, b. Aug. 18, bap. Oct. 5, 1735.

Mawrice, Martha, dau. of John by Christjan, b. Aug. 5, 1679.

May, Allen, son of John by Elizabeth, b. March 6, 1744, bap. March 31, 1745.

May, Frances, dau. of Cornelius by Ann, b. June 8, 1691.

May, Henry, son of Cornelius by Ann, of Denbeigh Parish, b. May 27, 1697.

May, James, son of James by Elizabeth, b. Dec. 26, bap. Jan. 25, 1718.

May, James, son of Stephen by Rebecca, b. Feb. 8, bap. March 20, 1742.

May, James, son of James and Eliz". b. June 30, bap. July 24, 1774.

May, James, son of John and Anne, b. Oct. 12, bap. Nov. 26, 1775.

May, John, son of James by Elizabeth, b. Dec. 3, bap. Jan. 11, 1724.

May, John, son of John by Elizabeth, b. Oct. 13, bap. Nov. 8, 1747.

May, John Allen, son of John and Anne "(E. City)." b. March 17, bap. May 2, 1773.

May, Mary, dau. of Stephen by Rebecca, b. May 31, bap. June 28, 1741.

May, Nancy, dau. of John and Anne, b. April 27, bap. June 2, 1771.

May, Thomas, son of James by Elizabeth, b. ——— 4, bap. May 28, 1721.

McGregor, Elizabeth, dau. of William and Anne, b. Sept. 29, bap. Dec. 3, 1781. (Warwick).

Meekings, Elizabeth, [twin with Richard], dau. of Richard by Mary, b. Sept. 5, 1676.

Meekings, Richard, [twin with Elizabeth], son of Richard by Mary, b. Sept. 5, 1676.

Meekins, Elizabeth, [twin with Mary], dau. of Richard by Mary, b. July 17, 1667.

Meekins, Mary, [twin with Elizabeth], dau. of Richard by Mary, b. July 17, 1667.

Meholland, John, son of John and Mary, b. Aug. 17, 1771, "private Bap. 22^d pub. B. 24th Nov^r."

Mellington, James, son of Sarah, servant to Mr. Thos. Carson, b. March 20, 1690. [Father not named].

Mellis, Isaac, son of John by Pheba, b. July 4, 1713.

Mellis, Judith, dau. of Thomas by Ann, (of [illegible] City County), bap. May 20, 1677.

Melloe, James, son of John by Elizabeth, b. Feb. 1, bap. March 11, 1743.

Melloe, William, son of John and Elizabeth, b. June 19, bap. July 30, 174[9].

Mellow, Mary, dau. of John by Eliz^a. b. June 22, bap. July 19, 1741.

Mennes, Ann, dau. of Francis by Frances, b. Aug. 3, bap. Aug. 25, 1717.

Mennis, Benjamin, son of Callohill and Eliz^a. b. Nov. 1, 1756, bap. Feb. 6, 1757.

Mennis, Benjamin, son of Francis by Frances, b. Aug. 28, bap. Oct. 10, 1731.

Mennis, Callowhill, son of Francis by Frances, b. June 12, bap. July 12, 1719.

Mennis, Charles, son of Francis by Frances, b. Oct. 1, bap. Nov. 6, 1726.

Mennis, Charles, son of Francis by Frances, b. Dec. 31, 1728, bap. March 2, 1728/9.

Mennis, Charles, son of Francis and Mary, b. Sept. 22 bap. Dec. 4, 1785.

Mennis, Elizabeth, dau. of Francis by Frances, b. Dec. 16, bap. March 5, 1720.

Mennis, Frances, dau. of Francis by Frances, b. Jan. 26, bap. Feb. 27, 1724.

Mennis, Francis, son of Charles and Anne, b. Oct. 12, 1755, bap. May 2, 1756.

Mennis, Rebekah, dau. of Francis by Frances, b. Jan. 25, bap. March 10, 1722.

Mennis, Sally Sheilds, dau. of Francis and Mary, b. Dec. 21, 1783, bap. June 13, 1784.   (Warwick).

Merritt, Elizabeth, dau. of William by Elizabeth, bap. Sept. 5, 1687.

Merritt, Mary, dau. of John by Frances, b. Dec. 9, 170[4].

Merry, Hope, dau. of Willm. by Jane, b. March 21, 1669.

Merry(?), John, "son of John Merry by his second wife" [not naming her], b. Aug. 2, 1658.

Merry, Margarett, dau. of John by Sarah, b. Oct. 30, 1684.

Merry, Mary, dau. of William by Jane, b. Aug. 29, 1668.

Merry, Mary, dau. of William by Jane, b. Jan. 5, 1674.

Merry, Peter, son of William by Jane, b. Dec. 15, 1665.

Merry, Susan, dau. of William by Jane, b. Aug. 20, 1672.

Messor, Samuel, son of Sam'. by Dorothy, b. Dec. 5, bap. Jan. 25, 1735.

Metcalf, Ann, dau. of John by Elizabeth, b. July 6, 1686.

Metcalf, John, son of John by Bathsheba, b. June 12, 1672.

Metcalf, Mary, dau. of John by Elizabeth, b. Feb. 13, 1683.

Metcalph, Jaboe, son of John by Elinor, b. Feb. 6, 1694.

Miles, Elizabeth, dau. of Augustine by Mary, b. Nov. 20, bap. Dec. 23, 1721.

Miles, Jacob, son of Augustine by Sarah, b. Jan. 15, 171[3].

Miles, Mary, dau. of William by Elizabeth, b. Jan. 21, 1701.

Miles, Sarah, dau. of Augustine by Mary, b. March 13, 1710.

Miles, Sarah, dau. of Augustine by Sarah, b. Dec. 18, bap. Jan. 2, 1716.

Miller, Abigail, dau. of John by Ann, b. Dec. 17, 1688.

Miller, Ann, dau. of John by Ann, b. Feb. 5, [1699].

Miller, Dorithy, dau. of John by Ann, b. April 4, 169[6].

Miller, Elizabeth, dau. of John by Ann, b. Jan. 30, 1690.

Miller, John, son of John by Ann, b. Sept. 1, 1697.

Miller, Peter, son of John by Ann, b. Jan. 17, 1692.

Milloe, John, son of John by Elizabeth, b. Oct. 16, 1746, bap. Dec. 7, 174[6].

Millow, Anthony, son of John and Elizabeth, b. Nov. 22, 1755, bap. Jan. —, 1756.

    [Note: Following this entry is: "Returned to y* Secret* Office May 10ᵗʰ 1756"].

Mitchell, Abraham, son of Abraham by Mary, b. March 10, 1688.

Mitchell, James, son of Abraham by Mary, b. Jan. 9, 1683.

Mitchell, James Rule, son of Stephen and Margaret, b. Feb. 20, bap. March 9, 1783.

Mitchell, John, son of Abraham by Mary, b. July 17, 1685.

Mitchell, Mary, dau. of Abraham by Mary, b. Aug. 24, 1692.

Moore, Amee, dau. of John by Amee, b. Nov. 23, [1699].

Moore, Ann, [twin with John], dau. of John by Amee, b. July 20, 1695.

Moore, Ann, dau. of James by Elizabeth, b. May 16, 1697.

Moore, Ann, dau. of John and Elizabeth, b. ———, bap. Sept. 16, 1750.

Moore, Anne, dau. of Merritt and Anne, b. July 17, bap. Sept. 24, 1777.

Moore, Augustine, son of Daniel by Elizabeth, b. March 7, 1731, bap. April 23, 1732.

Moore, Augustine, son of Augustine and Lucy, b. Jan. 21, bap. Feb. 16, 1766.

Moore, Daniel, son of Dan¹. by Eliz*. b. Dec. 25, bap. Feb. 1, 1735.

Moore, Daniel, son of Augustine and Anne, b. Aug. 16, bap. Oct. 3, 1773.

Moore, Diana Tabb, dau. of William and Mary, b. Sept. 7, bap. Oct. 31, 1779.   (Eliz*. City).

Moore, Elizabeth, dau. of John by A[illegible], bap. Nov. 17, 1678.

Moore, Elizabeth, dau. of Grigs by Rebecca, b. Jan. 27, bap. March 8, 1723.

Moore, Griggs, son of John by Elizabeth, b. Oct. 18, 1693.

Moore, James, son of Alexander, of Old Poquoson, bap. June 1, 1669.

Moore, Jane, dau. of Augustine and Anne, b. Aug. 22, bap. Oct. 3, 1773.

Moore, John, [twin with Ann], son of John by Amee, b. July 20, 1695.

Moore, John, son of John by Amee, b. May 6, 1697.

Moore, John, son of Starkey by Ann, b. Feb. 16, bap. March 9, 1718.

Moore, John, son of Merrit and ———, b. Aug. 30, bap. Oct. 14, 1750.

Moore, John, son of Augustine and Anne, b. Feb. ———, bap. May 8, 1768.   ([ ]z* City).

Moore, John, son of William and Rebecca, b. Feb. 1, bap. March 24, 1776.

Moore, Martha, dau. of Starkey by Ann, b. Dec. 22, bap. Jan. 1, 1717.

Moore, Martha, dau. of Grigs by Rebekah, b. March 4, 1721, bap. Apr. 14, 1722.

Moore, Martha, dau. of Dan¹. by Eliz⁺. b. May —, bap. Aug. 24, 1734.

Moore, Martha, dau. of Merrit by Martha, b. April 9, bap. May 6, 1739.

Moore, Martha, dau. of Daniel by Mary, b. Aug. 1, bap. Aug. 21, 1741.

Moore, Mary, dau. of John by Amee[?] b. May 14, 1682.

Moore, Mary, dau. of Daniel by Elizabeth, b. Nov. 20, bap. Dec. 21, 1729.

Moore, Mary, dau. of Starkey and Mary, b. ———, bap. June 24, 1750.

Moore, Mary, dau. of Merritt and Anne, b. Nov. 14, bap. Dec. 16, 1779.

Moore, Merritt, son of Starkey by Ann, b. May 31, bap. July 31, 1729.

Moore, Phillip, son of Starkey by Ann, b. Oct. 25, bap. Nov. 28, 1731.

Moore, Sarah, dau. of John by Amie, b. Aug. 8, 1684.

Moore, Starkey, son of John by Amee, b. Oct. 30, 1692.

Moore, Starkey, son of Starkey by Ann, b. Oct. 26, bap. Nov. 24, 1722.

Moore, William, son of John and Elizabeth, b. Oct. 3, bap. Dec. 10, 1751.

Moore, William, son of Wm. and Mary, b. June 24, bap. Aug. 28, 1774.

Moreland, William, son of John and Fanny, b. March 18, bap. April 27, 1777. ([Nor]thampton).

Morfey, Frances, dau. of Glove, [No wife mentioned] bap. May 2, 1675.

Morgan, Charles, son of William by Ann, b. September 25, 1710.

Morgan, Elinor, dau. of Thomas by Elinor, b. Aug. 24, 1690.

Morgan, Gerrard, son of Humphrey and Anne, b. Dec. 15, 1762, bap. Jan. 15, 1763.

Morgan, John, son of William by Ann, b. May 24, 1714.

Morgan, Martha, dau. of Humphrey and Anne, b. Oct. 15, bap. Nov. 18, 1764.

Morgan, Mary, dau. of John by Ann, b. Dec. 8, 1734.

Morgan, Roger, son of Thomas by Elinor, b. Aug. 2, 1688.

Morgan, Samuel, son of Simon by Elizabeth, bap. April 30, [1703]. Denbeigh Parish.

Morgan, Sarah, dau. of Thomas by Elinor, b. March 10, 1684.

Morgan, Thomas, son of Thomas by Elinor, b. Jan. 1, 1679.

Morgan, Thomas, son of William by Ann, b. March 5, 1706.

Morgan, Thomas, son of John by Ann, b. Oct. 25, bap. Nov. 26, 1732.

Morgan, William, son of Thomas by Elizabeth, b. Nov. 17, 1677.

Morgan, William, son of William by Alice, b. July 12, 1690.

Morphew, Elinor, dau. of Richard by Izabel, b. Oct. 6, 1672.

Morphew, Richard, son of Richard by Izabell, b. Nov. 12, 1677.

Morphey, Mary, dau. of Richard by Izzab[ell], b. July 21, 1669.

Morris, Ambrose, son of Giles and Mary, b. Feb. 9, bap. April 4, 1773.

Morris, Anne, dau. of Nich[as]. by Mary, b. March 5, 1740/1, bap. April 5, 174[1].

Morris, Anne, dau. of William by Joyce, b. Nov. 12, bap. Dec. 22, 1742.

Morris, Anne, dau. of Wm. and Elizabeth, b. Aug. 11, bap. Oct. 31, 1784.

Morris, Anthony, son of John and Elizabeth, b. ———, bap. March 22, 1761.

Morris, Betsy Birdsong, dau. of Wm. and Eliz[a]. b. Oct. 22, bap. Dec. 19, 1779.

Morris, Conyers, son of John by Mary, b. March 12, 1740/1, bap. April 5, 1741.

Morris, Dianah, dau. of Nicholas by Mary, b. April 29, bap. May 29, 1743.

Morris, Elizabeth, dau. of John, Jun[r]. by Mary, b. Jan. 7, bap. Jan. 21, 1738/9.

Morris, Elizabeth, dau. of Giles and Mary, b. Sept. 8, bap. Oct. 10, 1756.

Morris, Elizabeth, dau. of John and Elizabeth, b. Jan. 12, bap. April 8, 1781. (Warwick).

Morris, Hannah, dau. of John Jun'. by Mary, b. Oct. 17, bap. Nov. 22, 1730.

Morris, Hannah, dau. of William by Ann, b. Jan. 1, bap. Jan. 28, 1731.

Morris, Hannah, dau. of John and Eliz*. b. Aug. 17, bap. Sept. 15, 1756.

Morris, John, son of Nicholas by Mary, b. June 22, bap. July 19, 1747.

Morris, John, son of John and Elizabeth, b. Feb. 18, 1754.

Morris, John, son of Giles and Mary, b. Feb. 14, bap. April 9, 1758.

Morris, John, son of William and Eliz*. b. Jan. 10, bap. April 6, 1777.

Morris, Martha, dau. of William by Joice, b. March 25, 1747, bap. April 26, 17[47].

Morris, Martha, dau. of Giles and Mary, b. Dec. 9, 1769, bap. Feb. 18, 1770.

Morris, Mary, dau. of John Junr. by Mary, b. July 23, bap. Aug. 27, 1732.

Morris, Mary, dau. of Nicholas by Mary, b. May 25, bap. June 25, 1738.

Morris, Mary, b. May 10, bap. July 14, 1765.
   [Note: The names of her parents are not given. The whole entry is as follows: "Mary Morris born 10ᵗʰ May, Bap. 14ᵗʰ July 1765."]

Morris, Nancy Hunt, dau. of Wm. and Eliz*. b. May 25, bap. July 2, 1786.

Morris, Rich⁴. M°Intosh, son of John and Eliz*. b. Feb. 25, bap. March 30, 1783.

Morris, Thomas, son of John by Elizabeth, bap. July 6, 1669.

Morris, Thomas, son of Nicholas and Mary, b. Nov. 22, bap. Dec. 23, 1751.

Morris, William, son of Nicholas by Mary, b. June 1, 1749, bap. July 2, 17[   ].

Morris, William, son of Giles and Mary, b. Nov. 18, 1767, bap. Jan. 31, 1768.

Morriss, Eliz*., dau. of Nich**. by Mary, b. June 11, bap. July 7, 1734.

Morriss, Elizabeth, dau. of John by Mary, b. Dec. 10, 1709.

Morriss, Elizabeth, dau. of William by Ann, b. Sept. 14, bap. Oct. 20, 1717.

Morriss, Giles, son of William by Ann, b. Aug. 7, bap. Sept. 22, 1722.

Morriss, Giles, son of William by Ann, b. Oct. 13, bap. Nov. 9, 1729.

Morriss, Goodlove, dau. of William by Ann, b. Jan. 6, bap. Feb. 14, 1724.

Morriss, John, son of John by Mary, b. March 20, 1705.

Morriss, John, son of William by Ann, b. Jan. 12, bap. Feb. 25, 1726.

Morriss, Mary, dau. of Nicholas by Mary, b. March 17, 1744, bap. April 14, 1745.

Morriss, Nicholas, son of John by Mary, b. Nov. 19, 1713.

Morriss, Sarah, dau. of John by Mary, b. Sept. 17, bap. Oct. 20, 1728.

Morriss, Susanna, dau. of John Jun*. by Mary, b. Sept. 23, bap. Oct. 10, 1736.

Morriss, Tavernor, son of Willm. by Ann, b. Sept. 12, bap. Oct. 12, 1735.

Morriss, William, son of William by Ann, b. Jan. 9, bap. Jan. 18, 1719.

Morriss, William, son of William by Ann, b. Nov. 13, bap. Dec. 3, 1720.

Morton, Elizabeth, dau. of Richard by Joan, b. Nov. 9, 1705.

Morton, John, son of Richard by Joan, b. Dec. 30, 170[9].

Moss, Benjamin, [twin with James], son of William by Elizabeth, b. Aug. 23, 1719, bap. Aug. 24, 172[0].

Moss, Benjamin, son of William and Mary, b. Sept. 18, 1781, bap. Aug. 16, 1782. (Yorkhptn).

Moss, Dinah, dau. of Edward, Jun'. by Elinor, b. Dec. 22, bap. Feb. 8, 1735.

Moss, Edward, son of William by Elizabeth, b. Oct. 8, 1710.

Moss, Elizabeth, dau. of Wm. Junr. and Frances, b. Feb. 26, 1761.

Moss, Francis, son of Wm. Junr. and Frances, b. May 28, 1759.

Moss, James, [twin with Benjamin], son of William by Elizabeth, b. Aug. 23, 1719, bap. Aug. 24, 172[0].

Moss, John, son of William by Elizabeth, b. Jan. 2, bap. Jan. 21, 1717.

Moss, John, son of Benjamin by Eliz'. b. Jan. 15, 1737/8, bap. Feb. 12, 1737/8.

Moss, Lewis, son of John and Anne, b. June 27, bap. July 5, 1772.

Moss, Lucy, dau. of W'". Junr. and Frances, b. Aug. 22, bap. Oct. 10, 1762.

Moss, Margaret Tabb, dau. of Sheldon and Mary, b. Aug. 10, bap. Sept. 27, 1783. ([   ] City).

Moss, Randolph, son of Benj'. by Isabella, b. Feb. 16, bap. March 24, 1748.

Mountain, Elizabeth, dau. of Thomas by Elizabeth, b. Oct. 16, 1693.

Muckendree, Dennis, son of John by Martha, b. April 18, 1707.

Muckendree, Elizabeth, dau. of John by Martha, b. May 9, 1692.

Muckendree, Martha, dau. of John by Martha, b. March 20, 1711.

Muckendree, Mary, dau. of John by Mary, b. Dec. 31, 1697.

Mumford, Elizabeth, dau. of Joseph by Elizabeth, b. Feb. 2, 1700.

Mundel, Elizabeth, dau. of John and Elve, b. Feb. 24, bap. May 17, 1767.

Mundell, Anne, dau. of John and Elvy, b. April 4, bap. May 16, 1773.

Mundell, Diana, dau. of John and Elvira, b. Nov. 2, 1775, bap. Jan. 7, 1776.

Mundell, James, son of John and Elvy, b. Nov. 28, 1769, bap. April 22, 1770.

Murrey, Anna, dau. of James by Mary, bap. June 1, 1669.

Mutty, Daniel, son of Daniel by Bridget, b. Sept. 5ᵗʰ, 1670.

Mutty, Mary, dau. of Daniel by Bridget, b. Feb. 14, 1673.

N

Needham, John, son of Joseph and Frances, b. July 27, bap. Sept. 18, 1774.

Needham, Molly, dau. of Joseph and Frances, b. March 14, bap. April 22, 1776.   ([Eli]zᵃ City).

Nettles, John, son of John and Sally, b. Nov. 17, bap. Dec. 8, 1776.

Newman, John, son of Edward by Margarett, b. Oct. 23, bap. Dec. 6, 1719.

Newman, Sarah, dau. of Edward by Margarett, b. May 24, bap. June 23, 1717.

Nickson, Ann, dau. of John by Mary, b. April 17, 1687.

Nickson, Hannah, dau. of John by Mary, b. June 19, 1672.

Nickson, Hannah, dau. of John by Mary, b. Sept. 19, 1682.

Nickson, Humphrey, son of John by Mary, b. March 9, 1677.

Nickson, John, son of Humphry by Susan, b. Feb. 27, 1711.

Nickson, Martha, dau. of Humphry by Suzan, b. May 1, bap. June 1, 1718.

Nickson, Mary, dau. of Humphry by Susan, b. April 19, 1709.

Nickson, Richard, son of John by Mary, b. Oct. 3, 1670.

Nickson, Thomas, son of John by Mary, b. March 17, 1679.

Nickson, William, son of John by Mary, b. June 21, 1674.

Nightingale, Ann, dau. of Charles by Ann, b. Jan. 11, 170[9].

Noblin, Samuel Simmons, son of Matthew by Ann, b. Sept. 3, bap. Oct. 18, 1724.

Norclan, Nathaniel, son of Abraham by Catherine, b. Dec. 12, 1709.

Northarn, Phillip, son of John by Elizabeth, b. Sept. 25, 17[03].

Northarn, Rachel, dau. of John by Elizabeth, b. July 6, 1690.

Northorn, John, son of John by Elizabeth, b. April 14, 1692.

Nutting, Ann, dau. of Thomas by Elizabeth, b. Feb. 1, 1694.

Nutting, Booth, son of Thomas by Elizabeth, bap. Feb. 14, 1680.

Nutting, Catherine, dau. of Thomas by Elizabeth, b. March 31, 1692.

Nutting, Elizabeth, dau. of Thomas by Elizabeth, b. Oct. 10, 1686.

Nutting, Hope, dau. of Thomas by Elizabeth, b. Jan. 19, 1688.

Nutting, Hope, dau. of Thomas by Elizabeth, b. Feb. 11, 1689.

Nutting, Jane, dau. of Thomas by Elizabeth, b. Aug. 23, 1698.

Nutting, Mary, dau. of Thomas by Elizabeth, b. Jan. 7, 1682.

O

Ohaven, Mary, dau. of Barnaby by Bridget, bap. Sept. 5, 1687.

Orver[?], Elizabeth, dau. of John by Mary, b. Sept. 6, 1693.

Orver[?], Matthew, son of John by Mary, b. July 23, 1695.

Osburn, Samuel, son of John and Sarah, b. Jan. 29, bap. March 9, 1783.

Oswald, Elizabeth, dau. of Eleazar and Elizabeth, b. July 23, bap. Aug. 9, 1772.

Owen, Bartholomew, son of Robert by Catherine, b. Oct. 28, 1692.

Owen, John, son of John by Mary, b. Nov. 15, 1691. [This name may be Owin].

P

Page, John, son of Thomas by Suzand, b. Sept. 24, [1703].

Page, Thomas, son of Thomas by Elizabeth, b. March 31, 1710.

Page, William, son of Thomas by Elizabeth, b. Jan. 17, 1707.

Pain, Ann, dau. of George by Mary, b. Nov. 22, 1717, bap. April 6, 1718.

Pain, George, son of William by Ann, b. Feb. 20, 1689.

Pain, William, son of William by Ann, b. Sept. 20, 1692.

Palmer, Charlotte Ballard, dau. of Benjamin and Charlotte, b. Aug. 31, 1780, bap. June 17, 1781. (York Hampton).

Parr, John, son of John by Ann, b. Oct. 26, 1677.

Parson, Claire, son of John by Anne, b. Sept. 5, 1685.

Parsons, Amy, dau. of John by Elizabeth, b. March 4, 1659.

Parsons, Ann, dau. of William by Ann, b. March 31, bap. April 28, 1723.

Parsons, Anne, dau. of James and Martha, b. March 27, bap. May 28, 1780.

Parsons, Armager, son of James by Dorothy, b. April 21, 169[8?].

Parsons, Armiger, son of James and Elizabeth, b. Nov. 19, 1772, bap. Jan. 24, 1773.

Parsons, Dorithy, dau. of Armager by Elizabeth, b. Sept. 9, bap. Oct. 15, 1720.

Parsons, Dorithy, dau. of Armager by Elizabeth, b. April 6, bap. May 24, 1724

Parsons, Dorothy, dau. of James and Martha, b. Dec. 3, 1767, bap. Jan. 24, 1768.

Parsons, Edmund, son of John and Mary, b. Aug. 6, 1770, bap. Feb. 3, 1771.

Parsons, Elizabeth, dau. of John by Elizabeth, b. April 4, 1656.

Parsons, Elizabeth, dau. of John by Ann, b. Aug. 30, 1692.

Parsons, Elizabeth, dau. of James by Dorothy, b. Aug. 13, 1700.

Parsons, Elizabeth, dau. of Armoger by Elizabeth, b. Dec. 29, bap. March 10, 1721.

Parsons, Elizabeth, dau. of James and Martha, b. April 7, bap. May 5, 1765.

Parsons, Frances, dau. of James by Dorithy, b. Dec. 29, 1706.

Parsons, Frances, dau. of James by Dorithy, b. May 10, 1712.

Parsons, James, son of John by Elizabeth, b. March 27, 1673.

Parsons, James, son of James by Dorithy, b. Aug. 30, 1702.

Parsons, James, son of John by Ann, b. Nov. 6, 1707.

Parsons, James, son of Armager by Elizabeth, b. Jan. 29, 1726, bap. April 27, 1727.

Parsons, James, son of Armager by Eliz⁴., b. Sept. 8, bap. Nov. 4, 1733.

Parsons, James, son of James and Martha, b. Feb. 17, bap. April 15, 1770.

Parsons, Jane, dau. of John by Elizabeth, b. Sept. 13, 1669.

Parsons, John, son of John by Elizabeth, b. August 12, 1664.

Parsons, John, son of John by Ann, b. Oct. 22, 1690.

Parsons, John, son of John by Sarah, b. July 12, bap. Aug. 8, 1731.

Parsons, John, son of James and Martha, b. Feb. 5, bap. April 2, 1775.

Parsons, Mary, dau. of James and Martha, b. Sept. 30, bap. Nov. 9, 1760.

Parsons, Mary, dau. of John by Sarah, b. Nov. 10, bap. Dec. 16, 1733.

Parsons, Priscilla, dau. of John by Sarah, b. ——, bap. May 8, 1737.

Parsons, Rachel, dau. of Armager by Eliz*., b. Sept. 15, bap. Sept. 22, 1732.

Parsons, Sarah, dau. of John by Elizabeth, b. July 12, 1662.

Parsons, Thomas, son of Armager by Elizabeth, b. Oct. 8, bap. Nov. 16, 1729.

Parsons, Thomas, son of John and Martha, b. May 4, bap. Aug. 8, 1784.

Parsons, Wayd, son of James by Dorithy, b. Aug. 25, 170[8].

[The name is indexed Parsons, Wade,—which is, of course, the correct rendering].

Parsons, William, son of John by Ann, b. April 25, 1700.

Parsons, William, son of James and Martha, b. Dec. 4, 1777, bap. Jan. 24, 1778.

Pasqui, Ann, dau. of Peter by Mary, b. Nov. 1, 1706.

Pasqui, Elizabeth, dau. of Peter by Mary, b. April 9, 1705.

Pasqui, John, son of Peter by Mary, b. Jan. 18, 1702.

Pasqui, Peter, son of Peter by Mary, bap. Aug. 9, 1696.

Patlin, John, son of John by Elinor, b. Aug. 27, 1676.

Patrick, Alice, dau. of John by Elizabeth, b. Aug. 4, bap. Sept. 26, 1725.

Patrick, Ann, dau. of John by Mary, b. Dec. 3, 1686.

Patrick, Betsy, dau. of Edmund and Mildred, b. Oct. 5, bap. Nov. 27, 1785.

Patrick, Clayton, son of Curtis and Martha, b. Feb. 9, bap. March 19, 1769.

Patrick, Curtis, son of John by Eliz*., b. Jan. 13, bap. Feb. 10, 1733.

Patrick, Edmund, son of John and Elizabeth, b. ——, bap. April 26, [1752].

Patrick, Edmund, son of Edmund and Mildred, b. Feb. 10, bap. April 17, 1778.

Patrick, Edmund Curtis, son of Edmund and Mildred, b. Oct. 22, bap. Nov. 5, 1780.

Patrick, Edmund Curtis, son of William and Lucy, b. April 29, bap. May 25, 1777.

Patrick, Elizabeth, dau. of Curtis and Martha, b. Feb. 12, 1761.

Patrick, Elizabeth, dau. of John by Elizabeth, b. June 3, 1689.

Patrick, Elizabeth, dau. of John by Sarah, b. Feb. 19, 1700.

Patrick, Elizabeth, dau. of John and Mary, b. Oct. 26, 1753.

Patrick, Elizabeth Topless, dau. of Wm. and Lucy, b. Dec. 23, 1772, bap. Jan. 31, 1773.

Patrick, Frances, dau. of John by Sarah, b. Oct. 5, 1711.

Patrick, Frances, dau. of John by Elizabeth, b. Oct. 28, 1746, bap. Nov. 16, 17[46].

Patrick, Frances Manson, dau. of Wm. and Eliz*., b. Nov. 9, bap. Dec. 11, 1768.

Patrick, Hannah, dau. of John by Sarah, b. Aug. 25, 1710.

Patrick, Hannah, dau. of Wm. Junr. and Eliz*., b. June 30, bap. Aug. 9, 1761.

Patrick, Hannah, dau. of John and Mary, b. April 27, bap. May 19, 1765.

Patrick, John, son of Walter by Elizabeth, b. Oct. 2, 1675.

Patrick, John, son of John by Sarah, b. July 26, 1703.

Patrick, John, son of John Junr. by Elizabeth, b. Oct. 16, bap. Nov. 20, 1726.

Patrick, John, son of Wm. and Eliz*., b. April 23, bap. May 29, 1757.

Patrick, John, son of John and Mary, b. Dec. 6, 1758, bap. Jany. 11, 1759.

Patrick, John, son of Edmond and Mildred, b. Aug. 22, bap. Oct. 4, 1772.

Patrick, Martha, dau. of John by Sarah, b. July 19, bap. Aug. 9, 1719.

Patrick, Mary, dau. of Walter by Elizabeth, bap. June 8, 1677.

Patrick, Mary, dau. of John by Sarah, b. March 21, 1705.

Patrick, Mary, dau. of John by Eliz*., b. July 26, bap. Aug. 27, 1738.

Patrick, Mary, dau. of John and Mary, b. Feb. 11, bap. March 8, 1755.

Patrick, Mary, dau. of Wm. Junr. and Eliz*., b. Jan. 25, bap. Feb. 21, 1765.

Patrick, Merrit, son of John by Elizabeth, b. Nov. 17, bap. Dec. 9, 1744.

Patrick, Nancy, dau. of John and Mary, b. April 12, bap. May 9, 1762.

Patrick, Nancy, dau. of Curtis and Martha, b. Nov. 12, 1773, bap. Feb. 20, 1774.

Patrick, Peter, son of John and Mary, b. Feb. 11, bap. March 13, 1757.

Patrick, Robert, son of Wm. and Eliz*., b. Feb. 11, bap. March 24, 1767.

Patrick, Sally Clayton, dau. of Edmund and Mildred, b. March 12, bap. April 14, 1775.

Patrick, Sarah, dau. of John by Sarah, b. Oct. 4, 17[08].

Patrick, Sarah, dau. of John Junr. by Elizabeth, b. April 12, bap. May 9, 1731.

Patrick, Sarah, dau. of Curtis and Martha, b. Nov. 16, 1758.

Patrick, Sarah, dau. of Wm. Senr. and Elizabeth, b. Oct. 10, 1759.

Patrick, Susanna, dau. of John by Eliz*., b. July 26, bap. Aug. 9, 1743.

Patrick, Susanna, dau. of Curtis and Martha, b. Nov. 29, 1755, bap. Jan. 18, 1756.

Patrick, Thomas, son of John by Elizabeth, b. Sept. 5, bap. Oct. 6, 1722.

Patrick, Thomas, son of John Junr., by Elizabeth, b. Dec. 6, 1728, bap. Jan. 12, 1728/9.

Patrick, Thomas, son of Wm. Junr. and Elizabeth, b. Jan. 14, bap. Feb. 6, 1763.

Patrick, Thomas Curtis, son of Curtis and Martha, b. May 5, bap. June 1, 1766.

Patrick, Walter, son of John by Elizabeth, b. Dec. 9, bap. Jan. 12, 1728/9.

Patrick, Walter, son of John Senr. by Eliz*., b. Jan. 20, bap. Feb. 21, 1730.

Patrick, William, son of John by Sarah, b. Jan. 16, bap. Feb. 16, 1716.

Patrick, William Loney, son of Eliz*. (an illegitimate), b. June 19, bap. Oct. 6, 1734.

Patrick, William, son of John by Elizabeth, b. March 30, 1740/1, bap. Apr. 26, 1741.

Patrick, William, son of Wm. and Lucy, b. June 17, bap. July 17, 1774.

Patrick, Willm., son of John by Eliz*., b. April 23, bap. May 23, 1736.

Pawmer, Ann, dau. of James by Catherine, b. March 7, 1692.

[This probably is the name we know today as Palmer].

Pebworth, John, son of Robert and "——— his wife," b. Aug. 25, 1767, bap. Jan. 10, 1768.

Pebworth, William, son of Robert and Margaret, b. March 25, bap. May 6, 1770.

Pemble, Mary, dau. of Thomas and Catharine, b. Oct. 12, bap. Oct. 15, 1752.

Pendrice, Temperance, dau. of Francis, by Elizabeth, b. Jan. 29, 1685.

Penrice, Elizabeth, dau. of Robert by Hannah, b. July 20, 1673.

Penrice, Francis, son of John by Perina, b. February 20, 1654.

Penrice, John, b. May 17, 1676.
    [Neither mother nor father named. The whole entry is: "John Penrice was born May 17th, 1676."]

Penrice, Mary, dau. of Francis, [Other parent not named], b. Jan. 10, 1688.

Penrice, Purina, dau. of Francis by Elizabeth, bap. March 6, 1680.

Penrice, Robert, son of Robert by Hannah, b. Aug. 16, 1671.

Penrice, Thomas, son of Francis by Elizabeth, b. June 6, 1683.

Penrice[?], Thomas, son of John, by P———, b. December 21, 1653.

Perkins, Elizabeth, dau. of Henry by Elizabeth, b. Aug. 21, 1683.

Perkins, Hannah, [twin with William], dau. of Henry by Elizabeth, b. Nov. 10, 1674.

Perkins, Henry, son of Henry by Elizabeth, b. May 29, 1677.

Perkins, John, son of Edward by Susannah, b. May 28, 1675.

Perkins, John, son of Edward by Susannah, b. May 28, 1679.

Perkins, John, son of Henry by Elizabeth, bap. April 11, 1680.

Perkins, William, [twin with Hannah], son of Henry by Elizabeth, b. Nov. 10, 1674.

Pescod, Elizabeth, dau. of Robert by Sarah, b. Jan. 23, 1701.

Pescod, Elizabeth, dau. of George by Mary, b. Jan. 17, bap. March 12, 1728/9.

Pescod, George, son of Robert by Sarah, b. Dec. 6, [1698].

Pescod, Peter, son of Thomas by Elizabeth, b. January 5, bap. Feb. 14, 1724.

Pescod, Rachell, dau. of Robert by Sarah, b. Feb. 9, 1695.

Pescod, Robert, son of Thomas and Ann, b. Aug. 6, bap. Aug. 23, 1752.

Pescod, Sarah, dau. of George by Mary, b. Oct. 31, bap. Dec. 18, 1726.

Pescod, Thomas, son of Rob⁺. by Sarah, b. April 21, 1691.

Pescod, Thomas, son of George by Mary, b. June 28, bap. July 26, 1724.

Pescod, Thomas, son of Thomas by Elizabeth, b. March 7, 1726, bap. April 2, 1727.

Pescud, Anna, dau of Tho˙. and Eliz˙., b. Nov. 9, 1769, "Bap. the week before Xmas."

[Note: On the margin is the entry: "Died 1ˢᵗ of Aug⁺. 1781."]

Pescud, Anna, dau. of Tho˙. and Elizabeth, b. July 21, privately bap. Aug. 21, 1781.

Pescud, Edward, son of Thos. and Eliz˙., b. Dec. 8, 1778, bap. Jan. 31, 1779.

Pescud, Elizabeth, dau. of Tho˙. and Eliz˙., b. Jan. 1, bap. Feb. 14, 1768.

Pescud, Elizabeth, dau. of Tho˙. and Eliz˙., b. March 18, bap. May 8, 1774.

Pescud, Robert, son of Thomas and Elizabeth, b. Oct. 5, bap. Dec. 3, 1776.

Pescud, Thomas, son of Thomas and Eliz˙., b. Nov. 25, bap. Dec. 22, 1771.

Peters, Rebecca, dau. of Tho˙. and Betty, "Baptized Nov⁺. 21ˢᵗ, 1773, at 9 weeks old."

Phillips, Anne Armistead, dau. of John and Patty, b. March 2, bap. May 26, 1782. (Eliz˙. City).

Phillips, Edmund, son of John and Martha, b. Nov. —, 1784, bap. Aug. 14, 1785. ([   ] City).

Phillips, Nicholas, son of Thomas by Rachell, b. Dec. 12, bap. Jan. 1, 1727.

Phillips, Thomas, son of Thomas by Rachell, b. Oct. 7, bap. Nov. 9, 1729.

Phillips, Thomas, ·son of Wm. and Elizabeth, b. Jan. 31, bap. April 16, 1770.

Phillips, William, son of Thomas by Rachel, b. Jan. 8, bap. Feb. 6, 1731.

Phips, Thomas, son of John by Elizabeth, bap. March 20, 1678.

Picket, Robert, son of Wm. Sandefer and Eliz⋆. b. Oct. 23, 1768, bap. Feb. 12, 1769.   (Warwick).

Picket, William, "bastard son of Eliz⋆. Picket," b. ———, bap. Nov. 24, 1765.   (Warwick).

Picket, William, (mulatto), son of John and Elizabeth, b. Aug. 7, 1784, bap. March 18, 1785.   (Warwick).

Pickett, George, son of George by Mary, bap. Dec. 4, 1681.

Pickett, Patsey, dau. of John and Eliz⋆., b. Sept. 18, bap. Nov. 3, 1782.   (Warwick).

Pickett, Samuel, son of George by Mary, b. Aug. 31, 1679.

Pierce, Becky, dau. of Peter and Rebecca Whitby, b. May 26, bap. July 13, 1783.   ([   ]wick).

Pierce, Elizabeth, dau. of Peter and Rebecca, b. March 15, bap. April 29, 1781.   (Warwick).

Platt, Ann, dau. of Lawrence by Faith, b. August 2, 1665.

Platt, Richard, son of Thomas by Frances, b. March 26, 1682.

Platt, Thomas, son of Thomas by Frances, b. May 19, 1680.

Pleasant, Ann, dau. of Bewford by Mary, b. Feb. 15, bap. March 17, 1733.

Pleasant, Buford, son of George by Dorithy, b. Dec. 1, 1696.

Pleasant, Buford, son of Buford by Mary, b. Sept. 15, bap. Oct. 17, 1731.

Pleasant, George, son of George, [Wife not named], b. Oct. 17, 1669.

Pleasant, George, son of Buford by Mary, b. Sept. 21, bap. Oct. 9, 1743.

Pleasant, John, son of George by Dorithy, b. Oct. 18, 1693.

Pleasant, John, son of Blewford by Elizabeth, b. May 26, bap. July 12, 1724.

Pleasant, Mary, dau. of Blewford, by Mary, b. Aug. 13, bap. Sept. 17, 1727.

Pleasant, Mary, dau. of Buford by [Ma]ry, b. Jan. 2, bap. Feb. 1, [17]35.

Pleasant, Peter, son of Buford by Mary, b. June 29, bap. July 23, 1738.

Pleasant, Sarah, dau. of Buford by Mary, b. Aug. 16, bap. Sept. 21, 1729.

Pond, Daniel, son of John by Elizabeth, b. Jan. 15, 171[5].

Pond, Daniel, [twin with Samuel], son of Daniel by Mary, b. Dec. 24, bap. Jan. 29, 1743.

Pond, Elizabeth, dau. of John by Elizabeth, b. Jan. 3, 17[03].

Pond, Elizabeth, dau. of Rich⁴. by Mar[   ], b. May 1, bap. June 4, 17 [49].

Pond, Esther, dau. of John by Elizabeth, b. March 31, 1714.

Pond, John, son of Stephen by Catherine, b. Nov. 6, 1672.

Pond, John, [twin with Mary], son of John by Elizabeth, b. Nov. 1, 1706.

Pond, John, son of Daniel by Mary, b. Oct. 1, bap. Nov. 8, 1741.

Pond, John, son of Richard and Martha, b. June 22, bap. Sept. 20, 1751.

Pond, Judith, dau. of John by Elizabeth, b. Aug. 27, 1700.

Pond, Mary, dau. of John by Elizabeth, b. March 17, 16[98].

Pond, Mary, dau. of Thomas by Agnes, b. March 1, 1700.

Pond, Mary, [twin with John], dau. of John by Elizabeth, b. Nov. 1, 1706.

Pond, Richard, son of John by Elizabeth, b. June 4, 1710.

Pond, Samuel, [twin with Daniel], son of Daniel by Mary, b. Dec. 24, bap. Jan. 29, 1743.

Pool, Anne, dau. of George and Sarah, b. May 16, bap. Sept. 5, 1779.

Pool, William, son of George and Mary, b. Aug. 16, 1782.

Poole, Sally, dau. of George and Sally, b. Feb. 5, bap. Aug. 29, 1781.

Potlin, Amidian, dau. of John by Elinor, b. March 9, 1693.

Potlin, Elinor, dau. of John by Elinor, b. Aug. 30, 1687.

Potlin, Elizabeth, dau. of John by Elinor, bap. March 20, 1678.

Potlin, Thomas, son of John by Elinor, b. Feb. 10, 1681.

Potlin, William, son of John by Elinor, b. Aug. 6, 1691.

Potlin, William, son of William by Elizabeth, b. March 26, bap. April 19, 1719.

Potter, Ann, dau. of Joseph by Elizabeth, b. Dec. 28, 1697.

Potter, Joseph, son of Joseph by Elizabeth, b. March 27, 1690.

Potter, Lydia, dau. of Joseph by Elizabeth, b. March 15, 1700.

Powell, Elizabeth, dau. of Isaac by Elizabeth, b. April 11, 1690.

Powell, William, son of Isaac by Elizabeth, b. Nov. 9, 1693.

Powers, Ann, dau. of John by Susanna, b. Jan. 27, bap. Feb. 24, 1733.

Powers, Charles, son of Charles by Mary, b. Feb. 23, 1706.

Powers, Charles, son of Charles by Sarah, b. Sept. 18, bap. Sept. 22, 1743.

Powers, Charles, son of Charles by Sarah, b. Oct. 23, bap. Nov. 22, 1747.

Powers, Edward, son of Charles by Mary, b. Oct. 19, bap. March 2, 1717.

Powers, Elinor, dau. of Charles by Sarah, b. Sept. 17, bap. Oct. 16, 1737.

Powers, Elizabeth, dau. of John by Elizabeth, b. Nov. 30, 1710.

Powers, Elizabeth, dau. of Charles by Elizabeth, b. Nov. 1, bap. Dec. 22, 1720.

Powers, Elizabeth, dau. of Charles by Sarah, b. Oct. 10, bap. Nov. 23, 1740.

Powers, Jane, dau. of Edward by Mary, of Denbeigh Parish, bap. April 4, 1671.

Powers, Jane, dau. of Charles by Sarah, b. Oct. 13, bap. Dec. 16, 1744.

Powers, John, son of Edward by Mary (of Denbeigh), b. April 15, 1677.

Powers, John, son of Edward by Sarah, b. July 9, 1707.

Powers, John, son of John by Margaret, b. Aug. 6, bap. Sept. 4, 1748.

Powers, Susanna, dau. of John by Susanna, b. Sept. 12, 1736.

Powil, Jane, dau. of William by Henri[   ], b. Feb. 26, bap. March 26, [1749].

Powmer, John, son of James by Hannah, b. July 31, 1714.

Pratt, William, son of Griffin, of Denbeigh, bap. Oct. 14, 1677.

Pressey, Elizabeth, dau. of Nicholas by Jane, b. Jan. 11, 1690.

Pressey, John, son of Nicholas by Jane, b. Feb. 28, 1701.

Pressey, Mary, dau. of Nicholas by Elizabeth, b. Dec. 25, 1700.

Pressey, Mary, dau. of Nicholas by Elizabeth, b. Sept. 24, 1707.

Pressey, Rachell, dau. of Nicholas by Jane, b. Aug. 20, 1693.

Pressey[?], Richard, son of Nicholas by Jane, b. Aug. 19, 1696.

Pressey, Thomas, son of Nicholas by Jane, b. Dec. 7, 170[3].

Presson, Anne, dau. of Thomas by Mar[   ], b. Nov. 11, 1746, bap. Dec. 14, 17[46].

Presson, Anne, dau. of James and Anne, b. Feb. 24, bap. April 9, 1773.

Presson, Benjamin, son of Rob‘. and Mary, b. Dec. 22, 1768, bap. March 19, 1769.

Presson, Callohill, son of Robert and Mary, b. Sept. 4, bap. Dec. 4, 1774.

Presson, Daniel, son of Nicholas by Elizabeth, b. Oct. 18, bap. Dec. 13, 1719.

Presson, Daniel, son of Daniel and Rebekah, b. Oct. 21, bap. Dec. 20, 1760.

Presson, Dorithy, dau. of William by Mary, b. Sept. 7, bap. Oct. 10, 1731.

Presson, Elizabeth, dau. of Richard by Hannah, b. July 22, bap. Aug. 24, 1723.

Presson, Elizabeth, dau. of John by Elizabeth, b. Aug. 13, bap. Sept. 5, 1725.

Presson, Elizabeth, dau. of John by Elizabeth, b. Sept. 23, bapt. Dec. 18, 1726.

Presson, Elizabeth, dau. of Robert by Frances, b. Oct. 15, bap. Oct. 20, 1744.

Presson, Elizabeth, dau. of Sam‘. and Mary, b. Dec. 18, 1749, bap. April 13, 1750.

Presson, Elizabeth, dau. of Daniel and Rebekah, b. June 27, bap. July 25, 1756.

Presson, Elizabeth, dau. of Rob‘. and Mary, b. Sept. 3, bap. Dec. 8, 1782.

Presson, Fanny, dau. of Samuel and Frances, b. Jan. 29, bap. March 21, 1784.

Presson, Frances, dau. of Daniel and Rebecca, b. Jan. 28, bap. Feb. 6, 1763.

Presson, Hannah, dau. of Richard by Hannah, b. Nov. 30, bap. Jan. 17, 1730.

Presson, James, son of Nicholas by Eliz‘. [?], b. Aug. 28, 1712.

Presson, James, son of James and Anne, b. Dec. 26, 1776, bap. Feb. 20, 1777.

Presson, James, son of Nicholas and Mary, b. March 8, bap. April 18, 1784.

Presson, James, son of Robert and Mary, b. Feb. 22, bap. April 30, 1786.

Presson, John, son of Richard by Hannah, b. Nov. 15, bap. Dec. 19, 1725.

Presson, John, son of Robert by Frances, b. Feb. 17, bap. March 29, 1740/1.

Presson, John, son of Wm. and Anne, b. Feb. 25, bap. March 30, 1766.

Presson, John, son of Robert and Mary, b. Oct. 1, bap. Nov. 17, 1771.

Presson, John, son of Thomas and Susanna, b. Jan. 8, bap. March 1, 1778.

Presson, Margett, dau. of John by Elizabeth, b. Dec. 13, bap. Jan. 21, 1732.

Presson, Martha, dau. of John by Eliz'., b. Dec. 11, 1741, bap. Jan. 24, 17[41].

Presson, Mary, dau. of John by Elizabeth, b. Sept. 12, bap. Oct. 25, 1730.

Presson, Mary, dau. of Willm. by Mary, b. Oct. 28, bap. Dec. 8, 1734.

Presson, Mary, dau. of Thomas by Marg^{tt}., b. Jan. 31, bap. Feb. 27, 1742.

Presson, Mary, dau. of Samuel by Mary, b. Dec. 31, bap. Feb. 17, 1744.

Presson, Mary, dau. of Robert by Frances, b. Jan. 26, bap. March 13, 1747.

Presson, Mary, dau. of Robert and Mary, b. Feb. 12, bap. Feb. 22, 1781.

Presson, Nancy, dau. of Thomas and Martha, b. Sept. 19, bap. Nov. 12, 1786.

Presson, Nicholas, son of Sam¹. by Mary, b. Oct. 28, 1746, bap. Dec. 7, 174[6].

Presson, Polly, dau. of Samuel and Frances, b. May 25, bap. July 1, 1781.

Presson, Rachel, dau. of Thomas by Marg"., b. Feb. 25, 1744, bap. April 7, 1745.

Presson, Rachel, dau. of Samuel Junr. and Frances, b. Jan. 6, bap. Feb. 19, 1777.

Presson, Robert, son of Will". by Mary, b. Feb. 22, 1736/7, bap. Apr. 24, 1737.

Presson, Robert, son of Robert and Mary, b. July 21, bap. Aug. 24, 1766.

Presson, Robert, son of Wm. and Ann, b. March ——, bap. May 7, 1769.

Presson, Samuel, son of Nicholas by Elizabeth, b. March 5, 1709.

Presson, Samuel, son of Nicholas by Elizabeth, b. Oct. 15, bap. Nov. 30, 1717.

Presson, Samuel, son of Thos. by Margt., b. July 27, bap. Sept. 1, 1734.

Presson, Samuel, son of Nicholas and Anne, b. March 6, bap. July 30, 1775.

Presson, Sarah, dau. of Thomas Junr. and Martha, b. Jan. 20, bap. April 17, 1785.

Presson, Thomas, son of Richard by Hannah, b. Sept. 12, bap. "8ber" 14, 1733.

Presson, Thomas, son of Thomas by Marg"., b. Dec. 20, bap. Feb. 18, 1740/41.

Presson, Thomas, son of Daniel and Rebekah, b. Oct. 6, bap. Nov. 26, 1758.

Presson, Thomas, son of Samuel and Frances, b. Aug. 22, bap. Sept. 20, 1778.

Presson, Thomas, son of Thomas and Susanna, b. Dec. 15, 1780, bap. Jan. 14, 1781.

Presson, Tomer, son of Robert and Frances, b. July 23, bap. Aug. 26, 1750.

Presson, William, son of Nicholas by Elizabeth, b. Jan. 5, 1705.

Presson, William, son of John by Eliz*., b. July 3, bap. Aug. 21, 1737.

Presson, William, son of Wm. and Anne, b. July 22, "private Bap. 28ᵗʰ 1771, pub. Bap. 17ᵗʰ Novʳ."

Presson, William, son of Robert and Mary, b. Jan. 14, bap. March 8, 1778.

Presson, Wm. son of James and Anne, b. Jan. 9, bap. Feb. 18, 1770.

Price, Dorithy, dau of James, [No wife mentioned], b. November 18, 1664.

Price, John, son of James, of York Parish, bap. April 6, 1669.

Price, Judith, dau. of Charles by Elizabeth, b. Sept. 5, 1687.

Prittiman, Thomas, son of Thomas by Aphia, bap. Oct. 3, 1687.

Proorst[?], Elizabeth, dau. of James by Phebe, b. Feb. 17, 1665.

Provo, Betsy, dau. of Matthew and Joanna, b. Oct. 8, bap. Dec. 10, 1769.

Provo, James, son of Mark by Sarah, b. May 2, bap. June 12, 1726.

Provo, John, son of Mark by Sarah, b. Feb. 28, 1733, bap. April 28, 1734.

Provo, Lewis, son of Mark by Dianah, b. March 27, bap. May 5, 1745.

Provo, Mariana, dau. of Matthew and Hannah, b. Feb. 15, bap. April 12, 1772.

Provo, Mark, son of Mark by Sarah, b. March 23, 1728/9, bap. Apr. 24, 1729.

Provo, Mark, son of Mark by Dinah, b. Sept. 2, bap. Oct. 30, 1737.

Provo, Matthew, son of Mark by Diana, b. June 1, bap. Aug. 1, 1742.

Provo, Sukey, dau. of Matthew and Joanna, b. April 22, bap. May 29, 1774.

Provo, William, son of Mark by Dinah, b. May 9, bap. July 8, 1739.

Provo, William, son of Matthew and Joanna, b. Oct. 9, bap. Nov. 17, 1776.

Purvo, Alice, dau. of James by Martha, b. March 12, 1681.

Purvo, Ann, dau. of James by Martha, b. Nov. 25, 1690.

Purvo, James, son of James by Martha, b. Feb. 16, 1692.

Purvo, Mark, son of James by Martha, b. March 10, 1685.

Puryear, Peggy, dau. of Samuel and Margaret, b. May 15, bap. June 8, 1766. (Warwick).

Q

Quarles, Anne Stith, dau. of John and Charlotte, b. Aug. 26, bap. Oct. 23, 1767. (Eliz⁴. City).

R

Ragdel, Thomas, son of Thomas, by Elinor, b. Oct. 2, 1675.

Ragdell, Ann, dau. of Thomas by Elinor, bap. June 6, 1687.

Ragdell, Anthony, [son of] Thomas by Ursella, b. Aug. 16, 1706.

[The name "Anthony" is supplied from the index—it is mutilated so as to be illegible in the body of the book].

Ragdell, Elias, son of Thomas by Ursella, b. Sept. 16, 170[9].

Ragdell, Elinor, dau. of Thomas by Ursella, b. Aug. 16, 1712.

Ragdell, Elizabeth, dau. of Thomas by Ursella, b. Jan. 11, 17[03].

Ragdell, Hannah, dau. of Thomas by Ursilla, b. Feb. 15, 1701.

Ragdell, James, son of Thomas by Elinor, b. Oct. 27, 1671.

Ragdell, John, son of Thomas by Elinor, b. Jan. 20, 1683.

Randle, Anne, dau. of John and Mary, b. July 19, bap. Oct. 11, 1774.

Randy, Mary, dau. of William by Elizabeth, b. Nov. 19, 1695.

Randy, Mary, dau. of William by Mary, b. Feb. 11, 1697.

Ransom, Jerimiah, son of John Sampson Ransom by Jane, b. July 2, bap. Sept. 2, 1722. Elizabeth City.

  [This name is not indexed under Ransom at all. It is indexed Jeremiah *Samson*].

Ratcliff, John, son of Richard by Elizabeth, b. June 16, 1706.

Rawlings, Anne, dau. of Vincent and Betsy[?], b. Oct. 8, 1775, bap. Jan. 7, 1776.

Rawlings, Anne, dau. of Vincent and Betsy, b. June 23, bap. Aug. 28, 1785.

Rawlings, Disey, dau. of Vincent and Betsy, b. Feb. 11, bap. April 13, 1783.

Rawlings, Edward, son of Vincent and Betsey, b. Feb. 24, bap. March 28, 1766.

Rawlings, John Baptist, son of Vincent and Patsey, b. Sept. 11, bap. Nov. 14, 1779.

Rawlings, Rebecca, dau. of Vincent and Susanna, b. Oct. 30, 1763, bap. Jan. 8, 1764.

Rawlins, Betsy, dau. of Vincent and Betsy, b. Oct. 15, bap. Dec. 5, 1773.

Rawlins, Joseph, son of Vincent and Betsy, b. Sept. 5, bap. Oct. 29, 1769.

Rawlins, Mary, dau. of Vincent and Betty, b. Sept. 20, bap. Oct. 25, 1767.

Rawlins, Mary, dau. of Joseph and Anne, b. March 22, 1741/2, bap. April 25, 1742.

Rawlins, Samuel, son of Vincent and Betsy, b. Oct. 4, bap. Nov. 17, 1771.

Ray, Chrismas, son of Chrismas by Sarah, b. Feb. 5, 1686.

Ray, John, son of Thomas by Sarah, b. Oct. 5, bap. Oct. 11, 1718.

Ray, Rebekah, dau of Thomas by Sarah, b. Nov. 3, 1712.

Ray, Sarah, dau. of Thomas by Sarah, b. March 19, 1719, bap. April 10, 1720.

Ray, Thomas, son of Chrismas by Sarah, bap. Nov. 13, 1684.

Ray, Thomas, son of Thomas by Sarah, b. July 14, 1710.

Reade, Elizabeth, dau. of Hawkins and Rachel, b. Oct. 19, 1782, bap. April 13, 1783. (James [City?]).

Reade, John, son of Hawkins and Rachel, b. March 15, Priv. bap. Sept. 22, 1784.

Reade, Mary, dau. of Hawkins and Elizabeth, b. May 27, 1789 "1 o'C in the afternoon."

Reade, Richard Hawkins, son of Hawkins and Eliz*., b. March 18, bap. April 19, 1787.

Reynolds, William, son of Wm. and Rebekah, b. July 9, bap. Aug. 16, 1772.

Richards, Dinah, dau. of Tho*. by Eliz*., b. Dec. 15, bap. Jan. 18, 1735.

Richards, Martha, dau. of Thomas by Eliz*., b. Sept. 15, bap. Oct. 17, 1731.

Richards, Mary, dau. of Thomas by Elizabeth, b. Oct. 26, bap. Nov. 30, 1729.

Richards, Rachel, dau. of Thomas by Eliz., b. Sept. 9, bap. Oct. 7, 1733.

Richardson, William, son of John and Abigale, b. Oct. 29, bap. Dec. 14, 1755.

Rideout, Giles, son of Giles by Frances, b. Feb. 8, bap. March 13, 1742.

Ridiout, William, son of Giles by Frances, b. July 10, bap. Aug. 31, 1740.

Ridout, Mary, dau. of Giles by Frances, b. May 20, bap. June 18, 1732.

Roberts, Ann, dau. of Gerard by Ann, b. Sept. 25, bap. Nov. 2, 1718.

Roberts, Ann, dau. of Thomas by Rose, b. July 12, 1674.

Roberts, Ann, dau. of Thomas by Rose, b. Sept. 22, 1676.

Roberts, Anne, dau. of Thomas and Lucy, b. June 12, bap. Sept. —, 1777.

Roberts, Anne Butts, dau. of Tho'. Junr. and Sarah, b. Feb. 24, bap. July 9, 1780.

Roberts, Butts, son of Thomas by Ann, b. Nov. —, bap. Jan. 13, 1733.

Roberts, Constant, dau. of Thomas by Rose, bap. July 5, 1669.

Roberts, Damazinah, dau. of Gerard by Ann, b. Dec. 31, 1728, bap. March 30, 1729.

Roberts, Dixon, son of Gerard by Ann, b. June 14, bap. Aug. 1, 1731.

Roberts, Elizabeth, dau. of Thomas by Rose, b. June 5, 1679.

Roberts, Elizabeth, dau. of Gerard by Ann, b. Nov. 30, bap. Dec. 25, 1724.

Roberts, Elizabeth, dau. of Thos. by Anne, b. Aug. 10, bap. Sept. 11, 1737.

Roberts, Elizabeth, dau. of Thos. and Lucy, b. Nov. 4, 1774, bap. Jan. 17, 1775.

Roberts, Elizabeth, dau. of Elizabeth, b. March 13, bap. May 21, 1783.

Roberts, Frances, dau. of Gerard, Ju'. by Eliz'., b. June 2, bap. July 30, 1738.

Roberts, Frances, dau. of Tho'. and Lucy, b. Jan. 21, bap. Feb. 18, 1770.

Roberts, Gerard, son of Thomas by Damazinah, b. Jan. 9, bap. Feb. 12, 1714.

Roberts, Gerrard, son of Thomas by Rose, b. May 5, 1687.

Roberts, James, son of James and Jane (Mulattoes), b. June 20, bap. Aug. 1, 1773.

Roberts, James, son of Thos. Senr. and Lucy, b. May 24, bap. Aug. 13, 1780.

Roberts, John, son of Thomas by Damazinah, b. Aug. 29, 1712.

Roberts, John, son of Gerard by Ann, b. Nov. 16, bap. Dec. 23, 1726.

Roberts, John, son of Thos. and Lucy, b. April 2, bap. April 20, 1766.

Roberts, John, son of Thos. Jun'. and Sarah, b. Oct. 15, 1777, bap. Jan. 4, 1778.

Roberts, Lazarus, son of Thomas by Rose, b. Nov. 24, 1684.

Roberts, Lazarus, son of Gerard Sen'. by Ann, b. ——, bap. March 24, 1733.

Roberts, Lucy, dau. of Thomas and Lucy, b. May 1, 1764.

Roberts, Mary, dau. of Thomas, Senr. and Lucy, b. March 27, bap. Oct. 23, 1783.

Roberts, Polly, dau. of Butts and Elizabeth, b. Dec. 24, 1779, bap. Feb. 20, 1780.

Roberts, Rookesby, son of Butts and Sarah, b. March 19, bap. May 19, 1765.

Roberts, Samuel, son of Thomas by Rose, b. Feb. 20, 1681.

Roberts, Samuel, son of Gerard by Ann, b. Nov. 6, bap. Jan. 7, 1722.

Roberts, Sarah, dau. of Thomas Junr. and Sarah, b. Oct. 9, 1783, bap. Jan. 1, 1784.

Roberts, Thomas, son of Thomas by Rose, b. March 5, 1671.

Roberts, Thomas, son of Thomas by Demazinah, b. Nov. 29, 1709.

Roberts, Thomas, son of Gerard, Junr. by Elizabeth, b. April 27, bap. June 1, 1740.

Roberts, Thomas, son of Thomas by Anne, b. Sept. 14, bap. Sept. 21, 1748.

Roberts, Thomas, son of Thomas and Ann, b. April 4, bap. June 2, 1751.

Roberts, Thomas Powell, son of Tho'. and Lucy, b. May 27, bap. June 26, 1768.

Roberts, William, son of Thomas and Lucy, b. March 24, bap. May 3, 1772.

Robertson, Susanna Thruston, dau. of Capt. Moses and Anne, b. May 21, bap. July 17, 1785. ([   ] City).

Robins, Frances, dau. of Anthony by Mary, b. Jan. 5, 1689.

Robins, Jane, dau. of Anthony by Jane, b. Nov. 29, 1713.

Robinson, Ann, dau. of Anthony by Jane, b. Oct. 28, 1707.

Robinson, Ann, dau. of William by Ann, b. July 26, bap. Aug. 27, 1732.

Robinson, Anne, dau. of Anthony by Dianna, b. Sept. 3, bap. Oct. 14, 1739.

Robinson, Anne, dau. of Wm. and Frances, b. Sept. 29, bap. Dec. 18, 1774.

Robinson, Anne, dau. of Anthony and Mary, b. March 2, bap. July 2, 1775.

Robinson, Anthony, son of John by Elizabeth, b. February 11, 1661.

Robinson, Anthony, son of Anthony by Mary, b. Oct. 23, 1697.

Robinson, Anthony, son of John by Frances, b. Sept. 9, 1711.

Robinson, Anthony, son of Wil^m. by Ann, b. Nov. 30, bap. Dec. 27, 1728.

Robinson, Anthony, son of John, Junr. by Frances, b. June 18, 1735.

Robinson, Anthony, son of Anth°. by Mary, b. June 15, bap. July 17, 1737.

Robinson, Anthony, son of Anth°. and Mary, b. Aug. 12, bap. Sept. 23, 1770.

Robinson, Diana, dau. of Anthony by Diana, b. Sept. 12, bap. Sept. 12, 1726.

Robinson, Elizabeth, dau. of Anthony by Mary, b. Dec. 14, 1687.

Robinson, Elizabeth, dau. of John by Frances, b. Dec. 3, 170[9].

Robinson, Elizabeth, dau. of William by Ann, b. Feb. 17, 1739/40, bap. April 4, 1740.

Robinson, Elizabeth, dau. of Anth°. and Mary, b. July 19, bap. Aug. 30, 1767.

Robinson, Everard, son of John and Martha, b. May 20, bap. July 2, 1769.

Robinson, Frances, dau. of Anthony by Diana, b. Aug. 1, bap. Aug. 9, 1729.

Robinson, Frances, dau. of William by Ann, b. Oct. 16, bap. Feb. 21, 1730.

Robinson, Frances, dau. of Anthony by Mary, b. Aug. 26, bap. Oct. 5, 1735.

Robinson, James, son of Anthony by Jane, b. June 5, [1699].

Robinson, James, son of Anthony by Jane, b. Nov. 23, 17[03].

Robinson, John, son of Anthony by Mary, b. Aug. 25, 1685.

Robinson, John, son of John by Frances, b. Sept. 4, 1714.

Robinson, John, son of Anthony by Dianah, b. Aug. 29, bap. Oct. 3, 1731.

Robinson, John, son of William by Anne, b. May 19, bap. June 27, 1742.

Robinson, John, son of Starkey and Susanna, b. Dec. 19, 1752 "and Baptized the 2ᵈ day of Janʳ. following."

Robinson, John, son of Anthony and Mary, b. Feb. 13, bap. April 4, 1773.

Robinson, Martha, dau. of John by Frances, b. Oct. 12, bap. Nov. 7, 1717.

Robinson, Martha, dau. of Capt. Anthʳ. by D[———], b. March 11, 1733.

Robinson, Mary, dau. of Anthony by Mary, b. May 14, 1694.

Robinson, Mary, dau. of John by Francis, b. Oct. 24, 1707.

Robinson, Mary, dau. of Anthony Junr. by Diana, b. April 18, bap. May 26, 1723.

Robinson, Mary, dau. of Anthony by Diana, b. Sepr. 16, bap. Octr. 30, 1737.

Robinson, Mary, dau. of Anth°. and Frances, b. Dec. 2, bap. Dec. 22, 1759.

Robinson, Mildred, dau. of William by Anna, b. Feb. 6, bap. March 7, 1744.

Robinson, Peter, son of Anthony by Jane, b. Dec. 28, 1700.

Robinson, Peter, son of Anthony by Mary, b. March 10, bap. March 18, 1733.

Robinson, Peter, son of Willm. by Ann, b. Feb. 17, bap. March 9, 1734.

Robinson, Peter Manson, son of W^m. and Hannah, b. Oct. 20, bap. Dec. 18, 1768.

Robinson, Rachel, dau. of Anthony by Diana, b. Oct. 4, bap. ———, 1732.

Robinson, Sarah, dau. of Anthony by Mary, b. Aug. 17, 1696.

Robinson, Starkey, son of Anthony by Mary, b. Dec. 10, 1691.

Robinson, Starkey, son of John by Frances, b. April 10, bap. June 4, 1720.

Robinson, Starkey, son of Anthony by Dianah, b. Feb. 14, bap. March 14, 1724.

Robinson, Starkey, son of Anthony Junr. and Mary, b. Dec. 7, 1763.

Robinson, Thomas, son of Anthony Junr. by Dianah, b. Dec. 25, bap. Jan. 6, 1721.

Robinson, William, son of Anthony by Jane, b. Aug. 20, 1705.

Robinson, William, son of Willm. by Anne, b. Nov. 10, bap. Dec. 18, 1737.

Robinson, William, son of Starkey and Susanna, b. April 12, bap. April 30, 1754.

Robinson, William Cole, son of Thomas and Elizabeth, b. Feb. —, bap. May 7, 1785. ([   ] City).

Roes, Mary, dau. of William and Martha, b. March 14, bap. April 12, 1754.

Rogers, Adenstone, son of Adustone by Kathrine, b. April 26, bap. May 23, 1731.

> [Note: The spelling of the names of father and son is different and perfectly distinct—in the register the son's name is spelled: "Adenstone," the father's "Adustone."]

Rogers, Anthony, son of James by Marg⁺⁺., b. Dec. 17, bap. Jan. 31, 1741.

Rogers, Elizabeth, dau. of James by Marg⁺⁺., b. ———, bap. Dec. 17, 1738.

Rogers, Elizabeth, dau. of Thomas by Sarah, b. May —, bap. June 24, 1739.

Rogers, John, son of James by Margarett, b. Sept. 1, bap. Oct. 17, 1736.

Rogers, John, son of Addenston and Mary, b. May 9, 1760.

Rogers, John Adenstone, son of Adduston by Kathrine, b. March 27, bap. April 22, 1733.

Rogers, Mary, dau. of Adduston by Kathrine, b. Aug. 19, bap. Sept. 21, 1735.

Rogers, Molly, dau. of John Aduston and Eliz⁺. Bernard, b. Dec. 3, 1775, bap. Feb. 11, 1776. ([York H]ampton).

Rogers, Susanna, dau. of William and Eliz⁺., b. Feb. 10, bap. April 17, 1778. ("Ykhpton").

Rogers, Thomas, son of Thomas by Sarah, b. Sept. 13, bap. Oct. 17, 1742.

Rogers, Thomas Adenston, son of Clayton by ——— "his wife," b. May 18, bap. June 11, 1738.

Rogers, William, son of James by Marg⁺⁺., b. Feb. 9, bap. March 10, 1733.

Rogers, William Addenston, son of Addenston and Mary, b. Jan. 23, 1759.

Rogers, Wm. Aduston, son of John and Eliz⁺. Bernard, b. July 15, bap. July 27, 1769. (York Hampton).

Rose, Elizabeth, dau. of William by Martha, b. Feb. 1, bap. March 16, 1745.

Rose, John, son of William and Martha, b. Aug. 24, bap. Oct. 19, 1760.

Rose, John, son of Wm. and Martha, b. Aug. 24, 1761.
[Note: "entered before page 77." This is on p. 78.]

Rose, Samuel, son of William by Martha, b. March 14, 1743, bap. April 8, 174[4].

Rose William, son of William by Marth[a], b. June 1, 1749, bap. July 2, 174[9].

Ross, Ann, dau. of Robert by Margarett, b. Aug. 20, 1690.

Ross, Anne, dau. of James Lebby and Sarah, b. April 2, bap. May 30, 1766.

Ross, Elizabeth, dau. of John, [wife not named], b. July 20, 1670.

Ross, Hannah, dau. of Robert by Margarett, b. April 2, 1669.

Ross, Izabel, dau. of Robert by Margarett, b. Nov. 3, 1681.

Ross, James, son of Robert by Elizabeth, b. Jan. 22, 1678.

Ross, Margarett, dau. of Robert by Margarett, b. Jan. 25, 1675.

Ross, Mary, dau. of Robert by Margarett, b. Oct. 1, 1667.

Ross, Robert, son of Robert by Margarett, b. Jan. 14, 1673.

Ross, William, son of Robert by Margaret, b. March 14, 1665.

Rowan, Lydia, dau. of Charles by Lydia, b. Aug. 31, bap. Sept. 10, 1727.

Russell, Aaron, son of John and Martha, b. Feb. 28, bap. April 1, 1770.

Russell, Adam, son of John and Frances, b. April 14, bap. June 9, 1754.

Russell, Benjamin (Bastard), "Benjamin, son of John Sandefur & Eliz⁸. Russell (wid°.) born Feby 7ᵗʰ Baptiz'd June 26ᵗʰ, 1784." (Eliz⁸. City).

Russell, Betsy, dau. of John and Martha, b. Oct. 1, bap. Nov. 8, 1772.

Russell, Betsy Birdson, dau. of Adam and Rebecca, b. March 18, bapt. April 25, 1779.

Russell, Elizabeth, dau. of John and Hannah, b. Oct. 7, bap. Nov. 14, 1779.

Russell, Frances, dau. of John and Martha, b. Jan. 4, bap. Feb. 14, 1768.

Russell, Hannah, dau. of James by Frances, b. April 25, 1710.

Russell, Hinde, son of John and Martha, b. Sept. 18, bap. Nov. 20, 1785.

Russell, James, son of James by Jane, (of Denbeigh), bap. Dec. 31, 1676.

Russell, James, son of James by Angellat, bap. Oct. 22, 1682.

Russell, John, son of Adam by Ann, b. Dec. 29, bap. Feb. 1, 1730.

Russell, John, son of Adam and Rebecca, b. Feb. 18, bap. March 17, 1776.

Russell, Martha, dau. of John and Hannah, b. March 15, bap. March 16, 1782.

Russell, Mary, dau. of Adam by Ann, b. March 22, 1728/9, bap. May 18, 1729.

Russell, Pennuel, son of Pennuel and Eliz*., b. May 7, bap. June 11, 1780.

Russell, Robert Sandefur, son of Rob*. Sandefur and Anne, b. May 25, bap. July 24, 1768. ([   ]liz*. City).

Russell, Sally, dau. of Adam and Rebecca, b. Feb. 19, bap. March 23, 1783. ([Eliz*.] City).

Russell, Thomas, son of James by Frances, b. Feb. 4, 1707. Denbeigh Parish.

Russell, Thomas, son of Penuel and Elizabeth, b. Feb. 17, bap. May 17, 1778.

Russell, William, son of John and Martha, b. Feb. 15, bap. March 19, 1775.

Russell, William, son of Adam and Rebecca, b. May 6, bap. July 1, 1781.

Russell, William, son of John and Hannah, b. Feb. 29, bap. March 28, 1784.

S

Sabee, Walter, son of John by Patience, b. May 12, 1689. [This name is indexed Sabbe].

Sable, Mary, dau. of Mary, b. Aug. 10, 1693. [Father not named].

Sallet, Ann, dau. of George by Catherine, b. May 12, 1674.

Sallet, Thomas, son of George by Catherine, b. April 19, 1676.

Sandefer, Ann, dau. of Rob'. and Ann, of "Eliz. County," b. Nov. 3, 1748.

Sandefer, Elizabeth, dau. of Rob'. and Ann, of "Eliz. County," b. Nov. 26, 1750.

Sandefer, Elizabeth, dau. of John, Junr. and Patience, b. Jan. 24, bap. March 6, 1763.

Sandefer, John, son of John and Patience, b. Sept. 28, bap. Nov. 3, 1765, (of Warwick).

Sandefur, Betsy, dau. of William and Eliz*., b. March 3, bap. April 26, 1778. ([Eli]z* City).

Sandefur, James, son of John Junr. and Patience, b. Nov. 30, 1758, bap. Jan. 14, 1759.

Sandefur, John, son of John and Mary, b. Oct. 17, bap. Nov. 20, 1757.

Sandefur, John, son of John and Patience, b. March 3, bap. April 6, 1760.

Sandefur, Martha, dau. of John and ——, b. Nov. 1, 1753.

Sandefur, Mary, dau. of John and Patience, b. Sept. 14, bap. Oct. 25, 1761.

Sandefur, Molly, dau. of William and Elizabeth, b. April 30, bap. June 11, 1775, (Eliz*. City).

Sandefur, Patsey, dau. of William and Eliz*., b. Aug. 26, bap. Oct. 21, 1781. (Warwick).

Sandefur, Peter, son of Peter and Frances, b. July 13, bap. Sept. 8, 1765. (of Warwick).

Sandefur, Sally, dau. of Wm. and Eliz*., b. March 23, bap. June 9, 1771.

Sandifer, Dunning, dau. of John by Mary, b. Oct. 5, 1695.

Sandifer, Elizabeth, dau. of John by Mary, b. July 18, 1696.

Sandiford, Ann, dau. of John by Elizabeth, b. Jan. 20, 17[09].

Sandiford, Ann, dau. of Thomas by Elizabeth, b. Aug. 8, bap. Sept. 4, 1720.

Sandiford, Elizabeth, dau. of John by Elizabeth (of Elizabeth City), b. Aug. 31, 1699.

Sandiford, Elizabeth, dau. of William by Elizabeth, b. March 11, 1709.

Sandiford, Elizabeth, dau. of John by Mary, b. Aug. 17, 1712.

Sandiford, Frances, dau. of John by Mary, b. July 17, 1702.

Sandiford, Mary, dau. of John by Mary, b. May 7, 1705.

Sandiford, Mary, dau. of William by Elizabeth, b. Aug. 11, 1705.

Sandiford, Robert, son of John by Mary, b. June 23, 170[9].

Sandiford, Samuel, son of John by Elizabeth, b. March 27, 1707.

Sandiford, Thomas, son of John by Mary, b. Aug. 31, 1699.

Sandifur, Anne, dau. of Jonathan by Constant, b. Nov. —, 1741, bap. Jan. 10, 17[41].

Sandifur, Anne, dau. of Robert by Anne, b. ———, bap. Jan. 22, 1748.

Sandifur, Anthony, son of Jonathan by Constant, b. March 18, 1744, bap. April 21, 1745.

Sandifur, Elizabeth, dau. of John by Mary, b. Jan. 9, bap. Feb. 12, 1743.

Sandifur, Martha, dau. of John by Mary, b. Nov. 19, 1746, bap. Dec. 28, 17[46].

Satterwhite, Ann, dau. of Mann and Ann, b. Nov. 8, bap. Dec. 31, 1749.

Saunders, ———, b. March 9, bap. [May] 24, 1785.

[Note: The entry at the top of page 111 partly torn away; only the family name Saunders, and the dates remain. The page of the index which would have contained this name is likewise torn and over half of it missing.]

Sava[?], Patience, dau. of John by Patience, b. May 5, 1701.

Savee, Jane, dau. of John Savee by Ann Combs, b. Dec. 10, 1722, bap. July 13, 1723.

Savee[?], Mary, dau. of John by Patience, b. Oct. 1, 17[03]. Elizabeth City County.

Savee, Sarah, dau. of John by Ann Combs, b. Feb. 24, 1724, bap. Oct. 3, 1725.

Saver, Hannah, dau. of John by Patience, b. Feb. 11, 1705.

Savidge, Mary, dau. of Edward by Martha, b. Dec. 29, bap. Feb. 8, 1722.

Savie[?], Janet, dau. of John by Sarah, b. Feb. 1, 1697.

Savill, Richard, son of Richard by Mary, b. Dec. 16, 1660.

Savory, Elizabeth, dau. of Henry by Isabella, b. Feb. 20, 1683.

Savory, Hannah, dau. of Henry by Isabella, b. June 27, 1680.

Savory, Lidia, dau. of Henry by Mary, b. Oct. 6, [1698].

Savory, Mary, dau. of Henry by Mary, b. June 1, 1702.

Savoy, Abraham, son of John by Patience, b. May 2, 1695.

Savy, Mary, "Mary Savy daughter of Ann Combs a bastard Child was born March 30, 1721 baptized May The 6ᵗʰ 1721."

[This entry seems to be indexed Mary Stacy].

Saxton, John, son of Robert by Abigail, b. Feb. 2, 1699.

Schlater, William Shelldon, son of James by Elizabeth, b. Jan. 8, bap. Feb. 16, 1724.

Sclater, Agnes, dau. of Richard by Mary, b. May 26, 1707.

Sclater, Alice, dau. of Thomas by Sarah, b. Feb. 11, 1697.

Sclater, Elizabeth, dau. of Richard by Mary, b. Oct. 4, 170[3?].

Sclater, Elizabeth, dau. of Richard by Eliz*., b. April 22, bap. May 6, 1744.

Sclater, Elizabeth, dau. of James by Mary, b. Nov. 10, 1688.

Sclater, Elizabeth, dau. of John and Mary, b. March 11, bap. May 29, 1782.

Sclater, James, son of James by Mary, b. Dec. 6, 1697.

Sclater, James, son of James by Elizabeth, b. Dec. 8, bap. Dec. 14, 1723.

Sclater, James, son of John and Mary, b. Aug. 11, 1783, bap. April 5, 1785.

Sclater, John, son of James by Mary, b. May 10, 1691.

Sclater, John, son of Richard by Martha, b. Jan. 9, bap. March 10, 1747.

Sclater, John, son of John and Mary, b. June —, 1777, bap. May 24[?], 1778.

Sclater, Martha, dau. of "Mr. James Sclater by Mary." b. July 22, 1700.

Sclater, Martha, dau. of John and Mary, b. Dec. 17, 1775, bap. Feb. 18, 1776.

Sclater, Mary, dau. of James by Mary, b. April 2, 1692.

Sclater, Mary, dau. of James by Mary, b. Oct. 16, 1702.

Sclater, Mary, dau. of Richard by Mary, b. March 9, 1712.

Sclater, Mary, dau. of Will. Sheldon and Sarah, b. Oct. 28, bap. Nov. 28, 1752.

Sclater, Mary, dau. of John and Mary, b. Oct. 3, bap. Nov. 14, 1773.

Sclater, Mary, dau. of John and Mary, b. July 11, bap. Oct. 1, 1780.

Sclater, Mildred, dau. of John and Mary, b. Dec. 22, 1786, bap. April 9, 1787.

Sclater, Richard, son of James by Elizabeth, b. Jan. 8, bap. Feb. 9, 1721.

Sclater, Richard, son of John and Mary, b. Feb. 23, bap. June 13, 1779.

Sclater, Sally, dau. of Rich⁴. and Martha, b. Nov. 26, bap. Dec. 16, 1740 [1750?].

Sclater, Sally, dau. of John and Mary, b. Dec. 27, 1771, bap. Jan. 26, 1772.

Sclater, Sarah, dau. of James by Mary, b. Jan. 11, 1695.
    [This name is indexed, it seems, Slater. In the text it looks like it might be Selater.]

Sclater, Sarah, dau. of Richard by Mary, b. Dec. 8, bap. Dec. 9, 1716.

Sclater, Thomas, son of Thomas by Sarah, b. Aug. 13, 1693. [The name is indexed Slater].

Sclater, Thomas, son of Thomas by Sarah, b. Nov. 29, 1700.

Sclater, William Sheldon, son of John and Mary, b. Feb. 7, bap. April 5, 1785.

Sclater, Wᵐ. Sheldon, son of Wᵐ. Sheldon, and Sarah, b. Oct. 17, bap. Nov. 28, 1756.
    [Note: Marginal entry as follows:
        "Died 26 Nov. 77
        Born   56
                    —
                    21."]

Scott, Catherine Middleton, b. Dec. 2, [1704]. The entry is as follows: "Catherine Middleton daughter of Catherine Scott to Jnº. Doswell born December 2ᵈ, 170[4]."

Scott, Mary, dau. of James by Jane, b. Oct. 22, 1682.

Searles, Elizabeth, dau. of Stephen by Abigail, bap. Nov. 27ᵗʰ, 1676.

Sexton, Ann, dau. of Samuel by Mary, b. July 21, 1713.

Sexton, Anna, dau. of Robert by Dorithy, b. May 15, 1676.

Sexton, Edward, son of Samuel by Ann, b. Feb. 3, 1709.

Sexton, John, son of Robert by Dorithy, bap. Sept. 4, 1681.

Sexton, Mary, dau. of Robert by Abigail, b. July 19, 1702.

Sexton, Mary, dau. of Samuel by Mary, b. Nov. 3, bap. Dec. 23, 1716.

Sexton, Samuill, son of Robert by Dorithy, b. March 20, 1678.

Seymour, Anne Ellison, dau. of Wm. and Rachel, b. Nov. 21, 1784, bap. June 5, 1785. ([   ]City).

Sheild, ———, son of Robert and Mary, b. [March] 23, bap. May 13, 1781.

    [Note: The first name here is wholly gone and that part of the index containing the entry is also torn away].

Sheild, Eleanor, dau. of John and Eleanor, b. March 23, bap. May 16[?], 1752.

Sheild, Patrick, son of Robert and Mary, b. Sept. 30, bap. Nov. 11, 1776.

Sheild, Robert, son of Robert and Mary, b. May 13, bap. June 26, 1774.

    [Note: "Died 1776"].

Sheild, Robert, son of Robert and Mary, b. April 4, bap. May 15, 1779.

Sherrington, Elizabeth, dau. of Robert and Amy, b. July 17, bap. Aug. 23, 1778.

Sherrington, James, son of Robert and Amy, b. Aug. 11, Privately bap. Oct. 5, 1781.

Sherrington, John son of Robert and Amy, b. Dec. 2, 1774, bap. Jan. 15, 1775.

Sherrington, Mary, dau. of Robert and Amy, b. Aug. 2, bap. Aug. 31, 1766.

Sherrington, Merrit, son of Robert and Amy, b. Feb. 12, bap. March 29, 1772.

Sherrington, Robert, son of Robert and Amy, b. July 7, bap. Aug. 27, 1769.

Sherrington, William, son of Robert and Amey, b. Sept. 28, bap. Oct. 21, 1764.

Shield, Ana, dau. of Robert by Mary, b. Jan. 25, [1698].

Shield, Ann, dau. of Robert by Sarah, b. Aug. 22, 1714.

Shield, Charles, son of Robert by Mary, b. April 12, 170[9].

Shield, Dunn, son of Robert by Mary, b. Jan. 2, 1695.

Shield, Elizabeth, dau. of Robert by Mary, b. Jan. 18, 1690.

Shield, Frances, dau. of Dunn by Susanna, b. Nov. 24, bap. Dec. 10, 1725.

Shield, ———, "Hercules a boy belonging to John Shield was born Ap^l. 20 & Phillip a boy belong^r to D^o. born June 27th 1754."

Shield, John, son of Robert by Mary, b. April 19, 1706.

Shield, John, son of Robert by Sarah, b. Nov. 24, bap. Jan. 18, 1719.

Shield, John, son of John and Elinor, b. Nov. 29, 1757, bap. Feb. 5, 1758.

Shield, Martha, dau. of Dun by Hope, b. May 12, bap. June 13, 1731.

Shield, Mary, dau. of Robert Junr by Sarah, b. Dec. 21, bap. Jan. 12, 1721.

Shield, Mary, dau. of Robert Junr. by Sarah, b. Jan. 2, bap. Feb. 2, 1722.

Shield, Mary, dau. of John by Elinor, b. Oct. 16, bap. Nov. 29, 1747.

Shield, Robert, son of Robert by Elizabeth, b. April 26, 1667.

Shield, Robert, son of Robert by Mary, b. April 18, 1693.

Shield, Robert, son of Robert by Sarah, b. Dec. 1, bap. Jan. 19, 1717.

Shield, Robt., son of John and Eleanor, b. March 12, bap. April 13, 1750.

Shield, Sarah, dau. of Robert by Sarah, b. Aug. 25, bap. Sept. 3, 1725.

Shield, Sarah, dau. of John by Elinor, b. Dec. 21, 1745, bap. Feb. 5, 174[ ].

Shield, Thomas, son of Robert by Mary, bap. April 12, 1702.

Shipworth, Alexander, son of Alexander by Ann, b. October 16, 1662.

Singleton, Anne, dau. of Rich^d. Hunt, by Mary, b. Nov. 29, bap. Jan. 11, 1746.

Singleton, Frances, dau. of Ambrose by Frances, b. Jan. 13, bap. March 17, 1716.

Singleton, Mary, dau. of Ambrose by Frances, b. May 31, bap. July 2, 1732.

Singleton, Rachel, dau. of Richard Hunt and Mary, b. Dec. 23, bap. Jan. 5, 1747.

Singleton, Samuel, son of Ambrose by Frances, b. Jan. 5, bap. Feb. 13, 1724.

Sladd, John, son of Samuel and Mary, b. Dec. 30, 1754.

Sladd, Sarah, dau. of Samuel and Mary, b. Nov. 9, 1752.

Slade, Margarett, dau. of Joshua by Sarah, b. March 3, 1721, bap. April 31, 1722.

Slade, Samuel, son of Joshua by Sarah, b. July 14, bap. Aug. 10, 1723.

Slade, Sarah, dau. of Joshua by Sarah, b. Jan. 13, bap. Feb. 27, 1725.

Slade, Sarah, dau. of Joshua by Sarah, b. Nov. 14, bap. Jan. 13, 1727.

Slate, Elizabeth, dau. of Robert by Elizabeth, b. Dec. 15, 1690.

Slate, Rachell, dau. of Robert by Elizabeth, b. June 9, 1692.

Slater, Elizabeth, dau. of Thomas by Sarah, b. Feb. 1, 1694.

Slater, John, son of Thomas by Sarah, b. February 12, 1705.

Slater, Mary, dau. of Thomas by Sarah, b. Sept. 15, 1702.

Slater, William, son of Thomas by Sarah, b. April 5, 1691.

Smith, Abraham (Mulatto), son of Thos. and Mary, b. Nov. 20, 1785, bap. March 12, 1786.

Smith, Colethorp, son of Robert and Mary, b. Sept. 14, 1767, bap. May 8, 1768.

Smith, Eliz*. Reade, dau. of Wm. and Eliz*., b. Dec. 1, priv. bap. Dec. 13, 1784.

Smith, George, [twin with Lucy], son of Robert and Mary, b. Oct. 4, 1769, bap. May 27, 1770.

Smith, John, son of John by Ann, b. Aug. 6, bap. Sept. 29, 1717.

Smith, John, son of William and Elizabeth, b. April 4, bap. April 14, 1783.

Smith, Lucy, [twin with George], dau. of Robert and Mary, b. Oct. 4, 1769, bap. May 27, 1770.

Smith, Mary, dau. of Howard and Eliz*., b. May 3, bap. June 14, 1767.

Smith, Mary, dau. of Robert and Rachel, b. Aug. 29, bap. Oct. 20, 1777.

Smith, Wm. Stafford, son of Wm. and Amy, b. ————, bap. Aug. 3, 1766.

Snignal, John, son of Samuel by Elizabeth, b. Aug. 29, 1686.

Soloway, Samuel, son of Richard by Elizabeth, b. July 27, bap. Aug. 25, 1728.

Southerland, Betty, dau. of Jno. and Mary, b. Feb. 14, bap. April 18, 1762.

Southerland, Mary, dau. of John and Margaret, b. Oct. 4, 1759.

Southerland, William, son of John and Margaret, b. March 10, bap. April 23, 1758.

Sparr, Samuel, son of Samuel by Elizabeth, b. Nov. 27, 1707.

Spruce, John, son of W^m and Betty, b. Aug. —, bap. Sept. 25, 1768.

Spruce, Sally, dau. of Wm. and Rebecca, b. Sept. 1, bap. Nov. 3, 1765.

Spurr, Benjamin, son of Samuel by Elizabeth, b. April 14, bap. May 12, 1723.

Spurr, Elizabeth, dau. of Samuel by Elizabeth, b. April 22, 1714.

Spurr, Elizabeth, dau. of John by Elizabeth, b. May 11, bap. May 15, 1730.

Spurr, Elizabeth, dau. of John by Elizabeth, b. ———, 1732, bap. Oct. 15, 1732.

Spurr, John, son of Samuel by Elizabeth, b. Dec. 15, 1705.

Spurr, John, son of Samuel by Anne, b. Dec. 22, 1740, bap. May 17, 1741.

Spurr, Mary, dau. of Samuel by Elizabeth, b. Oct. 1, 1711.

Spurr, Mary, dau. of John by Eliz*., b. Nov. 7, bap. Dec. 14, 1735.

Spurr, Mary, dau. of Samuel by Anne, b. ———, bap. Dec. 26, 1742.

Stacey, John, son of Joseph, by Mary, b. Dec. 15, bap. Jan. 12, 1722.

Stacey, John, son of Simon by Katherine, b. July 16, bap. Aug. 9, 1741.

Stacey, Simon, son of Simon by Katherine, b. March 20, 1742, bap. April 17, 1743.

Stacy, Elizabeth, dau. of Joseph by Mary, b. Jan. 11, 1713.

Stacy, Elizabeth, dau. of John and Anne, b. Nov. 27, 1766, bap. Jan. 18, 1767.

Stacy, Joseph, son of Simon by Elizabeth, b. July 24, 1690.

Stacy, Joseph, son of Joseph by Mary, b. April 6, bap. May 7, 1726.

Stacy, Joseph, son of Joseph and Faith, b. Oct. 13, 1767, bap. March 27, 1768.

Stacy, Mary, dau. of Joseph by Mary, b. June 17, bap. July, 15, 1720.

Stacy, Sarah, dau. of Joseph by Mary, b. Feb. 17, bap. March 19, 1716.

Stacy, Simon, son of Joseph by Mary, b. Jan. 29, 1711.

Staige, Ann, dau. of Rev⁴. Theodosius by Ann, b. March 26, bap. Apr. 4, 1731.

Staige, Gulielma, dau. of Theodosius by Ann, b. Nov. 1, bap. Dec. 25, 1739.

Staige, Letitia Theodora, dau. of Theodosius by Ann, b. Feb. 13, 1728/9, bap. March 30, 1729.

Staige, Lucia, dau. of Rev. Theod⁰. by Ann, b. Nov. 8, bap. Dec. 14, 1735.

Staige, Margareta, dau. of Rev. Theodosius by Ann, b. July 25, bap. Aug. 6, 1732.

Staige, Willm., son of Rev. Theodosius by Ann, b. Sept. 21, bap. 8ber 21, 1733.

Starkey, James, a mulatto, belonging to Peter Starkey, bap. April 28, 1700.

Starkey, Mary, dau. of Peter by Bridget, b. Oct. 14, 1668.

Starkey, Peter, son of Peter by Bridget, b. May 13, 1662.

Stevens, Elinor, dau. of "William, by Mary his wife of Maryland," b. Sept. 24, 1690.

St[   ], Molly, dau. of William and Martha, b. Nov. 20, 1782, bap. Jan. 12, 1783.

St Ledger, Samuel Cooper, "son of Sarah Lewis St Ledger (an illegitimate)," b. Aug. 29, bap. Nov. 19, 1769.

St Ledger, Sarah, dau. of Abraham by Mary, b. June 27, bap. July 25, 1736.

Stroud, William, son of Thomas and Eliz^a., b. March 13, bap. April 5, 1765.
        [Note: On margin is entry: "York Hampton."]

Stuckey, Edmond, [twin with John], son of Edm^d. and Elizabeth, b. Sept. 3, bap. Oct. 27, 1771.

Stuckey, John, [twin with Edmond], son of Edm^d. and Elizabeth, b. Sept. 3, bap. Oct. 27, 1771.

Stuckey, Mary, dau. of Edmund by Kathrine, b. Jan. 24, bap. Feb. 18, 1738/9.

Stuckey, Nancy, dau. of Edm^d. and Eliz^a., b. Novr. 14, 1773, bap. Jan. 23, 1774.

Stuckey, Simon, son of Edm^d. and Elizabeth, b. Nov. 12, bap. Dec. 31, 1769.

Sweny, Daniel, son of Edmund by Frances, b. July 28, 170[9].

Sweny, Daniel, son of Merrit by Mary, b. May 10, bap. July 17, 1743.

Sweny, Edmund, son of Edmund by Frances, b. Sept. 2, 1710.

Sweny, Martha, dau. of Edmund by Frances, b. March 4, 1711.

Sweny, Martha, dau. of Merit by Mary, b. July 28, bap. Aug. 14, 1741.

Swiny [Sweny], Frances, dau. of Merrit by Mary, b. June 21, bap. July 8, 1744.

T

Tabb, Anne, dau. of Thomas by Lockey, b. March 6, 1745, bap. May 11, 1746.

Tabb, Diana, dau. of Edward by Margarett, b. Oct. 3, 1711.

Tabb, Diana, dau. of Edward by Margarett, b. March 27, bap. May 4, 1718.

Tabb, Edward, son of Edward by Margarett, b. ———— 1712.

Tabb, Edward, son of Thomas by Lockey, b. Sept. 9, bap. Oct. 12, 1742.

Tabb, Edward, son of Edward by Elizabeth, b. Nov. 4, bap. Dec. 8, 1745.

Tabb, Elizabeth, dau. of Edward by Margarett, b. June 7, bap. Aug. 6, 1721.

Tabb, Elizabeth, dau. of Edward by Eliz*. b. Dec. 6, bap. Jan. 3, 1743.

Tabb, Henry, son of Edward by Margarett, b. March 28, 1707.

Tabb, Henry, son of Edward by Margarett, b. Jan. 18, 1715.

Tabb, John, son of Thomas of Old Paquason, bap. Nov. 12, 1676.

Tabb, John, son of Edward by Margarett, b. Dec. 23, bap. Jan. 22, 1722.

Tabb, John, son of William by Elizabeth, b. March 19, 1710.

Tabb, John, son of Edward by Elizabeth, b. Jan. 1, bap. Feb. 5, 1741.

Tabb, John, son of Thomas by Lockey, b. Dec. 31, 1747, bap. March 13, 17[47].

Tabb, Langhorne, son of Tho°. and Lockey, b. Jan. 22, bap. March 11, [1749].

Tabb, Margaret, dau. of Capt. Edward by Margaret, b. Oct. 13, 1724, bap. ——— 1724.

Tabb, Margaret, dau. of Thomas by Lockey, b. April 4, bap. May 11, 1744.

Tabb, Martha, dau. of Edward by Margarett, b. Jan. 24, 1709.

Tabb, Martha, dau. of Edward by Margarett, b. Dec. 15, bap. Dec. 22, 1726.

Tabb, Mary, dau. of Edward by Elizabeth, b. Oct. 6, bap. Nov. 16, 1740.

Tabb, Mary, dau. of Thomas by Lockey, b. Dec. 19, 1740.

Tabb, Mary, dau. of John and Diana, b. August 9, 1755.

Tabb, Thomas, son of Edward by Margarett, b. Sept. 5, 1719.

Tabb, William, son of William by Elizabeth, b. Dec. 30, 1712.

Tavennor, Elizabeth, dau. of William by Ann, b. March 12, 1670.

Tavernor, Ann, dau. of William by Margarett, b. Aug. 11, 1683.

Tavernor, Ann, dau. of Giles by Ann, b. July 20, 1691.

Tavernor, Giles, son of William by Ann, b. July 26, 1673.

Tavernor, Giles, son of Giles by Ann, b. Nov. 12, 1693.

Tavernor, Giles, son of Giles by Suzannah, b. June 24, bap. July 24, 1720.

Tavernor, Hannah, dau. of Giles by Ann, b. May 16, 1695.

Tavernor, Mary, dau. of Willm. by Ann, b. June 20, 1676.

Tavernor, Mary, dau. of Giles by Ann, b. Aug. 27, 1698.

Tavernor, Mary, dau. of Giles by Ann, b. Aug. 24, 1702.

Tavernor, William, son of William by Ann, bap. Nov. 1, 1685.

Tavernor, William, son of Giles by Ann, b. May 3, 1700.

Tavernor, William, son of William by Joyce, b. Nov. 12, bap. Dec. 9, 1744.

Taylor, Daniel, son of Henry by Elizabeth, b. March 24, 1695.

Taylor, Elizabeth, dau. of Henry by Elizabeth, b. Aug. 25, 1693.

Taylor, Elizabeth, dau. of Thomas by Sarah, b. Nov. 11, 170[4].

Taylor, Elizabeth, dau. of Daniel by Ann, b. Aug. 28, bap. Sept. 22, 1721.

Taylor, Frances, dau. of Henry by Elizabeth, b. Dec. 18, [1698].

Taylor, Henry, son of Henry by Elizabeth, b. Aug. 11, 1688.

Taylor, John, son of Henry by Elizabeth, b. June 5, 1691.

Taylor, Mary,, dau. of Thomas by Sarah, b. Nov. 11, 1701.

Taylor, Rachel, dau. of Henry by Elizabeth, b. Oct. 16, 1702.

Ten[?], Robert, "Robert son of Alice Ten [?], servant to John Doswell born June 14, 1705."

Thomas, James, son of Samuel and Eliz⁴. b. Aug. 6, bap. Sept. 6, 1778. (Warwick).

Thompson, James, son of Bartholomew by Mary, b. Dec. 9, bap. Jan. 6, 1716.

Thompson, John, son of Bartholomew by Margarett, bap. May 4, 1684.

Thorolow, Elizabeth, dau. of Jeremy [?], by Ann, b. July 18, bap. Aug. 19, 1721.

Todd, Angelina Mallory, dau. of Mallory and Anne, b. March 9, bap. June 6, 1786.

Todd, Anne, dau. of Mallory and Anne, b. April 17, bap. July 18, 1779. (Isle of Wight).

Todd, John Robinson, son of Mallory and Anne, b. April 3, bap. July 1, 1781. ([I]sle of Wight).

Todd, Mallory, son of Mallory and Anne, b. Jan. 16, bap. April 24, 1783.

Tomer, Ann, dau. of John by Constant, b. July 24, 1698.

Tomer, Charles, son of Thomas and Mary, b. Jan. 16, bap. March 12, 1758.

Tomer, Constant, dau. of Thomas by Elizabeth, b. Dec. 6, bap. Feb. 16, 1720.

Tomer, Eliz[?], dau. of James by Mary, b. Jan. 6, bap. Feb. 13, 1736.

Tomer, Elizabeth, dau. of Thomas by Elizabeth, b. March 19, 1722, bap. Apr. 19, 1723.

Tomer, Elizabeth, dau. of Thomas and Mary, b. Sept. 5, bap. Sept. 11, 1751.

Tomer, Frances, dau. of John by Mary, b. Nov. 1, 1713.

Tomer, Frances, dau. of James by Mary, b. Dec. 3, bap. Jan. 13, 1733.

Tomer, Frances, dau. of Thomas and Mary, b. Jan. 6, bap. Feb. 10, 1760.

Tomer [?], Hope, dau. of John by Constant, b. March 29, 1693.

Tomer, Hope, dau. of John by Mary, b. April 25, 1711.

Tomer, James, son of John by Mary, b. Oct. 18, 170[9].

Tomer, James, son of Thomas and Mary, b. Jan. 12, bap. Feb. 20, 1763.

Tomer, John, son of John by Hope, b. Aug. 2, 1685.

Tomer, John, son of James by Mary, b. Feb. 2, 1740/41, bap. March 15, 1740/41.

Tomer, Mary, dau. of John by Hope, b. June 30, 1683.

Tomer, Mary, dau. of Thomas and Mary, b. Aug. 2, bap. Aug. 9, 1768.

Tomer, Robert, son of Thomas and Mary, b. April 29, bap. June 7, 1767.

Tomer, Sally, dau. of Thomas and Mary, b. Jan. 24, bap. Feb. 21, 1773.

Tomer, Samuel,
    "Samuel son of Ann Tomer by Samuel Tompkins was born December the 5th 1716 baptized January the 4th 1716."

Tomer, Sheldon, son of Thomas and Mary, b. Dec. 29, 1769, bap. Feb. 11, 1770.

Tomer, Thomas, son of Thomas by Elizabeth, b. Feb. 8, bap. Feb. 9, 1726.

Tomer, Thomas-Frayser, son of Thomas and Mary, b. Sept. 16, 1753, bap. Jan. 13, 1754.

Tompkins, Ann, dau. of Humphry by Hannah, b. May 12, 1668.

Tompkins, Anne, dau. of Saml. by Martha, b. Feb. 5, 1736/7, bap. March 4, 1736/7.

Tompkins, Anne, dau. of Bennet and Anne, b. July 23, bap. Aug. 29, 1756.

Tompkins, Bennet, son of Samuel by Elizabeth, b. March 1, 1683.

Tompkins, Bennet, son of Bennet by Hope, b. March 31, 1711. [1710?]

Tompkins, Bennet, son of William and Anne, "(Of Eliz^a. City County)," b. Dec. 22, 1758.

Tompkins, Bennet, son of Bennet and Anne, b. Jan. 24, 1759.

Tompkins, Edith, dau. of Humphry by Hannah, b. February 2, 1651.

Tompkins, Edmund, son of Bennet by Mary, b. Dec. 11, bap. Jan. 14, 1721.

Tompkins, Elizabeth, dau. of Humphry by Hannah, b. Feb. 22, 1666.

Tompkins, Elizabeth, dau. of Samuel by Sarah, b. Jan. 16, 1702.

Tompkins, Elizabeth, dau. of Bennet, by Hope, b. Sept. 29, 1713.

Tompkins, Elizabeth, dau. of Saml. by Martha, b. Aug. 13, bap. Sept. 9, 1739.

Tompkins, Elizabeth, dau. of Bennet and Anne, b. Jan. 3, 1753.

Tompkins, Frances, dau. of Samuel by Sarah, b. Nov. 5, [1699].

Tompkins, Frances, dau. of Bennet by Mary, b. Jan. 14, bap. Feb. 15, 1729/30.

Tompkins, Frances, dau. of Samuel by Martha, b. Oct. 23, bap. Dec. 6, 1730.

Tompkins, Hannah, dau. of Humphry by Hannah, b. September 4, 1664.

Tompkins, Hannah, dau. of Samuel by Elizabeth, b. Dec. 23, 1681.

Tompkins, Humphry, son of Humphry by Hannah, b. Dec. 4, 1662.

Tompkins, James, son of Samuel by Martha, b. May 27, bap. July 15, 1733.

Tompkins, James, son of William and Anne, "(of Eliz⁑. City County)." b. Jan. 9, 1757.

Tompkins, John, son of Humphry by Hannah, b. June 5, 1670.

Tompkins, John, son of Bennett by Hope, b. May 25, bap. June 29, 1718.

Tompkins, Lazarus, son of Samuel by Martha, b. July 7, bap. Sept. —, 1725.

Tompkins, Martha, dau. of Sam". by Martha, b. Oct. 1, bap. Nov. 14, 1722.

Tompkins, Martha, dau. of Bennet by Mary, b. Nov. 22, bap. Dec. 19, 1725.

Tompkins, Martha, dau. of William and Anne, ("Of Eliz⁑. City County"). b. March 4, 1754.

Tompkins, Mary, dau. of Umphry by Hannah, b. March 7, 1649.

Tompkins, Mary, dau. of Samuel by Sarah, b. July 29, 1690.

Tompkins, Mary, dau. of Samuel by Martha, b. Feb. 12, bap. March 12, 1719.

Tompkins, Mary, dau. of Bennett by Mary, b. Sept. 26, bap. Oct. 29, 1720.

Tompkins, Mary, dau. of Bennet by Mary, b. Dec. 17, bap. Jan. 14, 1727.

Tompkins, Mary, dau. of Bennet and Ann, b. Sept. 2, bap. ————, 1749.

Tompkins, Miles, son of Bennet by Anne, b. Aug. —, 1746, bap. Aug. — 174[6].

Tompkins, Rebecca, dau. of Bennet by Anne, b. Oct. 6, bap. Nov. 11, 1744.

Tompkins, Samuel, son of Humphry by Hannah, b. March 13, 1658.

Tompkins, Samuel, son of Samuel by Sarah, b. June 19, 1697.

Tompkins, Samuel, son of Bennet by Mary, b. Jan. 15, bap. Feb. 12, 1723.

Tompkins, Sarah, dau. of Samuel by Sarah, b. July 26, 1692.

Tompkins, Sarah, dau. of Samuel by Martha, b. Feb. 1, bap. Mar. 10, 1727. [Elizabeth] City County.

Tompkins, William, son of Humphry by Hannah, b. Dec. 30, 1660.

Tompkins, William, son of Samuel by Sarah, b. May 15, 1695.

Tompkins, William, son of Bennet by Mary, b. April 13, bap. May 16, 1731.

Tompson, Bartholomew, son of Bartholomew by Elizabeth, b. Sept. 10, 1690.

Tompson, Elizabeth, dau. of Bartholomew by Margarett, bap. July 24, 1681.

Toomer, Elizabeth, dau .of Tho°. and Mary, b. April 12, bap. May 5, 1765.

Toomer, James, son of John and Eliz°. b. May 24, bap. June 30, 1771.

Toomer, James, son of John and Elizabeth, b. Feb. 14, bap. March 23, 1773.

Toomer, John, son of Thomas and Mary, b. Sept. 22, bap. Oct. 26, 1755.

Toomer, John, son of John and Elizabeth, b. Jan. 26, bap. March 13, 1768.

Toomer, Mary, dau. of John and Elizabeth, b. Oct. 21, bap. Dec. 2, 1764.

Toplady, Ann, dau. of Robert by Isabel, b. Aug. 11, 1696.

Towell, Margarett, dau. of Nicholas by Susannah, b. Dec. 14, 1685.

Towell, Mary, dau. of Nicholas by Suzan, b. Jan. 7, 1682.

Townzen, Mary, dau. of William by Frances, b. Jan. 17, 1707.

Travilian, Elizabeth, dau. of John by Jane, b. Dec. 16, 1697.

Travilian, John, son of John by Jane, b. Aug. 8, 1694.

Travilian, Samuel, son of John by Jane, b. May 18, 1696.

Travilian, Sarah, dau. of Samuel by Mary, b. Oct. 5, 1670.

Travilian, Sarah, dau. of John by Elizabeth, b. July 25, 1688.

Trevillian, Elizabeth, dau. of Samuel by Mary, b. March 3, 1667.

Trotter, Armager, son of William by Ann, b. Dec. 10, 1701.

Trotter, Elizabeth, dau. of William by Ann, bap. March 21, 1697.

Trotter, John, son of William by Ann, b. Nov. 22, 1694.

Trotter, William, son of William by Ann, b. Jan. 15, [1698].

Truman, Martha, dau. of Matthew by Martha, b. Aug. 16, bap. Sept. 23, 1744.

Tucker, Ann, dau. of Thomas by Elizabeth, b. Oct. 20, [1698].

Tucker, Mary, dau. of Thomas by Elizabeth, b. May 20, 1694.

Tucker, Thomas, dau. of Thomas by Elizabeth, b. April 22, 1701.

Tucker, William, son of Thomas by Elizabeth, b. Sept. 17, 1696.

V

VanDoverag, Henry Fason, son of Henry Fason and Rebekah, b. February 14, 1656.

Vanson, Arthur, son of Arthur by Mary, bap. Dec. 21, 1684.

Vanson, Elizabeth, dau. of Arthur by Mary, b. Oct. 3, 1679.

Vanson, Margarett, dau. of Arthur by Margarett, b. March 18, 1672.

Vanson, Mary, dau. of Arthur by Mary, b. Oct. 6, 1682.

Vanson, Richard, son of Arthur by Mary, b. June 1, 1677.

Vanson, Sarah, dau. of Arthur by Mary, b. Jan. 9, 1680.

Vansum, John, son of Arthur by Margarett, b. March 8, 1674.

Varnum, Elizabeth, dau. of Lewis by Elizabeth, b. March 22, [1698].

Varnum, Francis, son of Lewis by Elizabeth, b. March 28, 1707.

Varnum, John, son of Lewis by Elizabeth, b. Aug. 20, 17[04].

Varnum, William, son of Lewis by Elizabeth, b. Dec. 8, 1700.

Vergett, Job, son of Job, of York Parish, bap. Jan. 2, 1671.

W

Wade, Ann, dau. of Armager by Elizabeth, b. April 5, 1674.

Wade, Dorithy, dau. of Armager, Jun., by Elizabeth, b. Jan. 31, 1669.

Wade, Dorithy, [twin with Elizabeth], dau. of Armager by Elizabeth, b. May 14, 1678.

Wade, Dorithy, [twin with Elizabeth], dau. of Armager by Elizabeth, b. June 3, 1679.

Wade, Elizabeth, [twin with Dorithy], dau. of Armager and Elizabeth, b. May 14, 1678.

Wade, Elizabeth, [twin with Dorithy], dau. of Armager by Elizabeth, b. June 3, 1679.

Wade, Frances, dau. of Armager, Jun., by Elizabeth, b. August 1, 1668.

Wade, Frances, dau. of Armager by Elizabeth, b. March 31, 1691.

Wade, Mary, dau. of Armager by Elizabeth, b. May 16, 1683.

Waire, Mary, dau. of George and Martha, b. Sept. 28, bap. Oct. 28, 1764.

Walker, Ann, dau. of Thomas by Elizabeth, b. Sept. 23, 17[04].

Walker, Elizabeth, dau. of Thomas by Elizabeth, b. April 26, 170[9].

Walker, Martha, dau. of Robert and Rebecca, b. Aug. 6, bap. Aug. 7, 1780. (Eliz⁴. City).

Walker, Patrick, son of Robert and Rebecca, b. Oct. 24, bap. Dec. 30, 1778. (Eliz⁴. City).

Ward, Edward, son of Planey by Mary, b. April 23, bap. May 13, 1726.

Ward, Pasca, son of Edward by Elizabeth, of Elizabeth City County, b. Oct. 1, 1688.

Ward, Plany, son of Edward by Elizabeth, b. Nov. 6, 1690.
   [This name is indexed Planey Ward].

Ware, William, son of George and Martha, b. Dec. 29, 1760.

Warrington, Francis Spencer, son of the Rev^d. Thomas Warrington by Elizabeth, b. January 20, 1749/50, bap. Feb. 11, 1749/50.

Warrington, Rachel, dau. of Rev^d. Thomas and Elizabeth, b. Jan. 20, bap. Feb. 2, 1753.

Watkins, Ann, dau. of Henry by Ann, b. May 6, 1695.

Watkins, Elizabeth, dau. of William by Sarah, b. Jan. 6, bap. Feb. 13, 1724.

Watkins, Henry, son of Henry by Ann, b. June 27, 1692.

Watkins, Henry, son of Henry by Agnes, b. Nov. 22, bap. same day, 1718.

Watkins, John, son of Henry by Ann, b. Dec. 21, 1702.

Watkins, John, son of William by Sarah, b. Jan. 6, bap. Feb. 15, 1724.

Watkins, Mary, dau. of Henry by Ann, b. March 14, 1697.

Watkins, Thomas Aduston, son of Henry and Sarah, b. Oct. 18, bap. Dec. 3, 1786. (Warw^k.)

Watkins, William, son of Henry by Ann, b. Feb. 9, 1689.

Watkins, William, son of William by Sarah, b. Oct. 13, bap. Nov. 12, 1721.

Watson, John, son of John by Sarah, b. April 1, 1678.

Watts, Everett, son of Anthony by Rebekah, b. April 6, 1694.

Watts, Mary, dau. of Anthony by Rebekah, b. March 4, 1696.

Watts, Thomas, son of Anthony by Rebekah, bap. March 31, 1700.

Webb, Edgar, son of Terrance by Mable, b. March 2, 1710.

Webb, Elizabeth, dau. of Armager and Sarah, b. Feb. 18, bap. March 31, 1765.

Webb, Henry, son of John by Mary, b. September 9, 1691.

Webb, John, son of John, [wife not named], b. Sept. 22, 1666.

Webb, John, son of John by Mary, b. Nov. 27, 1693.

Webb, John, son of Terrance by Mabel, b. July 17, 1705.

Webb, John, son of William by Elizabeth, b. ———, bap.

[Note: Entry preceding this is dated March 16, 1745; that immediately following is dated April 13, 1745.].

Webb, Mary, dau. of John by Mary, b. April 20, 1697.

Webb, Mary, dau. of Tarrence by Mabel, b. March 24, 1706.

Webb, Wentworth, son of John by Mary, b. March 23, 1699.

Webb, William, son of Tarrence by Mabel, b. Nov. 14, bap. Dec. 21, 1718.

Webb, William, son of Amager and Sarah, b. Aug. 19, bap. Sept. 25, 1768.

Welch, Elizabeth, dau. of John by Ann, b. Aug. 12, bap. Sept. 10, 1720.

Weldon, Rebecca, dau. of Robert by Prudence, b. July 9, bap. Aug. 10, 1723.

Wellings, Charles, son of Robert and Anne, b. Feb. 9, bap. March 27, 1774.

Wellings, John, son of Robert and Anne, b. July 3, bap. July 31, 1768.

Wellings, Mary, dau. of Robert and Anne, b. May 20, bap. June 17, 1764.

Wellings, Nancy, dau. of Robert and Anne, b. April 13, bap. May 14, 1758.

Wellings, Robert, son of Robert and Anne, b. October 11, 1761.

Wellings, Thomas, son of Robert and Anne, b. Nov. 17, 1770, bap. Jan. 27, 1771.

Wellings, William, son of Robert and Anne, b. Sept. 29, bap. Oct. 27, 1765.

Wellons, Anna Mireah, dau. of John by Anna Mireah, b. May 30, bap. July 3, 1743.

Wellons, Barbara, dau. of John by Ann, b. March 10, 1734, bap. Apr. 13, 1735.

Wellons, Elizabeth, dau. of John by Annamariah, b. Sept. 25, bap. Oct. 19, 1740.

Wellons, Mary, dau. of John by Anna Mireah, b. March 18, bap. April 13, 1745.

Wellons, Willm. son of John by Anna Miriah, b. Feb. 10, bap.
March 12, 1737/8.

Wells, Anthony, son of Peter by Abigail, b. Nov. 18, 16[98].

Wells, Pate, son of John by Elizabeth, b. Sept. 30, 1710.

Wells, Thomas, son of John by Elizabeth, b. June 23, 1702.
[This name may possibly be Wills].

Weymouth, Katy, dau. of John and Mary, b. Feb. 25, bap. May
26, 1782. (Eliz^a. City).

White, Alexander, "son of John White by Frances Bartless,"
b. Dec. 17, 1691.

White, Ann, dau. of John by Elizabeth, b. May 17, 1690.

White, Dennis, son of John by Elizabeth, b. Sept. 10, 1695.

White, James, son of John by Mary, b. May 26, bap. July 13,
1723.

White, John, son of John by Elizabeth, b. Oct. 11, 1692.

White, John, son of John by Mary, b. Oct. 10, bap. Dec. 12,
1719.

White, Mary, dau. of John by Elizabeth, b. Feb. 25, 1697.

White, Mary, dau. of John by Mary, b. Dec. 24, bap. Feb. 5,
1720.

White, Mary, dau. of Mary,
"Mary daughter of Mary White a legitimate was born
May the 19th 1722 baptized June the 30th 1722."

White, Samuell, son of George by Mary, b. May 29, 1679.

Whiteing, Ann, dau. of "Ann, being a mullatto," b. Dec. 14,
1701.

Whitfield, Martha,
"Martha daugh^r. of Sarah Whitfield born July the 28th
1729."

Whitifield, John, son of John by Sarah, b. Feb. 28, 1702.
[This name is indexed, "Whitfield"].

Whitifield, Mary, dau. of John by Sarah, b. Nov. 4, 1705.

Whiting, Catherine, dau. of Sarah Whiting by John Combs, b.
Feb. 14, 170[4].

[The entire entry is as follows: "Catherine daughter of Sarah Whiting by John Combs was born February 14ᵗʰ 170[4.]"]

Whiting, Mary, dau. of Sarah a mulatto, b. April 16, 1694.

Wild, James, son of Thos. Junr. and Anne, b. Oct. 18, 1783, bap. June 16, 1784. (Warwick).

Wild, James Sclater, son of Thomas and Sarah, b. Nov. 19, 1774, bap. Feb. 1, 1775.

Wilkinson, Elizabeth, dau. of George, [wife not named], b. Jan. 29, 1678.

Wilkinson, George, son of George by Mary, b. July 11, 1681.

Wilkinson, Mary, dau. of George by Mary, b. Sept. 24, 1685.

Wilkinson, Thomas, son of George by Mary, b. Feb. 6, 1676.

Wilkinson, Thomas, son of George by Mary, b. Feb. 22, 1679.

Williams, Elizabeth, dau. of William and Hannah, b. May 12, bap. June 10, 1750.

Williams, Frances, dau. of William and Hannah, of "Elizabeth County," b. May 23, bap. June 28, 174[9].

Williams, Richard, son of Peter by Dorcas, b. May 20, bap. June 25, 1738.

Williams, Robert, son of John by Hester, b. Aug. 18, 1688.

Williams, William, son of Peter by Dorcas, b. Aug. —, bap. Dec. 29, 1728.

Williamson, John, son of George Williamson by Mary Durgin, b. Nov. 24, 1683.

Willis, James, son of James by Mary, b. July 7, 1684.

Willis, Mary, dau. of James by Mary, b. Sept. 20, 1688.

Willons, Henry, son of John by Ann, b. July 30, bap. Aug. 8, 1728.

Willons, John, son of John by Ann, b. Oct. 19, bap. Nov. 21, 1725.

Willons, William, son of Robert by Prudence, b. May 1, 1720, bap. same day.

Wills, John, son of John by Elizabeth, b. Nov. 29, 1705.

Wills, John, son of John and Elizabeth, b. Oct. 1, bap. [Oct.] 27, 1765. (Of Warwick).

Wills, John Pate, son of John by Elizabeth, b. Nov. 13, 1712. [This name may be Wells.]

Wills, Martha, dau. of John and Elizabeth, b. Dec. 29, 1763. (Of Warwick).

Wills, Samuel, son of Miles and Martha, b. Nov. 1, 1784, bap. March 21, 1785. (Warwick).

Wills, Thomas, son of John and Elizabeth, b. Nov. 11, bap. Dec. 13, 1767. (Warwick).

Wilson, Anne, an illegetimate dau. of Mary Wilson, b. Jan. 14, 1744, bap. May 5, 1745.

Wilson, Elizabeth, dau. of John by Mary, b. Nov. 1, bap. Nov. 30, 1729.

Wilson, Henry,
> "Henry a Child belonging to Coll°. Wilson was baptized April 1, 1704" Elizabeth City

Wilson, Mary, dau. of John by Mary, b. March 6, 1725, bap. April 24, 172[6].

Wilson, Mary, dau. of Edward and Susanna, b. July 8, bap. Sept. 24, 1775.

Wilson, Sally, dau. of Tho°. Combs and Anne, b. June 24, bap. July 28, 1765.

Wilson, Sally, dau. of John and Mary, b. Feb. 19, bap. May 12, 1782. ([Elizabeth?] City).

Wilson, Sarah, dau. of Willis and Martha, b. March 26, bap. May 7, 1780.

Wilson, William, son of Thomas by Grissle, b. Aug. 30, 1688.

Wilson, William, son of Edward and Eliz°. b. Nov. 30, 1764, bap. April 14, 1765.

Wilson, William, son of Wilson [?], and Martha, b. Jan. 29, bap. April 28, 1782.

Wilson, Willis, son of Edward and Susanna, b. Aug. 14, bap. Sept. 26, 1773.

Wise, Ann, dau. of Robert and Ann, b. ———, bap. Jan. 19, 1752.

Wise, Anne, dau. of Robert by Anne, b. Oct. 10, 1748, bap. Nov. 24, [1748?].

Wise, Charles, son of William by Sarah, b. March 17, 1689.

Wise, Charles, son of William by Elizabeth, b. Aug. 19, bap. Sept. 25, 1720.

Wise, Elizabeth, [twin with Frances], dau. of William by Mary, b. Sept. 2, 1674.

Wise, Frances, [twin with Elizabeth], dau. of William by Mary, b. September 2, 1674.

Wise, Frances, dau. of Charles by Rachell, b. Oct. 21, 1712.

Wise, Gerard, son of Robert by Anne, b. Dec. 8, 1741, bap. Jan. 17, 174[1].

Wise, John, son of William by Elizabeth, b. Feb. 20, bap. March 6, 1722.

Wise, John, son of William by Ann, b. ———, bap. Dec. 22, 1734.

Wise, John, son of Robert by Anne, b. April 15, bap. June 8, 1746.

Wise, Mary, dau. of William by Mary, b. Dec. 27, 1678.

Wise, Mary, dau. of William by Sarah, b. December 30, 170[4].

Wise, Mary, dau. of Willm. by Ann, b. Nov. 3, baptized priv. Nov. 11, 1732.

Wise, Polly, dau. of John and Mary, b. March 25, bap. June 4, 1769.

Wise, Robert, son of William by Elizabeth, b. June 6, bap. June 10, 1718.

Wise, Robert, son of John and Mary, b. Oct. 18, 1771, bap. Jan. 19, 1772.

Wise, "Thomas, son of Anne Wise Born July 1769 Baptized June 12th, 1774."

Wise, William, son of William by Mary, b. June 10, 1677.

Wise, William, son of William by Sarah, b. Nov. 20, 170[8].

Wise, William, son of William by Ann, b. Jan. 8, 1730, bap. April 4, 1731.

Wise, William, son of Robert by Anne, b. Dec. 29, bap. Feb. 6, 1743.

Wislin, Edith, [twin with George], dau. of John by Margarett, b. Aug. 31, 1669.

Wislin, George, [twin with Edith], son of John by Margarett, b. Aug. 31, 1669.

Wood, Bennett, son of John and Anne, b. Oct. 2, bap. Dec. 15, 1776. (Eliz⁴. City).

Wood, Charles, son of Charles by Judith, b. Dec. 17, 17[08].

Wood, Humphry, son of Edward by Elizabeth, b. Aug. 3, [1703]. Elizabeth City.

Wood, James, son of John and Hannah, b. June 11, bap. Dec. 11, 1785. ([ ] City).

Wood, John, son of John and Hannah, b. Dec. 15, 1773, bap. March 27, 1774.

Wood, Martha, dau. of William by Mary, b. June 14, bap. July 26, 1741.

Wood, Martha, dau. of John and Hannah, b. Feb. 28, bap. April 18, 1779. (Eliz⁴. City).

Wood, Meade, son of Meade and Susanna, b. May 6, bap. June 19, 1774.

Wood, Rebecca, dau. of Mead and Susanna, b. Feb. 2, bap. March 31, 1776.

Wood, Robert, son of John and Hannah, b. April 27, bap. July 14, 1782. (Eliz⁴. City).

Wood, Samuel, son of Charles by Judith, b. Aug. 26, 1711.

Wood, Sukey, dau. of John and Susanna, b. March 14, bap. May 11, 1777. ([Wa]rwick).

Wood, Thomas, son of Mead and Rebecca, b. July 6, bap. Aug. 3, 1766. (Warwick).

Wood, Thomas, son of Thomas and Elizabeth, b. Jan. 14, bap. March 24, 1776.

Wood, William, son of John by Elinor, b. Aug. 17, 1707.

Wood, William, son of Thos. [?], and B[?] [———]. b. April
—, bap. May 31, 1778. (Warwick).

Woodhouse, Ann, dau. of Edward by Sarah, b. June 30, 1665.
(A note says: "by the book 1695.").

Woodhouse, Anne, [twin with John], dau. of Charles by Elizabeth, b. Nov. 9, bap. Nov. 12, 1740.

Woodhouse, Charles, son of Charles by Eliz⁴. b. ———, bap.
Dec. 17, 1738.

Woodhouse, Edward, son of Edward by Sarah, b. Feb. 14,
1700.

Woodhouse, Henry, son of Charles by Elizabeth, b. Jan. 18,
bap. Jan. 22, 1742.

Woodhouse, John, son of Edward by Elizabeth, b. June 15,
1711.

Woodhouse, John, [twin with Anne], son of Charles by Elizabeth, b. Nov. 9, bap. Nov. 12, 1740.

Woodhouse, Sarah, dau. of Edward by Sarah, b. Jan. 25, 1702.

Woodman, Mary, dau. of William by Frances, b. Dec. 17, 1688.

Woodman, William, son of William by Mary, bap. Feb. 10,
1674.

Woodman, William, son of William by Frances, b. May 6, 1690.

Woolph, Robert, son of Thomas by Alice, b. Jan. 9, 170[4].

Wooten, Elizabeth, dau. of Thomas by Judith, b. June 29, 1680.

Wooton, Ann, dau. of Thom by Elizabeth, b. March 9, 1726,
bap. April 30, 1727.

Wootten, Edward, son of William and Sally, b. Dec. 25, 1776,
bap. March 16, 1777.

Wootton, Elizabeth, dau. of Wm. and Sarah, b. Oct. 14, 1773,
bap. Jan. 2, 1774.

Word, Benjamin, son of Cuthb⁴. by Mary, b. Nov. —, bap.
Dec. 23, 1733.

Word, Thomas, son of Cuthbert by Mary, b. March 22, 1736.

Worley, Edward, son of Edward by Mary, b. Feb. 21, 1713.

Worley, Edward, son of Nicholas, by [   ], his wife, b.
Jan. 18, bap. Feb. 25, 1738/9.

Worley, Hayward, son of Edward by Margarett, b. May 9, bap. June 5, 1720.

Worley, Mary, dau. of Nich⁹. by Anne, b. March 13, 1736/7, bap. April 24, 1737.

Worley, Nicholas, son of Edward by Mary, b: Aug. 25, 1711.

Worley, Thomas, son of Edward by Mary, b. March —, 17[08].

Worley, Thomas, son of Nich°. by Ann, b. March 19, 1733, bap. April 14, 1734.

Wright, Augustine, son of John by Elizabeth, b. Nov. 29, 1683.

Wright, Benjamin, son of Benjamin and Lucy, b. Aug. 13, bapt. Sept. 19, 1775.

Wright, Betsy, dau. of John and Eliz⁴. b. Jan. 10, bap. Feb. 21, 1768.

Wright, Dudley, [twin with William], son of John and Eliz⁴. b. March 1, bap. privately March 11, publicly April 4, 1773.

Wright, Eliz⁴. Curtis, dau. of Benj⁴. and Lucy, b. Nov. 20, 1768, bap. Jan. 1, 1769.

Wright, Fanny, dau. of Benj⁴. and Lucy, b. Feb. 12, bap. March 15, 1778.

Wright, John, son of John and Elizabeth, b. March 7, bap. April 5, 1765.

Wright, John, son of John by Mary, bap. April 5, 1770.

Wright, Kathrine, dau. of Edward by Kathrine, b. Dec. 30, bap. Feb. 1, 1735.

Wright, Mary, dau. of John and Eliz⁴. b. Feb. 13, bap. April 8, 1770. (York Hampton).

Wright, Nancy, dau. of William and Elizabeth, b. March 3, bap. April 17, 1778. ("Ykhpton").

Wright, Peter, son of John and Eliz⁴. b. June 16, bap. July 23, 1775.

Wright, William, [twin with Dudley], son of John and Eliz⁴. b. March 1, bap. privately March 11, publicly April 4, 1773.

Wyatt, Richard, son of Richard and Rhoda, b. May 1, bap. June 18, 1775.

Y

Yargan, Patience, dau. of John by Patience, b. Aug. 3, bap. Sept. 6, 1724. Denbeigh Parish.

Yeargain, Elizabeth, dau. of William and Mary, b. June 24, bap. July 30, 1780. (Eliz*. City)..

Young, Frances, dau. of William by Marg"., b. March 14, 1740/1, bap. April 26, 1741.

Young, James, son of Richard and Elizabeth, b. July 23, bap. Nov. 7, 1778. (Warwick).

Young, Matthew, son of William by Marg". b. March 14, 1740/1, bap. Apr. 12, 174[1].

Young, Nightingale, son of John by Ann, b. April 19, bap. May 19, 1728.

Young, Sarah, dau. of William by Marg". b. June 11, bap. July 16, 1738.

CHAPTER V

The method of arranging the material of the Register of Deaths is the same as that followed in presenting the Register of Births. In other words, the names of the persons who died have been arranged alphabetically, in the manner of an index. These names, being thus arranged in a self-indexing list, do not appear in the index. All other names, however, are indexed in the usual way.

A

Acust, John, servant to Richard Trotter, d. May 19, 1672.
Albritton, Benjᵃ., d. Aug. 29, 1702.
Albritton, Charles, d. Jan. 18, 1692.
Albritton, Edward, buried Sept. 6, 1688.
Albritton, John, d. Aug. 25, 1689.
Albritton, Ralph, d. Jan. 21, 1701.
Albritton, William, d. Dec. 6, 1692.
Allen, William, "being a dutch Man," d. Sept. 16, 1672.
Allen, William, d. Nov. 3, 1697.
Allman, William, d. Oct. 4, 1750.
Andrews, Henry, Mr., d. Nov. 10, 1705.
Ann, servant to Edward Phelps, d. Oct. 17, 1677.
Armistead, Jane, wife of Edward, d. Feb. 24, 1756.
Armistead, Robert, son of Edwᵈ. and Jane, d. Nov. 15, 1757.
Arnold, William, buried, Feb. 24, 1681.
Arnolds, Hannah, d. June 6, 1693.
Avery, Ann, wife of John, d. Oct. 5, 1729.
Avory, Edee, d. June 25, 1697.
        [Note: Indexed "Edith Avory"].
Avory, Elizabeth, wife of John, d. Dec. 21, 1732.
Avory, James, d. Oct. 24, 1707.

Avory, James, d. Feb. 22, 1716.
Avory, John, d. June 26, 1694.
Avory, Mary, wife of John, d. Jan. 14, 1676.
Avory, Mary, widow, d. Jan. 10, 1711.

B

Badgett, John, son of John and Margt., d. July 2, 1751.
Bailey, Mary, wife of John, d. Aug. 2, [1749].
Baker, Hannah, dau. of Samuel, d. Jan. 14, 1677.
Baker, Thomas, buried, Jan. 18, 1681.
Barber, Thomas, d. Jan. 10, 1711.
Barker, Arrabella, servant to John Clarke, d. Jan. 13, 1701.
Barnal, Gimmon, d. April 7, 1718.
Barnes, Anna Maria, d. May 2, 1702.
Barnes, Brian, d. April 27, 1679.
Barnes, Bridget, wife of John, d. April 14, 1744.
Barnes, Bryan, son of Matthew, d. Dec. 3, 1726.
Barnes, Elizabeth, dau. of Brian, d. March 11, 1678.
Barnes, Elizabeth, dau. of John, d. Oct. 27, 1741.
Barnes, Frances, dau. of Matthew, d. Dec. 25, 1726.
Barnes, John, son of Matthew, d. Oct. 13, 1744.
Barnes, Johnson, Singleman, d. April 2, 1744.
Barnes, Martha, d. Dec. 24, 1706.
Barnes, Martha, dau. of Matth^w., d. Oct. 18, 1713.
Barnes, Mary, wife of Matthew, d. Sept. 23, 1706.
Barnes, Matthew, infant, d. Nov. 9, 1732.
Barnes, Matthew, d. May 23, 1734.
Barns, John, son of Nathl. and Diana, d. Oct. 4, 1753.
Barradall, Thos., d. Jan. 18, 1749.
Barradel, Henry, "of Yk [York] parish," d. May 7, 1743.
Barradel, Susannah, widow, d. Feb. 7, 1750.
Barradell, John, d. Dec. 1, 1751.
Bartlet, Alexander, d. April 28, 1720.
Bartlett, Alexander, son of Alex^r., d. Dec. 9, 1720.

Bartlett, John, d. May 7, 1675.
Bartlett, Michael, son of John, d. Nov. 5, 1689.
Bartlett, Michael, d. June 19, 1713.
Bartlett, Samuel, d. March 1, 1700.
Barwick, Thomas, servant to John Hay, d. Oct. 20, 1665.
Batts, Anthony, d. Dec. 24, 1718.
Batts, John, servant to John Moore, d. Nov. 15, 1699.
Beane, Ann, servant to Peter Manson, d. Dec. 25, 1694.
Belvin, Mary, dau. of John, d. Sept. 14, 1719.
Belvin, Thomas, d. July 18, 1783.
Bennet, Catharine, d. March 4, 1700.
Bennet, Charles, son of Charles, d. Jan. 20, 1736.
Bennet, Charles, d. Aug. 16, 1736.
Bennet, Elizabeth, wife of James, d. Dec. 29, 1709.
Bennet, Elizabeth, d. Jan. 12, 1719.
Bennet, James, d. Feb. 15, 1719.
Bennet, James, d. Nov. 25, 1724.
Bennet, Martin, d. March 18, 1725.
Bennett, James, Junr., d. Sept. 14, 1713.
Bennice, Edward, buried, March 21, 1685.
Bentley, Ann, d. March 19, 1700.
Berry, John, d. Dec. 21, 1693.
Berry, Margarett, wife of John, d. Sept. 17, 1692.
Berry, Mary, d. March 12, 1700.
Berry, Mary, wife of James, d. Oct. 8, 1784.
Berry, William, d. Feb. 5, 1717.
Bevens, John, buried, Feb. 26, 1687.
Bevens, Thomas, d. Dec. 8, 1678.
Bevens, Thomas, son of Thomas, d. March 2, 1677.
Bigling, Rebekah, widow, d. July 8, 1671.
Bircher, Bartho, d. March 9, 1735.
Bircher, Martha, wife of James, d. Aug. 23, 1748.
Bircher, Sarah, dau. of Barth°., d. March 17, 1717.
Bircher, Sarah, dau. of James, d. Oct. 19, 1748.
Bircher, William, d. Sept. 14, 1736.

Birdsong, Bennet, son of John, d. Jan. 3, 1744.

Birdsong, Elizabeth, wife of James, d. Jan. 6, 1737.

Birdsong, Enos, son of John, d. Jan. 14, 1735.

Birdsong, Hannah, d. Dec. 30, 1729.

Birdsong, Mary, d. Nov. 18, 1732.

Birdsong, Mary, wife of Charles, d. Jan. 10, 1744.

Birdsong, Mary, wife of John, d. Aug. 26, 1748.

Birdsong, Sarah, d. March 18, 1735.

Blackey, Sarah, drowned in a well, d. Nov. 9, 1742.

Blackston, Elizabeth, d. Aug. 22, 1724.

Blackston, Thomas, d. Oct. 8, 1725.

Blackston, William, d. March 31, 1720.

Blackstone, James, "of York prsh," d. Oct. 14, 1706.

Blith, Edith, dau. of Henry, d. Nov. 21, 1689.

Blith, Jane, d. Oct. 28, 1693.

Blyth, Henry, d. Dec. 5, 1700.

Bond, Elizabeth, d. Jan. 9, 1703.

Bond, Elizabeth, dau. of John, d. Sept. 28, 1737.

Bond, James, son of John, d. Jan. 30, 1732.

Bond, John, Senr., d. Jan. 8, 1742.

Bond, Mary, dau. of John, d. March 11, 1717.

Bond, Thomas, son of John, d. Aug. 17, 1738.

Bond, William, d. Aug. 1, 1696.

Bond, William, a youth, d. July 15, 1743.

Booth, Margarett, d. June 26, 1697.

Booth, William, d. May 16, 1692.

Borrodell, Ann, dau. of Henry, d. March 3, 1717.

Borrodell, Elizabeth, d. March 15, 1717.

Borrodell, Henry, son of Henry, d. Aug. 31, 1710.

Borrodell, Mary, d. April 27, 1720.

Bowen, Walter, d. July 3, 1693.

Bowen, William, d. Nov. 24, 1781.

Bowin, Lewis, servant to Henry Freeman, d. Aug. 30, 1665.

Bowler, John, d. Jan. 21, 1704.

Branford, Elizabeth, d. Jan. 24, 1688.

Branton, Deborah, d. Sept. 20, 1697.

Bridges, Edward, d. Feb. 10, 1686.

Bridges, Mary, buried Feb. 22, 1686.

Brighting, Samuel, d. Nov. 2, 1671.

Brodie, Alexander, son of Doc^r. Jn°., d. March 19, 1726.

Brodie, "James, son of Alexr. and ———— Brodie (S. Carolina)," d. Jan. 11, 1782.

Broster, Agitha, d. Feb. 23, 1735.

Broster, Elizabeth, d. Sept. 29, 1700.

Broster, John, d. Nov. 12, 1689.

Broster, John, "Clark of the Parish," d. Dec. 18, 1705. [Note: Not mentioned in *The Colonial Church in Virginia*.)

Brown, Ann, d. April 17, 1726.

Brown, Cathrine, wife of James, d. Dec. 24, 1753.

Brown, Constant, d. Oct. 19, 1724.

Brown, Francis, d. Feb. 3, 1678.

Brown, James, buried, Jan. 27, 1686.

Brown, James, d. April 11, 1769.

Brown, Richard, d. Nov. 13, 1706.

Brown, Thomas, son of Francis, d. June 17, 1676.

Brown, Thomas, d. Feb. 11, 1695.

Brown, William, d. March 7, 1717.

Bryan, Elizabeth, d. May 20, 1718.

Bullen, Thomas, buried, Feb. 11, 1686.

Burcher, Elizabeth, wife of Barth°., d. Feb. 20, 1710.

Burcher, Lewis, d. Nov. 17, 1724.

Burkett, Sarah, d. May 12, 1724.

Burkhead, Samuel, d. Jan. 18, 1719.

Burkhead, William, d. Oct. 30, 1697.

Burnet, Mary, dau. of Thos., d. March 9, 1667.

Burnham, Thomas, son of Thomas, d. Aug. 26, 1711.

Burnham, Thomas, d. March 31, 1718 [1717?].

Burroughs, Elizabeth, d. April 9, 1758.

Burroughs, John, d. Nov. 25, 1750.

Burrows, Nicholas, d. April 17, 1709.

Burton, Edward, d. June 17, 1705.
Burton, Elizabeth, dau. of James, d. Oct. 24, 1713.
Burton, Elizabeth, wife of James, d. Nov. 3, 1717.
Burton, Elizabeth, dau. of Mary, d. June 11, 1732.
Burton, James, d. June 10, 1725.
Burton, John, d. Sept. 16, 1725.
Burton, Joseph, servant to Armager Wade, d. Dec. 8, 1677.
Burton, Lewis, d. June 21, 1701.
Burton, Lewis, d. April 14, 1718.
Burton, Phillip, d. Nov. 15, 1727.
Burton, Ursella, d. July 11, 1701.
Butler, Henry, d. Feb. 20, 1692.
Butts, Anthony, buried Nov. 1, 1687.
Butts, Eliz*., d. Nov. 3, 1733. "Eliz*. Robinson relict of Anth°.
    Butts & late wife of Jn°. Robinson."

C

Cable, Edward, d. March 19, 1674.
Callowhill, Ann, d. Jan. 25, 1722.
Callowhill, Francis, d. July 23, 1692.
Callowhill, James, d. May 15, 1718.
Callowhill, Mary, d. Nov. 18, 1688.
Calthorp, Ann, the widow, d. Dec. 9, 1667.
Calthorp, Ann, dau. of James, d. Dec. 7, 1673.
Calthorp, Ann, buried April 7, 1685.
Calthorp, Anthony, son of Elistrange, d. Oct. 2, 1712.
Calthorp, Barbara, buried July 28, 1680.
Calthorp, Charles, d. Dec. 16, 1718.
Calthorp, Christopher, d. June 27, 1694.
Calthorp, Elistrange, son of Charles, d. July 22, 1718.
Calthorp, Elistrange, d. Oct. 4, 1726.
Calthorp, Elizabeth, d. Sept. 14, 1697.
Calthorp, Elizabeth, dau. of James, d. Aug. 21, 1698.
Calthorp, Elizabeth, dau. of Eliz*., d. Aug. 7, 1726.

Calthorp, James, d. Aug. 3, 1689.

Calthorp, James, d. Dec. 21, 1711.

Calthorp, James, son of Elimelech, d. Oct. 14, 1732.

Calthorp, John, son of Elimelech, d. Feb. 26, 1732.

Calthorp, Mary, wife of James, d. Aug. 24, 1698.

Calthorpe, Ann, wid°., d. March 31, 1734.

Calthorpe, Butts, son of Charles, d. Oct. 17, 1739.

Calthorpe, Elimelech, son of James, d. Jan. 14, 1733.

Calthorpe, James, Singleman, d. Nov. 2, 1744.

Calthorpe, Mary, wife of Elistrange, d. Oct. 24, 1718.

Canthwall, Joan, servant to Henry Hayward, decd., d. Dec. 9, 1705.

Canurs, Ann, d. Feb. 14, 1726.

Carey, Jane, d. Feb. 28, 1735.

Carrell, Cornelius, d. Dec. 1, 1670.

Carter, Hope, d. Oct. 14, 1699.

Cary, Mary, wife of John, d. May 17, 1761.

Catesby, George, d. May 7, 1675.

Cattilla, Ann, d. Oct. 13, 1729.

Cattilla, Catharine, d. Nov. 7, 1718.

Cattilla, Edward, son of Matthew, d. Nov. 6, 1748.

Cattilla, Judith, d. Dec. 10, 1735.

Cattilla, Mary, d. Dec. 10, 1703.

Cattilla, Mary, wife of Abraham, d. May 3, 1750.

Cattilla, Matthew, d. March 15, 1700.

Cattilla, Matthew, d. Nov. 13, 1748.

Chairington, William, d. March 1, 1667.

Chapman, Walter, son of Walter, d. April 7, 1678.

Chapman, Walter, buried Oct. 1, 1685.

Chapman, Willm., d. Feb. 15, 1700.

Chappell, John, d. May 6, 1736.

Charle, William, son of Francis, d. Oct. 29, 1700.

Charlesworth, Godfrey, buried Oct. 10, 1684.

Charter, John, d. May 3, 1679.

Cheatham, Margarett, wife of Thomas, d. April 6, 1670.

Cheley, Joseph, d. Feb. 19, 1694.

Cheviston, John, d. Dec. 12, 1723.

Chisman, Edmund, d. April 13, 1784.

Chisman, Elizabeth, dau. of John, d. March 16, 1717.

Chisman, Elizabeth, d. Nov. 18, 1717.

Chisman, Elizabeth, dau. of John, d. July 27, 1737.

Chisman, Eliz*., wife of Tho*., d. April 23, 1757.

Chisman, George, son of Thomas, d. Oct. 6, 1710.

Chisman, John, d. June 13, 1679.

Chisman, John, d. Sept. 19, 1728.

Chisman, John, Junr., d. Sept. 4, 1735.

Chisman, John, son of Thomas and Diana, d. Feb. 14, 1782.

Chisman, Mary, widow, d. Dec. 11, 1678.

Chisman, Mary, dau. of Thomas, d. Jan. 22, 1719.

Chisman, Mary, dau. of Henry and Mary, d. Feb. 5, 1749.

Chisman, Mary, widow of John, d. Dec. 18, 1760.

Chisman, Mary, wife of Edmund, d. Nov. 19, 1781.

Chisman, Mildred Dowsing, d. Sept. 25, 1748.

Chisman, Thomas, Capt., d. Dec. 11, 1722.

Chisman, Thomas, d. April 7, 1727.

Chrismas, Isabel, widow, d. March 24, 1669.

Christjan, Henry, servant to Mr. Trotter, d. July 2, 1678.

Clark, Ann, d. April 9, 1718.

Clark, Frances, widow, d. April 6, 1751.

Clark, Francis, son of John, d. Oct. 15, 1719.

Clark, Henry, d. Nov. 25, 1724.

Clark, John, Senr., d. June 17, 1689.

Clark, John, d. May 9, 1710.

Clark, Margarett, wid°., d. Jan. 26, 1710.

Clark, Mary, dau. of Francis, d. Sept. 11, 1703.

Clarke, Alexander, d. July 14, 1724.

Clarke, Ann, wife of Henry, d. March 11, 1701.

Clarke, Elizabeth, wife of John, d. Jan. 19, 1698.

Clarke, Elizabeth, d. March 13, 1724.

Clarke, Francis, d. March 19, 1717.

Clarke, Grace, d. Dec. 13, 1720.

Clarke, Henry, d. Sept. 16, 1726.

Clarke, James, d. Sept. 9, 1729.

Clarke, John, son of John, d. July 26, 1678.

Clarke, John, d. Feb. 11, 1680.

Clarke, John, d. March 22, 1717.

Clarke, John, son of Henry, d. Jan. 9, 1736.

Clarke, John, parish orphan, d. Nov. 10, 1731.

Clarke, Mary, d. March 24, 1717.

Clarke, Mary, parish orphan, d. April 21, 1731.

Clarke, Mildred, "an illegetimate infant," d. June 26, 1744.

Clarke, Nicholas, d. Sept. 25, 1694.

Clarke, Sarah, servant to Martha Freeman, d. April 20, 1676.

Clarke, Stephen, d. Jan. 19, 1698.

Clarke, William, d. March 19, 1698.

Clifford, John, d. Nov. 7, 1693.

Clifford, Martha, d. Dec. 8, 1693.

Clifton, Benjamin, d. March 28, 1728.

Clifton, Elinor, d. Sept. 4, 1693.

Clifton, Elinor, d. March 22, 1717.

Clifton, Elizabeth, d. March 26, 1696.

Clifton, John, d. Sept. 8, 1702.

Clifton, John, d. March 21, 1726.

Clifton, Mary, d. Nov. 11, 1724.

Clifton, Mary, dau. of Thomas, d. Oct. 14, 1739.

Clifton, Richard, d. Aug. 6, 1718.

Clifton, Samuel, d. Sept. 21, 1700.

Clifton, Samuel, d. March 24, 1717.

Clifton, Sarah, d. Feb. 16, 1719.

Clifton, Sarah, dau. of Benj., d. July 16, 1734.

Cockerhill, Elizabeth, dau. of Sam'., d. May 14, 1714.

Cockerhill, Mary, d. June 26, 1735.

Colbert, Robert, d. Feb. 2, 1692.

Coleman, Thomas, buried Oct. 31, 1685.

Coleson, William, son of Issa: d. April 5, 1737.

Collison, Ann, widow, d. Sept. 21, 1731.

Colvert, William, d. July 26, 1666.

Combs, Sarah, d. Jan. 16, 1752.

Conner, Ann, wife of Gerald, d. Jan. 23, 1668.

Conner, Elizabeth, dau. of Gerald, buried Oct. 7, 1684.

Conner, Gerrald, d. Nov. 28, 1693.

Conner, Mary, d. June 17, 1689.

Conner, Richard, d. July 19, 1696.

Conners, Thomas, d. Oct. 31, 1668.

Conyers, Elizabeth, d. April 10, 1737.

Conyers, John, d. March 9, 1710.

Cook, Anabella, dau. of William, d. July 4, 1671.

Cook, Ann, dau. of William, buried Sept. 27, 1670.

Cook, Anne, wife of Wm., d. May 19, 1762.

Cook, John, d. Aug. 23, 1695.

Cook, John, son of Francis and Mary, d. Feb. 12, 1779.

Cook, Mary, dau. of Francis and Rachel, d. July 3, 1757.

Cook, Mary, wife of John, d. May 8, 1761.

Cook, Rachel, wife of Francis, Junr., d. Dec. 27, 1760.

Cook, William, d. Nov. 7, 1671.

Cooke, Elizabeth, dau. of James, d. Oct. 3, 1748.

Cooke, Frances, d. March 17, 1700.

Cooke, James, son of Francis, d. Oct. 24, 1732.

Cooke, Martha, dau. of James, d. Nov. 15, 1742.

Cooke, Mary, "a twin daugh'. of Fran'. Cooke," d. March 24, 1748.

Cooke, Samuel, d. June 22, 1700.

Cooke, Sarah, d. April 14, 1717.

Cooke, Thomas, son of James, d. Dec. 26, 1737.

Cooper, Elizabeth, d. Feb. 12, 1716.

Cooper, Mary, d. Dec. 3, 1692.

Corlew, Wᵐ., son of Edward [?], of Yorkhampton Parish, d. Sept. 21, [1749].

Coudart, Bernard, "Clark of this parish," d. March 30, 1723.

Coudart, Lidia, d. Jan. 13, 1718.

Coudert, John, d. Nov. 16, 1736.

Coudert, Mary, singlewoman, d. Sept. 10, 1739.

Cowdert, John, son of Wm. and Dianah, d. Sept. 10, 1756.

Cox, Constant, wife of David, d. Dec. 5, 1741.

Cox, David, d. April 4, 1758.

Cox, Dorcas, wife of David, d. Dec. 26, 1749.

Cox, Elizabeth, dau. of Tho'., d. Oct. 9, 1737.

Cox, Elizabeth, dau. of David, d. April 10, 1740.

Cox, James, son of Thomas and Amy, d. May 18, 1787.

Cox, Jane, dau. of Thomas, d. Jan. 29, 1716.

Cox, Jane, wife of David, d. Jan. 28, 1737.

Cox, John, d. Oct. 14, 1713.

Cox, John, d. Dec. 29, 1724.

Cox, John, son of David, d. May 24, 1735.

Cox, Joseph, d. Aug. 16, 1696.

Cox, Mary, d. Feb. 14, 1726.

Cox, Mildrick, d. March 10, 1716.

Cox, Richard, son of David, d. Feb. 21, 1748.

Cox, Thomas, d. Feb. 27, 1692.

Craddock, John, d. Nov. 16, 1750. "Killed by the Kick of a Horse."

Craddock, William, d. Oct. 15, 1741.

Crandall, Thomas, d. Jan. 29, 1674.

Crane, Mary, wife of Richard, d. Aug. 29, 1678.

Crawford, James, servant to John Drewry, d. July 7, 1722.

Crocker, Paul, d. March 10, 1674.

Crofts, John, Merchant of London, d. July 23, 1709.

Croucher, Robert, d. Dec. 5, 1705.

Crow, Thomas, buried April 23, 1681.

Crupsey, John, Capt. of the Ship Catherine, d. June 2, 1691.

Culley, Jane, d. Feb. 9, 1720.

Cunningham, Jane, d. Aug. 12, 1696.

Curson, Thomas, d. March 25, 1704.

Curtis, Damazinah, dau. of Thos., d. Nov. 6, 1722.

Curtis, Edmund, d. Oct. 27, 1728.

Curtis, Elizabeth, wife of Edmund, d. Dec. 30, 1751.
Curtis, Mary, buried Jan. 26, 1687.
Curtis, Mary, dau. of Edmund, d. March 21, 1710.
Curtis, Robert, buried Jan. 15, 1687.
Curtis, Robert, d. Jan. 19, 1728.
Curtis, Thomas, d. Dec. 15, 1722.
Curtis, Thomas, son of Thomas, d. Jan. 16, 1730.

D

Daniel, Mary, d. Oct. 20, 1703.
Davies, Richard (and William Pescod, "sons of Rachell Kee"), d. Sept. 29, 1678.
Davies, Thomas (and Wil^m. Pescod "sons of Rachell Kee"), d. Oct. 6, 1678.
Davis, Elias, d. Nov. 25, 1688.
Davis, Elizabeth, wife of John, d. Oct. 7, 1781.
    "Elizabeth, wife of John Davis (York) at the House of her Brother Thomas Powell in this Parish."
Davis, Grace, wife of Owen, d. Feb. 18, 1677.
Davis, John, d. Jan. 25, 1719.
Davis, John, d. April 8, 1727.
Davis, John, d. Oct. 16, 1734.
Davis, Mary, buried Oct. 30, 1687.
Davis, Mary, dau. of John, d. April 20[?], 1720.
Davis, Owin, d. May 4, 1705.
Davis, Peter, son of John, d. Sept. 19, 1735.
Day, Edward, buried May 6, 1687.
Defeat, John, buried Feb. 21, 1687.
Defeat, Sarah, buried Jan. 15, 1687.
Delaney, Mary, d. March 34, 1717.
Delany, Susanna, wife of Thos., d. Nov. 23, 1733.
Dennis, Thomas, of Denbeigh Parish, d. Nov. 21, 1695.
Devonshire, Joshua, d. Oct. 22, 1688.
Dickason, Charles, buried Feb. 9, 1686.

Dickason, Elizabeth, wife of Richard, d. Feb. 12, 1677.

Dixon, Ann, dau. of James, d. March 25, 1733.

Dixon, James, d. March 14, 1752.

Dixon, Martha, wife of James, d. Feb. 4, 1752.

Dixon, Richard, d. Nov. 14, 1705.

Dixon, Richard, son of James, d. Feb. 21, 1744.

Dixon, William, son of James, d. Sept. 29, 1721.

Dixon, Willm., d. Jan. 17, 1701.

Doris, Judith, d. Oct. 17, 1693.

Dorithy, servant to Humphry Tompkins, d. June 30, 1673.

Doswell, Catherine, wife of John, Senr., d. March 4, 1710.

Doswell, Edward, d. March 7, 1739.

Doswell, Elizabeth, widow, d. Sept. 24, 1727.

Doswell, John, d. June 12, 1718.

Doswell, John, d. Nov. 13, 1732.

Doswell, John, Junr., d. Nov. 26[?], 1718.

Doswell, Nutting, d. Sept. 29, 1703.

Doswell, Richard, son of John Doswell by Elizabeth, d. Oct. 13, 1708.

    [Note: The full entry is as follows: "Richard & two more Male twins sons of John Doswell by Elizabeth his wife died all together October the 13th."].

Draper, Hester, wife of Robert, d. April 16, 1665.

Draper, Jane, wife of Robert, buried Feb. 10, 1684.

Draper, Josiah, d. Feb. 23, 1717.

Draper, Robert, buried Dec. 19, 1684.

Draper, Robert, d. Jan. 5, 1693.

Draper, Robert, d. Jan. 16, 1693.

Draper, Susanna, d. March 15, 1693.

Draper, Thomas, servant to Armoger Wade, Senr., d. Sept. 18, 1667.

Drewit [Duwit?], Jane, b. Feb. 13, 1686.

Drewry, Agnes, d. Feb. 11, 1723.

Drewry, Benjamin, d. March 3, 1784.

Drewry, Deborah, d. Sept. 17, 1735.

Drewry, Edward, d. Jan. 29, 1719.

Drewry, Elinor, widow, d. Dec. 2, 1748.

Drewry, Elizabeth, dau. of Saml., d. Oct. 17, 1739.

Drewry, Henry, d. Oct. 31, 1782.

Drewry, John, son of Rob'. decd., d. Nov. 13, 1694.

Drewry, John, Senr., d. July 28, 1714.

Drewry, John, son of John, Junr., d. July 7, 1722.

Drewry, John, d. Oct. 2, 1727. "drowned in Charles River a p. [as per?] Inquisition of a Jury sworn."

Drewry, John, son of John and Mary, d. Aug. 23, 1751.

Drewry, Mary, d. Nov. 27, 1717.

Drewry, Mary, dau. of Robert, d. Sept. 23, 1732.

Drewry, Rachel, d. Feb. 17, 1726.

Drewry, Rachel, widow, d. Nov. 24, 1751.

Drewry, Robert, buried Feb. 4, 1686.

Drewry, Robert, d. Jan. 17, 1717.

Drewry, Robert, Senr., d. March 25, 1744.

Drewry, Thomas, Senr., d. May 6, 1746.

Drewry, William, son of Edward, d. Jan. 14, 1719.

Drewry, William, Senr., d. Jan. 28, 1725.

Dunkley, Sarah, singlewoman, d. Feb. 15, 1743.

Dunn, Anne, wife of William, d. Nov. 20, 1739.

Dunn, Charles, d. March 16, 1678.

Dunn, Elizabeth, wife of Charles, d. Jan. 29, 1667.

Dunn, John, son of Charles, d. Dec. 18, 1673 .

Dunn, Rob'. son of Wil^m., d. Oct. 7, 1736.

Dunning, Mary, d. Sept. 9, 1696.

Dunning, Thomas, d. Oct. 14, 1692.

Dunsterfield, Dorithy, d. Jan. 6, 1694.

Dunsterford, Ann, d. Jan. 3, 1725.

Durgin, Moses, d. April 12, 1689.

E

Eaton, Ann, d. Dec. 29, 1719.

Edward, Aaron, d. Dec. 17, 1691.

Embrey, Isaac, d. Nov. 11, 1699.

Emmerry, John, d. April 29, 1679.

Ensworth, Elizabeth, wife of John, d. Nov. 7, 1666.

Ensworth, John, d. Sept. 26, 1674.

Evans, Elizabeth, wife of Thomas, d. Aug. 28, 1669.

Evans, Leonard, servant to Doctor Plovier, d. Sept. 28, 1676.

Evans, Mary, widow, d. May 25, 1679.

Evans, Thomas, d. Dec. 28, 1675.

Everit, Mary, wife of Robert, d. Jan. 15, 1670.

Everit, Mary, d. Dec. 24, 1693.

Everitt, Robert, buried March 8, 1681.

F

Faison, Elias, d. March 13, 1735.

Faison, Henry, d. March 31, 1735.

Faison, Mary, wife of James, d. April 12, 1734.

Faison, Thomas, d. Feb. 12, 1752.

Falconar, James, The Rev⁴. Mr., d. Feb. 2, 1727. [Minister Charles Parish 1725-1727].

Farmer, Thomas, buried April 12, 1681.

Farrell, John, servant to Danl. Holland, d. Nov. 2, 1700.

Farrell, William, d. Nov. 15, 1693.

Fason, Elizabeth, d. April 11, 1705 .

Fason, Elizabeth, dau. of James, d. Sept. 17, 1731.

Fason, Henry, d. Dec. 9, 1697.

Faulkner, Richard, buried March 15, 1679.

Fenn, Henry, buried Jan. 29, 1686.

Ferguson, Davis, d. Sept. 4, 1700.

Ferguson, John, d. Feb. 6, 1707.

Ferguson, John, d. Nov. 13, 1731.

Ferguson, Mary, widow, d. June 7, 1702.

Ferguson, William, buried Jan. 10, 1686.

Ferguson, William, d. Dec. 11, 1735.

Feukenbridge, Pheben, d. March 10, 1693.

Figg, Ann, dau. of John, d. Sept. 21, 1665.

Figg, Elizabeth, d. March 5, 1700.

Figg, Izabel, dau. of John, d. June 30, 1700.

Figg, John, d. March 5, 1667.

Figg, John, d. July 22, 1707.

Finck, Edith, d. Feb. 15, 1666.

Finney, Thomas, The Reverend Mr., d. Dec. 8, 1686, "and lyeth buried in the Chancel of New Poquoson Church."

Fisher, Elizabeth, widow, d. Sept. 16, 1676.

Fisher, Elizabeth, d. March 26, 1720.

Floyd, Thomas, a tanner, d. Nov. 17, 1677.

Foote, Purina, wife of Thomas, d. April 7, 1668.
     [Note: Buried in same coffin with her husband Thomas, who died April 6, 1668.]

Foote, Thomas, d. April 6, 1668.
     [Note: Buried in same coffin with his wife Purina, who died April 7, 1668.]

Foreman, Nicholas, d. March 9, 1667.

Foresyth, Elinor, d. June 5, 1698.

Foresyth, Grace, d. Jan. 27, 1705.

Foresyth, James, d. Feb. 14, 1695.

Fossett, Elizabeth, widow, d. March 18, 1732.

Foster, John, servant to Armager Wade, Jun., d. Jan. 31, 1670.

Foth, William, servant to Richard Trotter, d. Nov. 10, 1677.

Fowler, Tobias, d. April 1, 1701.

Fox, Dennis, d. May 8, 1718.

Fox, Mary, d. Feb. 18, 1717.

Fox, Mary, d. Jan. 25, 1719.

Francis, John, son of Abraham and Mary, d. Nov. —, 1782.

Francis, Susannah, wife of John, d. Jan. 24, 1750.

Francis, Thomas, son of John and Sarah, d. May 22, 1756.

Franklin, Anthony, d. Oct. 19, 1694.

Franklin, John, d. May 16, 1718.

Franklin, John, son of William, d. March 18, 1737.
Franklin, Mary, d. Oct. 9, 1693.
Franklin, Pheba, d. Feb. 29, 1667.
Freeman, Alice, buried Dec. 29, 1684.
Freeman, Barbara, wife of Henry, d. Dec. 22, 1711.
Freeman, Charles, son of Henry, d. Jan. 29, 1711.
Freeman, Elizabeth, dau. of Henry, d. Sept. 4, 1702.
Freeman, Elizabeth, d. April 17, 1705 .
Freeman, Henry, Junr., d. April 5, 1676.
Freeman, Henry, d. April 4, 1720.
Freeman, Henry, d. Jan. 14, 1752.
Freeman, John, d. Jan. 30, 1709.
Freeman, Mary, dau. of John, d. March 15, 1716.
Freeman, Robert, son of John, d. Feb. 18, 1699.
Freeman, Simon, buried Feb. 19, 1686.
Furner, Arabella, wife of Henry, d. Dec. 24, 1694.
    [Note: In the Register this name appears plainly
    written "Furner." It is indexed "Farner"].
Furner, Henry, d. Dec. 20, 1694.
    [Note: This name is indexed "Farner"].
Fussill, Mary, d. Feb. 17, 1678.

G

Gemmil, Elizabeth, wife of James, d. March 25, 1748.
Gemmill, Samuel Broster, an infant, d. Oct. 21, 1781.
Gibbons, Elizabeth, d. Oct. 2, 1700.
Gibbons, Jane, wife of Thomas, d. June 23, 1698.
Gibbons, John, son of John, d. Sept. 9, 1739.
Gibbons, Mary, d. Sept. 25, 1697.
Gibbons, Thomas, d. Dec. 3, 1695.
Gibbons, Thomas, son of Thomas, d. Oct. 16, 1697.
Gibbons, Thomas, d. Dec. 13, 1706.
Gibbons, Thomas, d. April 15, 1727.
Gibbs, Elizabeth, wife of John, d. Nov. 22, 1748.

Gibson, Priscilla, d. Jan. 6, 1701.

Gill, Ann, buried Oct. 12, 1679.

Gill, William, buried Aug. 16, 1680.

Gillet, Sarah, buried Jan. 20, 1686.

Gingill, Thomas, d. March 12, 1678.

Goodwin, Mary, wife of Peter, d. May 9, 1747.

Goodwin, Peter, son of Peter, d. Jan. 4, 1739.

Goodwin, Sheldon, d. Sept. 15, 1751.

Goodwin, Mrs., widow, d. Feb. —, 1782.

Gordon, Thomas, servant to Owen Davis "was found drowned in the River and was adjudged to have voluntarily drowned himself upon the 25th day of August," 1693.

Goulding, Elinor, wife of John, d. Aug. 10, 1738.

Goulding, Eliz*., d. April 8, 1736.

Grace, Richard, d. Dec. 12, 1670.

Gray, Ann, widow, d. Sept. 6, 1710.

Gray, Edward, d. April 14, 1720.

Gray, Elizabeth, d. Feb. 23, 1701.

Gray, John, d. Feb. 16, 1705.

Gray, Sarah, dau. of John, d. Dec. 5, 1702.

Gray, Sarah, d. Nov. 25, 1724.

Green, John, servant to William Colvert, d. July 20, 1665.

Green, John, son of John, d. June 17, 1721.

Green, John, d. Oct. 13, 1722.

Green, William, servant to Bartholomew Enalds, d. June 4, 1666.

Greenhill, Marg*. of London, d. Nov. 1, 1736.

Grey, Edward, d. Jan. 26, 1698.

Grey, Henry, d. Dec. 22, 1689.

Grey, Mary, servant to Robert Ross, d. Sept. 4, 1665.

Griggs, John, d. Dec. 9, 1678.

Griggs, Mary, wife of John, d. March 11, 1674.

Groome, Rebecca, singlewoman, d. June 15, 1745.

Groves, James, d. March 27, 1668.

Grubb, Ann, wife of Edward, d. Oct. 13, 1677.
Grubb, Edward, buried March 8, 1684.

H

Haline[?], Thomas, found drowned Aug. 24, 1695.
Hall, Elizabeth, d. May 9, 1689.
Hall, Elizabeth, d. Aug. 3, 1703.
Hall, John, son of John, buried Feb. 13, 1687.
Hall, John, son of John, d. July 27, 1689.
Hall, John, son of John, d. Sept. 14, 1693.
Hall, John, d. Dec. 28, 1695.
Hall, Mary, d. Oct. 27, 1689.
Hall, Thomas, d. Oct. 21, 1691.
Hansford, Edward, of Portsmouth, d. Aug. —, 1781.
Hansford, Thomas, d. Oct. 15, 1785.
Harding, Elizabeth, d. Dec. 20, 1708.
Harding, Thomas, d. Feb. 17, 1701.
Harman, William, d. July 24, 1669.
Harmer, Adam, d. Nov. 23, 1667.
Harriss, Beatriss, d. April 26, 1699.
Harrisson, William, d. April 4, 1675.
Harvie, Catharine, d. June 5, 1701.
Harwood, Lydia, "Killed by Thunder March the 16th, 1694.
    "Adjudged by a jury."
Harwood, Thomas, d. April 5, 1700.
Hawkins, Elizath., dau. of Thos., d. Nov. 9, 1734.
Hawkins, Elizabeth, relict of Thos., d. May 2, 1748.
Hawkins, John, d. March 10, 1717.
Hawkins, Matthew, d. July 2, 1734.
Hawkins, Sarah, d. Jan. 20, 1727.
Hawkins, Thomas, d. Dec. 17, 1743.
Hawkins, William, son of Matthew, d. March 12, 1730.
Hay, ———, "a female child [of] Robt. Hay," d. Feb. 8,
    1713.

Hay, Anne, second wife of Robert, d. Dec. 20, 1744.
Hay, Anthony, son of Nath¹., d. Oct. 27, 1737.
Hay, Armager, d. Sept. 4, 1696.
Hay, Dorithy, dau. of Robert, d. March 1, 1713.
Hay, Hannah, d. Dec. 9, 1726.
Hay, James, son of Robert, d. March 11, 1701.
Hay, James, son of Robert, d. Aug. 22, 1720.
Hay, John, buried Jan. 7, 1686.
Hay, John, d. Sept. 30, 1737.
Hay, Mary, wife of John, d. Dec. 6, 1675.
Hay, Mary, wife of Robert Hay, d. Oct. 7, 1739.
Hay, Mary, widow, d. Jan. 20, 1747.
Hay, Nathaniel, d. Sept. 10, 1739.
Hay, Rachel, dau. of Robert, d. Oct. 9, 1739.
Hay, Robert, d. April 12, 1717.
Hay, Robert, son of Robᵗ., d. Sept. 16, 1747.
Hay, Robert, d. Oct. 20, 1748.
Hay, Rochel, dau. of Robert, d. Oct. 26, 1748.
Hay, William, son of Capt. William, d. Oct. 9, 1666.
Hay, William, Capt., d. Jan. 23, 1668.
Hay, William, d. April 21, 1699.
Hay, William, son of Robert, d. Jan. 5, 1713.
Hayrick, Thomas, d. May 6, 1668.
Hays, Rachell, d. Jan. 19, 1703.
Hayward, Dianah, d. April 21, 1699.
Hayward, Edward, son of Henry, d. Jan. 13, 1709.
Hayward, Elinor, d. Jan. 14, 1735.
Hayward, Eliz*., wife of Willᵐ., d. Jan. 7, 1735.
Hayward, Elizabeth, dau. of Henry, d. June 24, 1693.
Hayward, Francis, d. Feb. 6, 1695.
Hayward, Francis, d. Nov. 3, 1698.
Hayward, Francis, "son of Franˢ. Hayward Gent." d.
    "8ber" 4, 1736.
Hayward, Groves, d. Oct. 10, 1700.
Hayward, Henry, Mr., Senr., d. Dec. 10, 1711.

Hayward, Henry, Mr., d. Nov. 18, 1720.

Hayward, John, son of Henry, d. March 22, 1700.

Hayward, John, d. Aug. 18, 1713.

Hayward, John, son of John, d. Nov. 8, 1735.

Hayward, Martha, dau. of Francis, Gent., d. March 3, 1738.

Hayward, Martha, wife of Francis, d. June 17, 1740.

Hayward, William, son of Henry, d. March 29, 1701
[1700?].

Hayward, William, d. Oct. 27, 1711.

Hayward, William, d. Dec. 5, 1719.

Hazelgrove, John, d. Nov. 7, 1673.

Hazelgrove, Mary, wife of James, d. March 16, 1665.

Hazelgrove, Mary, d. Sept. 27, 1708.

Hazelton, Constant, d. Nov. 6, 1703.

Hazelton, Duning, d. May 8, 1703.

Hazelton, Mary, d. July 19, 1691.

Hazelton, Thomas, d. Feb. 19, 1701.

Hearne, James, d. Oct. 7, 1700.

Hewit, John, son of John, d. Oct. 7, 1743.

Hewit, William, son of John and Martha, d. Sept. 12, 1751.

Hewlet, Agnes, buried Nov. 1, 1687.

[This name is bracketed with that of Stephen Hewlet, who also was buried Nov. 1, 1687.]

Hewlet, Stephen, buried Nov. 1, 1687.

[This name is bracketed with that of Agnes Hewlet,
who also was buried Nov. 1, 1687.]

Hill, Samuel, d. Sept. 11, 1697.

Hill, Samuel, d. April 4, 1698.

Hill, Sarah, dau. of Samuel, d. Nov. 28, 1694.

Hinde, Elizabeth, d. Sept. 26, 1729.

Hinde, Hannah, d. Oct. 22, 1692.

Hinde, James, d. Oct. 22, 1699, buried in grave with John
Hinde.

Hinde, John, d. Oct. 22, 1699, buried in grave with James
Hinde.

Hinde, Thomas, d. March 7, 1717.

Hinde, Thomas, d. Jan. 16, 1736/7.

Hobday, Ann, dau. of Richard and ———, d. Aug. 31, 1751.

Hodges, William, servant to Thomas Hinde, d. July 16, 1700.

Hoffman, Godfrey, a German, d. Oct. 29, 1733.

Holland, Mary, d. Nov. 20, 1701.

Holloway, Ann, dau. of David, d. Feb. 20, 1716.

Holloway, Anna, d. Oct. 20, 1701.

Holloway, David, d. July 13, 1698.

Holloway, David, Senr., d. May 27, 1732.

Holloway, Elizabeth, d. Nov. 4, 1700.

Holloway, Elizabeth, wid°., d. July 9, 1736.

Holloway, Elizabeth, dau. of James, d. July 26, [1749].

Holloway, George, son of George, d. Oct. 1, 1688.

Holloway, George, d. June 13, 1714.

Holloway, James, Senr., d. July 19, 1678.

Holloway, James, son of George, d. Nov. 27, 1705.

Holloway, Mary, wife of James, d. June 5, 1736.

Holloway, Mary, dau. of James, d. July 13, 1736.

Holloway, Mary, dau. of James, d. Oct. 4, 1749.

Holloway, Matthas, d. March 7, 1700.

Holloway, Robert Owen, son of James and Eliz*., d. Oct. 10, 1757.

Holloway, Sarah, dau. of George, d. April 13, 1714.

Holmes, Thomas, d. July 7, 1783.

Homes, James, servant to John Tomer, d. Nov. 9, 1702.

Homes, Jane, widow, d. Jan. 31, 1732.

Hooke, Rebecca, widow, d. Sept. 10, 1741.

Hopkins, Ann, dau. of Benj*., d. July 23, 1709.

Hopkins, Dorothy, wife of Joseph, d. Jan. 24, 1761.

Hopkins, Joseph, d. Oct. 26, 1764.

Hopkins, Samuel, son of Benj*., d. July 22, 1709.

Houghton, Elizabeth, d. March 16, 1689.

Houghton, John, son of William, d. Aug. 28, 1726.

Houghton, William, d. March 19, 1716.

Howard, Anne, Mrs. "Relict of Capt. Jno. Howard," d. March 6, 1782.

Howard, Anne, wife of Robert, d. Sept. 29, 1771.

Howard, Elinor, "of South Britain," d. Nov. 9, 1748.

Howard, Elizabeth, dau. of Frances, Gent., d. April 18, 1748.

Howard, Elizabeth, d. May 5, 1772.

Howard, Francis, son of John, d. March 16, 1745.

Howard, Francis, Gent., d. March 14, 1746.

Howard, Henry, son of Henry and Frances, d. March 2, 1756.

Howard, Henry, d. Dec. 2, 1781.

Howard, John, son of Henry and Frances, d. Aug. 22, 1751.

Howard, John, d. Dec. 1, 1770.

Howard, Mary, dau. of Henry, d. Oct. 2, 1747.

Hubbard, Mary, dau. of Mary, d. Jan. 4, 1689.

Hubbard, Matthew, d. Nov. 12, 1688.

Hudson, Edward, d. Feb. 16, 1678.

Hughes, Richard, d. Feb. 10, 1723.

Hughes, Thomas, an infant, d. June 3, 1744.

Hunley, Anthony, son of Charles, d. Oct. 15, 1732.

Hunt, Ann, wife of John, d. Feb. 15, 1752.

Hunt, Dinah, dau. of John, d. Nov. 1, 1739.

Hunt, Elinor, wife of Ralph, d. Oct. 26, 1671.

Hunt, Elizabeth, d. Nov. 7, 1718.

Hunt, George, d. April 28, 1679.

Hunt, John, Senr., d. April 12, 1679.

Hunt, John, Junr., d. Oct. 26, 1718.

Hunt, John, Senr., d. March 8, 1734.

Hunt, John, d. May 24, 1762.

Hunt, Margarett, wife of John, d. March 8, 1667.

Hunt, Mary, dau. of Richard, d. Nov. 5, 1718.

Hunt, Mary, d. Dec. 14, 1720.

Hunt, Mary, wife of Thomas, d. Dec. 27, 1781.

Hunt, Ralph, son of John, d. Jan. 6, 1675.

Hunt, Ralph, d. Dec. 19, 1675.
Hunt, Rebekah, d. March 24[?], 1720.
Hunt, Richard, son of John, d. April 18, 1679.
Hunt, Richard, son of Richard, d. Aug. 5, 1698.
Hunt, Richard, son of Richard, d. July 20, 1700.
Hunt, Richard, d. Feb. 16, 1719.
Hunt, Sarah, dau. of John, d. Sept. 27, 1665.
Hunt, Sarah, wife of George, d. Dec. 24, 1677.
Hunt, Susanna, wife of John, d. Nov. 1, 1744.
Hunt, William, d. Sept. 3, 1696.
Hunt, William, infant son of Thos. and Eliz'., d. Feb. 7, 1784.
Hyde, Dianah, d. Oct. 5, 1721.
Hyde, Mary, d. July 8, 1698.

I

Inglish, Mary, wife of Richard, d. Oct. 11, 1748.
Inglish, Sarah, dau. of Richard, d. Oct. 14, 1748.
Irwin, Jones, of Warwick County, d. Oct. 5, 1751.
Issard, John, buried Feb. 9, 1686.

J

Jacket, John, d. "about the latter End of July," 1673.
Jackson, Anthony, d. Aug. 15, 1688.
Jackson, Thomas, d. Jan. 12, 1701.
James, Elizabeth, dau of Sam'., d. Nov. 30, 1732.
James, Elizabeth, wife of John, d. Aug. 10, 1739.
James, Elizabeth, widow, d. March 3, 1741.
James, Emanuel, son of John, d. Dec. 4, 1711.
James, Enos, single man, d. March 23, 1743.
James, George, buried Jan. 23, 1681.
James, George, d. April 24, 1718.
James, George, Singleman, d. June 8, 1740.
James, John, Senr., d. Jan. 8, 1736.

James, John, Junr., d. May 12, 1736.

James, John, son of Sam¹., d. Sept. 16, 1739.

James, John, son of John, d. Aug. 26, 1740.

James, Mary, Singlewoman, d. June 3, 1691.

James, Mary, buried Jan. 10, 1687.

James, Mary, dau. of George, d. Oct. 1, 1717.

James, Mary, d. April 12, 1718.

James, Nathaniel, d. Nov. 19, 1696.

James, Temperance, d. Jan. 8, 1701.

James, William of England, d. March 25, 1736.

James, a servant to William Wetherall, d. April 8, 1676.

James, a servant to Mr. James Sclater, d. Aug. 29, 1698.

Jarvis, Eliz*., wife of George, d. Jan. 17, 1736.

Jarvis, Elizabeth, d. April 9, 1701.

Jarvis, Elizabeth, d. Jan. 10, 1724.

Jarvis, George, d. Nov. 17, 1751.

Jarvis, John, d. April 24, 1720.

Jarvis, Judith, wife of Christmas, d. Nov. 19, 1750.

Jarvis, Mary, dau. of George, d. Oct. 3, 1732.

Jarvis, Wilkinson, son of George, d. June 17, 1746.

Jeggits, Gardeen, d. Oct. —, 1783.

Jenkins, Henry, servant to Thos. Bevens, found dead
    March 9, 1674.

Jill, Elinor, dau. of William, d. April 29, 1678.

Johnson, Ann, wife of John, d. Jan. 4, 1709.

Johnson, Edward, buried March 2, 1684.

Johnson, Elizabeth, d. Nov. 15, 1699.

Johnson, Elizabeth, d. Feb. 21, 1726.

Johnson, Elizabeth, singlewoman, d. Feb. 23, 1748.

Johnson, Elizabeth, dau. of Joseph and Eliz*., d. Feb. 17,
    1762.

Johnson, George, d. April 6, 1679.

Johnson, John, son of John, d. June 23, 1689.

Johnson, John, a Miller, d. Aug. 5, 1734.

Johnson, John, Senr., d. Nov. 13, 1738.

Johnson, Martha, d. Jan. 22, 1727.

Johnson, Martha, [Wife or dau., — blotted and impossible to read], of James, d. Oct. 20, 1760.

Johnson, Mary, widow, d. Oct. 4, 1743.

Johnson, Mary, relict of Jno. Johnson, Miller, d. May 13, 1746.

Johnson, Rachel, dau. of Joseph, d. Aug. 11, 1748.

Johnson, Samuel, d. Sept. 2, 1701.

Johnson, Samuel, d. March 4, 1712.

Johnson, Sarah, d. May 1, 1699.

Johnson, Sarah, wife of Samuel, d. Nov. 20, 1699.

Johnson, Sarah, d. June 22, 1717.

Johnson, William, d. Feb. 6, 1724.

Johnson, William, son of John the Elder, d. June 18, 1731.

Jones, Charles, d. Feb. 9, 1717.

Jones, Evans, d. Nov. 9, 1701.

Jones, John, son of Job., d. Sept. 15, 1711.

Jones, Matthew, d. March 1, 1712.

Jones, Thomas, servant to Martha Freeman, d. July 29, 1677.

Jones, William, d. Jan. 1, 1677.

Joyce, a servant to George Johnson, d. June 21, 1670.

K

Kabell, Thomas, buried Jan. 7, 1687.

Kee, Thomas, d. Feb. 14, 1688.

Keeble, Thomas, son of Thomas, d. Jan. 28, 1677.

Kees, Elizabeth, d. June 19, 1692.

Kees, Honour, d. May 12, 1698.

Kees, William, son of William, d. Nov. 12, 1693.

Keith, John, d. Sept. 6, 1699.

Kendrick, Henry, buried Feb. 15, 1679.

Kerby, Arthur, son of Robert, d. June 27, 1702.

Kerby, Bennet, son of Bennet, d. April 9, 1730.

Kerby, Bennet, d. Aug. 19, 1780.
Kerby, Charles, son of Robert, d. Sept. 4, 1707.
Kerby, Elizabeth, wife of Rob'. Kerby Junr., d. Jan. 6, 1725.
Kerby, Elizabeth, dau. of Bennet, d. Oct. 2, 1748.
Kerby, Frances, wife of Thomas, d. July 23, 1718.
Kerby, Frances, dau. of Thomas, d. July 7, 1720.
Kerby, Henry, d. Aug. 4, 1718.
Kerby, James, son of Bennet, d. March 18, 1729.
Kerby, Katherine, widow, d. May 30, 1745.
Kerby, Martha, dau. of Bennet, d. Sept. 25, 1748.
Kerby, Martha, dau. of John and Mary, d. March 7, 1781.
Kerby, Mary, buried Feb. 8, 1686.
Kerby, Mary, d. June 14, 1693.
Kerby, Mary, dau. of Robt., d. Jan. 12, 1708.
Kerby, Rachel, dau. of Thom'., d. Aug. 13, 1734.
Kerby, Rachell, dau. of Rob'., d. April 21, 1714.
Kerby, Robert, Junr., d. April 12, 1727.
Kerby, Robert, Mr., d. April 25, 1727.
Kerby, Robert, d. May 14, 1785.
Kerby, Susanna, d. Jan. 6, 1725.
Kerby, Thomas, d. June 1, 1668.
Kerby, Thomas, d. Feb. 25, 1740.
Kerby, Thomas, son of Bennet, d. Nov. 26, 1742.
Kerby, William, d. Sept. 23, 1781.
Kettle, Elizabeth, d. Dec. 21, 1700.
Kibble, Ann, d. Feb. 28, 1678.
King, Mary, d. Dec. 17, 1717.
Kingston, Edward, d. June 29, 1705.
Knight, Bridget, d. July 11, 1717.
Knight, John, d. July 7, 1719.
Kniveton, Francis, d. Feb. 1, 1693.
Kniveton, Susannah, d. March 14, 1700.
Kunliving, John, d. Aug. 22, 1713.

L

Lamb, Anthony, d. Dec. 29, 1700.

Lamb, Anthony, Senr., d. Nov. 15, 1734.

Lamb, Anthony, son of [Thomas?] and Sarah, d. April 19, 1750.

Lamb, Anthony, d. March —, 1758.

Lamb, Daniel, d. July 4, 1744.

Lamb, Elizabeth, wife of Daniel, d. May 15th, 1756.

Lamb, Elizabeth, second wife of Anthony, d. Feb. 25, 1757.

Lamb, Hannah, d. April 3, 1735.

Lamb, John, d. March 28, 1733.

Lamb, Mary, wife of Anthony, d. Jan. 3, 1677.

Lamb, Rachel, wife of Anthony, d. May 31, 1751.

Lamb, Sarah, dau. of Daniel, d. Sept. 10, 1713.

Lamb, Sarah, d. April 18, 1736.

Lamb, Thomas, son of John, d. Oct. 6, 1746.

Lamb, William, d. Sept. 30, 1698.

Lambus, Elias, d. Dec. 4, 1716.

Langham, William, d. Aug. 3, 1667.

Larante, Chastean, Doctor, d. Sept. 22, 1786.

Latimer, Elizabeth, d. Jan. 1, 1729.

Layfield, Elizabeth, dau. of Elizabeth, servant to Terrence Webb, d. April 29, 1711.

Lee, Charles, d. Nov. 30, 1716.

Lee, Francis, d. Dec. 5, 1716.

Lewis, Ann, wife of Henry, d. Oct. 28, 1677.

Lewis, Ann, d. July 16, 1688.

Lewis, Ann, d. May 12, 1698.

Lewis, David, d. Feb. 8, 1669.

Lewis, David, Senr., d. March 9, 1702.

Lewis, David, Junr., d. May 2, 1703.

Lewis, Edmund, d. April 2, 1700.

Lewis, Elinor, d. April 8, 1694.

Lewis, Elizabeth, d. Oct. 9, 1702.

Lewis, Henry, d. Dec. 12, 1696.

Lewis, Roger, son of Roger, d. May 3, 1689.

Lewis, Sarah, d. Aug. 28, 1693.

Lewiss, Roger, d. March 16, 1693.

Lilbourne, John, d. March 27, 1744.

Lilburn, Amee [Amy], d. April 21, 1720.

Lilburn, Reuben, d. Aug. —, 1780.

Long, Rodger, a shoemaker, d. (drowned), June 21, 1670.

Long, Thomas, buried Jan. 20, 1686.

Longest, Thom*., "of Kingston in Gloster," d. Oct. 6, 1748.

Love, Elias, son of Elias and Eleanor, d. Sept. 16, 1750.

Love, Eliz*., Junr., d. Jan. 22, 1736.

Love, Elizabeth, wife of Silas, d. June 9, 1677.

Love, Elizabeth, wife of Elias, d. Nov. 21, 1707.

Love, Elizabeth, dau. of Elias, d. April 2, 1722.

Love, Elizabeth, dau. of Elias, d. Oct. 26, 1743.

Love, Henry, son of Elias and Eleanor, d. May 4, 1751.

Love, Justinian, son of Justinian, d. Dec. 2, 1723.

Love, Justinian, d. June 8, 1731.

Love, Martha, wife of Elias, d. Nov. 8, 1739.

Love, Mary, dau. of Eliz*., d. May 19, 1721.

Love, Sarah, widow, d. Oct. 12, 1706.

Love, Sarah, dau. of Elias and Eleanor, d. Oct. 26, 1750.

Love, Silas, d. Jan. 13, 1694.

Love, Silas, d. Jan. 26, 1712.

Love, Thomas, d. Oct. 18, 1729.

Lovell, Hugh, son of Benj*., d. Oct. 11, 1701.

Lovett, Catherine, d. Oct. 20, 1696.

Lovett, Elizabeth, d. Jan. 4, 1694.

Loyd, John, servant to Armager Wade, d. April 26, 1671.

Lucas, Edward, d. Feb. 11, 1700.

Lucas, James, d. April 5, 1705.

Lucas, Thomas, d. Feb. 27, 1703.

Lyell, James, d. April 14, 1720.

Lyell, John, d. Jan. 19, 1717.

M

Mackay, Mary, d. Sept. 12, 1700.

Mackentosh, Elizabeth, d. Sept. 6, 1695.

Mackentosh, Francis, d. June 25, 1700.

Mackentosh, Samuel, d. June 24, 1697.

Mackintosh, Enos, buried Feb. 10, 1686.

Mallicote, Frances, Wid°., d. April 22, 1727.

Mallicote, Mary, d. April 29, 1727.

Manders, James, d. Dec. 27, 1675.

Manson, Frances, dau. of Peter, d. Dec. 25, 1707.

Manson, Hannah, d. June 24, 1784.

Manson, Olis, d. Dec. 19, 1689.

Manson, Peter, d. Aug. 31, 1721.

Marcy, Gload, d. March 12, 1678.

Martin, Ann, d. July 17, 1719.

Martin, Jane, d. April 1, 1720.

Martin, Mary, d. May 26, 1702.

Martin, Nicholas, d. Jan. 13, 1719.

Mary, servant of Elias Davis, buried Oct. 5, 1685.

Mary, servant to Henry Freeman, d. May 19, 1672.

Mason, Arrabella, dau. of Thomas, d. Sept. 27, 1670.

Mason, Thomas, d. July 17, 1670.

Massington, David, of North Britain, d. Aug. 23, 1744.

Matthews, Ann, d. Dec. 31, 1695.

Matthews, Constant, d. April 26, 1679.

Matthews, Hope, d. Jan. 19, 1701.

Matthews, Joan, d. Feb. 18, 1701.

Matthews, John, d. March 22, 1701.

Matthews, Mary, d. June 17, 1703.

Matture, Thomas, d. Oct. 12, 1699.

Maurice, Thomas, son of John, d. April 4, 1671.

Mawrice, Christjan, buried Sept. 10, 1683.

Mawrice, Izabel, d. July 7, 1695.

Mawrice, Joan, servant to Francis Callowhill, d. Jan. 9, 1688.

Mawrice, John, d. Jan. 14, 1694.

Mawrice, Martha, buried Feb. 6, 1684.

May, Cornelius, d. Jan. 7, 1700.

May, James, d. Sept. 10, 1748.

May, John, d. Jan. 19, 1750.

May, Thomas, son of James, d. Sept. 5, 1721.

McClare, Thomas, d. Nov. 21, 1735.

McKenney, Elizabeth, d. Nov. 1, 1718.

McKenzie, Roger, of North Britain, d. Nov. 17, 1737.

Mecham, Rich⁴., Gloucester, d. Dec. 25, 1751.

Meddows, John, Junr., d. April 18, 1706.

Meddows, John, Senr., d. Jan. 9, 1707.

Meddus, Elizabeth, d. August 17, 1694.

Meddus, Sarah, d. April 8, 1705.

Meekings, Elizabeth, dau. of Richard, d. Aug. 12, 1668.

Meekings, Richard, son of Richard, d. Sept. 12, 1676.

Meekings, Richard, d. Jan. 4, 1677.

Mellie, Mary, d. Aug. 18, 1717.

Mellio, Elizabeth, d. Dec. 17, 1719.

Mellio, Isaac, d. Sept. 6, 1724.

Mellio, John, d. March 31, 1720.

Mellis, Phebe, wife of John, d. Aug. 5, 1714.

Mennis, Callohil, d. July 16, 1785.

Mennis, Charles, son of Francis, d. May 15, 1727.

Mennis, Frances, wife of Francis, d. April 13, 174[1].

Mennis, Rebecca, dau. of Francis, d. Aug. 27, 1732.

Merry, Elizabeth, dau. of William, d. Aug. 3, 1665.

Merry, Hope, buried Feb. 3, 1686.

Merry, Jane, widow, d. Oct. 18, 1699.

Merry, John, buried Aug. 20, 1686.

Merry, Margarett, dau. of John, buried Jan. 2, 1684.

Merry, Peter, d. Feb. 11, 1686.

Merry, Sarah, wife of John, buried Nov. 30, 1684.

Merry, William, Senr., d. Dec. 12, 1677.
Metcalf, Bathsheba, wife of John, d. June 18, 1672.
Metcalf, Grace, wife of John, d. March 3, 1670.
Metcalph, Ann, buried April 13, 1688.
Metcalph, John, Clerk of the Parish, buried Jan. 5, 1688.
Metcalph, Joseph, d. Dec. 29, 1694.
Millar, Anne, Singlewoman, d. Aug. 27, 1740.
Miller, Ann, d. Dec. 2, 1719.
Miller, Dorithy, d. Aug. 5, 1696.
Miller, John, d. Dec. 28, 1675.
Miller, Peter, son of John, d. July 31, 1700.
Mingham, Dorothy, d. Jan. 26, 1747.
Mingham, Mary, dau. of Thomas, d. Oct. 10, 1748.
Mingham, Thomas, of Elizabeth City, d. Oct. 19, 1748.
Mitchell, Abraham, d. Nov. 28, 1696.
Mitchell, Mary, wife of Abraham, d. Aug. 30, 1692.
Mitchell, Mary, d. Oct. 14, 1693.
Moore, Amee, buried Dec. 14, 1700.
Moore, Ann, dau. of James, d. Oct. 3, 1697.
Moore, Ann, d. Jan. 12, 1700.
Moore, Anne, dau. of Starkey, d. Sept. 22, 1748.
Moore, Daniel, son of Dan¹. Moore, Gent., d. Oct. 13, 1739.
Moore, Eliz*., relict of James Sclater and late wife of Dan¹.
    Moore, d. Dec. 30, 1735.
Moore, Elizabeth, wife of Alexander, d. April 12, 1668.
Moore, James, servant to James Calthorp, d. April 25, 1676.
Moore, James, d. Oct. 30, 1696.
Moore, John, son of John, d. Aug. 4, 1695.
Moore, John, d. April 25, 1700.
Moore, John, son of Starkey, d. Dec. 14, 1716.
Moore, John Grigs, d. Dec. 17, 1738.
Moore, Judith, widow, d. April 19, 1751.
Moore, Martha, dau. of Starkey, d. Jan. 9, 1717.
Moore, Martha, dau. of Dan¹., d. Jan. 18, 1734.
Moore, Martha, wife of Merrit, d. June 17, 1740.

Moore, Mary, wife of Dan¹. Moore Gent., d. Dec. 11, 1738.

Moore, Mary, dau. of Merritt and Anne, d. Oct. 31, 1781.

Moore, Starkey, d. April 20, 1733.

Morgan, Ann, wife of John, d. Feb. 19, 1732.

Morgan, Ann, 2nd wife of John, d. Feb. 23, 1734.

Morgan, Charles, son of William, d. Nov. 15, 1712.

Morgan, Elinor, d. Dec. 16, 1697.

Morgan, Mary, d. Oct. 18, 1726.

Morgan, Mary, d. Aug. 15, 1729.

Morgan, Mary, d. June 16, 1737.

Morgan, Roger, d. Feb. 17, 1703.

Morgan, Thomas, d. Jan. 21, 1691.

Morgan, Thomas, d. March 5, 1700.

Morgan, Thomas, son of Wilᵐ., d. Sept. 1, 1710.

Morgan, Thomas, son of John, d. Dec. 9, 1732.

Morgan, William, d. May 16, 1720.

Morphew, Izabel, wife of Richard, d. Dec. 21, 1677 .

Morphew, Mary, servant to Peter Starkey, d. Feb. 14, 1697.

Morril, Abraham, d. July 17, 1720.

Morris, John, Senr., d. Jan. 5, 1746.

Morris, Mary, wife of Nicholas, d. July 12, 1734.

Morris, Mary, d. Feb. 12, 1752.

Morris, Tavernor, son of William, d. Oct. 10, 1739.

Morriss, Elizabeth, wife of John, d. Jan. 8, 1670.

Morriss, Elizabeth, dau. of John, d. Nov. 29, 1709.

Morriss, William, d. June 29, 1670, "Willfully drowned himself."

Morriss, William, d. Oct. —, 1751.

Moss, ———, dau. of Edward, Junr., by Elizabeth, d. Oct. 18, 1749.

Moss, Bennet, son of Benjˢ. and Elizˢ., d. Aug. 31, 1751.

Moss, Edwd., son of Willᵐ., d. May 3, 1737.

Moss, Rebecca, dau. of Benjˢ. and Isabella, d. Oct. 29, 1751.

Moss, William, d. Jan. 27, 1718.

Mountain, Thomas, d. Sept. 30, 1695.

Muckendree, Elizabeth, "being drowned" March 2, 1693.
Muckendree, Elizabeth, d. March 31, 1697.
Muckendree, John, d. May 12, 1679.
Muckendree, John, d. Jan. 15, 1719.
Muckendree, Martha, dau. of John, d. Sept. 15, 1713.
Muckendree, Martha, d. April 18, 1718.
Muckendree, Mary, d. Sept. 3, 1700.
Muckindree, Martha, d. July 31, 1723.
Muttit, Daniel, buried May 23, 1685.
Mutty, Bridget, wife of Daniel, d. Dec. 31, 1678.
Mutty, Mary, d. Aug. 31, 1694.
Mutty, Thomas, d. March 12, 1691.

N

Nelson, John, (Eliz*. City), d. Feb. 14, 1700.
Newcomb, Joseph, buried Feb. 22, 1686.
Newman, James, d. Nov. 15, 1724.
Nickson, Frances, d. Nov. 8, 1700.
Nickson, Hannah, dau. of John, d. Dec. 9, 1677.
Nickson, Humphry, d. March 25, 1718, [1717?].
Nickson, John, d. Feb. 4, 1693.
Nickson, John, d. April 3, 1735.
Nickson, Sarah, d. Aug. 23, 1722.
Nickson, William, son of John, d. Dec. 8, 1677.
Nightingale, Charles, d. Jan. 15, 1717.
Nixon, Mary, buried March 28, 1687.
Northern, Rachell, d. Sept. 18, 1691.
Nutting, Ann, d. July 7, 1696.
Nutting, Booth, d. April 5, 1701.
Nutting, Hope, dau. of Thomas, d. Jan. 27, 1688.
Nutting, Thomas, d. July 31, 1717.

O

Oglesby, Lawrence, servant to Mr. James Sclater, d. Aug. 27, 1702.
Owen, Catherine, d. Sept. 20, 1697.
Owen, Mary, d. Dec. 10, 1701.
Ower, William, d. May 6, 1678.

P

Page, Elizabeth, d. Jan. 26, 1707.
Page, Jethro, buried April 19, 1688.
Page, John, d. Sept. 28, 1705.
Page, Susanna, d. Jan. 13, 1703.
Paine, Elizabeth, d. Aug. 15, 1696.
Pardo, James, d. Feb. 22, 1717.
Pardo, Jane, d. April 5, 1699.
Pardo, Mary, d. March 31, 1718 [1717?].
Parker, John, d. Jan. 10, 1676.
Parr, Ann, wife of John, d. Jan. 9, 1677.
Parsons, Ann, d. Jan. 24, 1724.
Parsons, Armager, d. Jan. 15, 1734.
Parsons, Dorithy, d. July 9, 1723.
Parsons, Elizabeth, d. Feb. 27, 1697.
Parsons, Elizabeth, dau. of James, d. Nov. 4, 1700.
Parsons, Frances, d. Jan. 3, 1706[?], [1708].
    [Note: The entry of this name is under the year 1706; but in the margin opposite is written "1708"].
Parsons, James, son of John, d. Jan. 20, 1726.
Parsons, James, son of Armager, d. Nov. 15, 1731.
Parsons, James, d. March 26, 1735.
Parsons, John, d. Jan. 8, 1699.
Parsons, John, d. Feb. 13, 1717.
Parsons, Rachel, dau. of Armager, d. Sept. 24, 1732.
Parsons, Sarah, wife of John, d. Jan. 9, 1743.
Parsons, Thomas, son of Armager, d. Nov. 1, 1731.

Pasque, Peter, d. Dec. 23, 1720.

Pasqui, Mary, d. Oct. 31, 1697.

Patrick, Curtis, d. Feb. 1, 1785.

Patrick, Elizabeth, d. Feb. 27, 1678.

Patrick, Elizabeth, dau. of John, d. July 1, 1718.

Patrick, John, the elder, d. Oct. 12, 1732.

Patrick, Sarah, dau. of John, d. Oct: 14, 1709.

Patrick, Sarah, d. March 31, 1720.

Patrick, Susanna, an infant, d. Aug. 26, 1743.

Patrick, Walter, d. March 3, 1678.

Patrick, Walter, d. March 20, 1729.

Patrick, William, son of John, d. Oct. 10, 1739.

Pawmer, Ann, d. Oct. 10, 1693.

Paxford, Richard, son of Thomas, decd., d. Feb. 19, 1674.

Penrice, John, d. Jan. 17, 1700.

Penrice, Robert, d. March 24, 1677.

Penrice, Robert, d. Jan. 21, 1700.

Penrice, Thomas, d. Aug. 18, 1667.

Penrice, Thomas, d. May 6, 1679.

Perkins, Edwards, d. Sept. 23, 1693.

Perkins, John, son of Henry, buried Nov. 9, 1684.

Perkins, Susanna, d. May 4, 1699.

Pescod, Elizabeth, d. Nov. 20, 1710.

Pescod, Elizabeth, d. Nov. 2, 1729.

Pescod, George, d. Dec. 11, 1734.

Pescod, James, son of Robert, d. Sept. 25, 1720.

Pescod, Mary, wife of George, d. Oct. 23, 1732.

Pescod, Peter, son of Thomas, d. March 4, 1726.

Pescod, Robert, d. Dec. 15, 1701.

Pescod, Robert, d. April 3, 1736.

Pescod, Thomas, d. Sept. 28, 1725.

Pescod, Thos., d. Sept. 19, 1751.

Pescod, Wilm. (and Richard Davies, "sons of Rachell Kee"), d. Sept. 29, 1678.

Pescod, Wil^m. (and Thomas Davies, "sons of Rachell Kee"), d. Oct. 6, 1678.

Pescud, Anna, dau. of Thos. and Eliz^a., d. Aug. 11, 1781.

Pescud, Thomas, d. Sept. 23, 1781.

Phelps, Edward, d. Feb. 10, 1677.

Phen, Stephen, d. Jan. 5, 1697.

Phillips, Mary, widow of Thos., d. Dec. 2, 1781.

Phillips, Nicholas, d. Nov. 21, 1702.

Phillips, Rachel, wife of Thomas, d. Nov. 30, 1732.

Phillips, Thomas, d. July 11, 1781.

Philpot, Samuel, buried May 1, 1687.

Phipps, John, d. April 15, 1679.

Phips, Elizabeth, wife of John, d. Feb. 8, 1678.

Platt, Faith, buried Nov. 10, 1685.

Platt, Frances, buried Feb. 22, 1686.

Platt, Richard, son of Lawrence, d. Nov. 3, 1677.

Platt, Thomas, buried Feb. 19, 1686.

Pleasant, Dorithy, d. Nov. 14, 1697.

Pleasant, Elizabeth, d. May 8, 1725.

Pleasant, George, d. Dec. 23, 1697.

Pleasant, George, son of Buford, d. Nov. 26, 1743.

Pleasant, John, d. Dec. 14, 1693.

Pleasant, John, d. July 22, 1735.

Pleasant, Mary, d. Nov. 21, 1735.

Plovier, John, Doctor, d. Jan. 13, 1677.

Pond, Catherine, d. Oct. 31, 1700.

Pond, Eliz., dau. of John, decd., "and Eliz^a. his wife now a widow," d. Feb. 13, 1734.

Pond, Elizabeth, widow, d. April 9, 1748.

Pond, Esther, dau. of John decd., "and Eliz^a. his wife now a widow," d. Jan. 28, 1734.

Pond, John, son of John, decd., "and Eliz^a. his wife now a widow," d. Feb. 2, 1734.

Pond, John, d. July 18, 1688.

Pond, John, d. Dec. 10, 1718.

Pond, John, son of Richard and Martha, d. Nov. 14, 1751.
Pond, Mary, dau. of John, d. March 9, 1698.
Pond, Mary, d. April 26, 1719.
Pond, Stephen, d. Sept. 20, 1717.
Pond, Thomas, d. Jan. 29, 1701.
Potlin, John, d. April 14, 1720.
Potlin, Willm., d. March 20, 1719.
Potling, Elinor, d. Oct. 2, 1704.
Potter, Elizabeth, wife of Joseph, d. Nov. 7, 1712.
Potter, Joseph, son of Joseph, d. June 13, 1693.
Potter, Joseph, d. Jan. 14, 1719.
Potter, Lydia, dau. of Joseph, d. Aug. 9, 1693.
Potyling, Elizabeth, buried Feb. 11, 1686.
Potyling, John, d. "In the month of June," 1674.
Potyling, John, d. Nov. 20, 1695.
Powel, Lewis, son of Tho'., d. Oct. 4, 1747.
Powell, Elizabeth, d. Dec. 21, 1705.
Powell, Isaac, d. Dec. 16, 1705.
Powell, Thomas, d. Oct. 13, 1781.
Powell, William, d. April 4, 1718.
Powers, Charles, d. April 14, 1720.
Powers, Charles, son of Charles, d. Sept. 25, 1743.
Powers, Edward, d. Dec. 3, 1678.
Powers, Elizabeth, dau. of Charles, d. March 20, 1719.
Powers, Elizabeth, d. 1722.
     [Note: No month or day is given. The entry is be-
     tween one of Aug. 23, and another of Oct. 15.].
Powers, John, Senr., d. Nov. 6, 1736.
Powers, John, d. Oct. 26, 1748.
Powers, Susanna, d. Jan. 15, 1736.
Powers, Willm., son [of] John, d. April 2, 1737.
Pratt, Elinor, buried Feb. 5, 1686.
Presson, Anne, dau. of Thomas and Margaret, d. Sept. 16,
     1770.
Presson, Anne, widow of William, d. Jany. —, 1781.

Presson, Daniel, d. Nov. 22, 1782.

Presson, Elizabeth, dau. of Nicholas, d. Sept. 19, 1694.

Presson, Elizabeth, wife of Richard[?], d. Feb. 6, 1718.

Presson, Elizabeth, dau. of John, d. Dec. 23, 1725.

Presson, Elizabeth, wife of John, d. Aug. 8, 1743.

Presson, Elizabeth, dau.of Robert, d. Nov. 13, 1744.

Presson, Frances, wife of Robert, d. May 13, 1757.

Presson, Jane, d. Nov. 3, 1699.

Presson, John, d. Nov. 5, 1767.

Presson, Margaret, dau. of John, d. July 14, 1738.

Presson, Margaret, wife of Thos. Senr., d. March 31, 1781.

Presson, Mary, d. Jan. 23, 1700.

Presson, Mary, wife of Samuel, d. Nov. 25, 1751.

Presson, Nicholas, d. April 4, 1738.

Presson, Rachel, dau. of Thomas [?] and Margaret, d. Sept. 28, 1750.

Presson, Robert, d. Sept. —, 1757.

Presson, Samuel, son of Nicholas, d. Sept. 15, 1717.

Presson, Samuel, son of Thos. and Margt., d. Nov. 7, 1751.

Presson, Thomas, son of Thomas,. Junr. and Susanna, d. Oct. 1, 1781.

Presson, Thomas, Senr., d. Oct. 28, 1785.

Price, Charles, buried May 5, 1688.

Prosser, John, The Reverend Mr., d. July 6, 1666.

Provo, Alice, dau. of James, buried Feb. 25, 1684.

Provo, Ann, d. Nov. 7, 1697.

Provo, James, d. Dec. 19, 1693.

Provo, Lewis, son of Mark, d. Sept. 17, 1748.

Provo, Mark, son of Mark, d. Oct. 13, 1732.

Provo, Mark, d. Nov. 11, 1748.

Provo, Martha, d. June 8, 1703.

Provo, Sarah, wife of Mark, d. March 4, 1735.

Provo, Susanna, d. Jan. 8, 1720.

Provoe, James, d. Feb. 23, 1692.

Provost, Elizabeth, dau. of James, d. May 30, 1670.

Provost, Pheba, wife of James, d. April 20, 1676.
Putland, Thomas, d. June 1, 1704.

R

Ragdell, Anthony, son of Thos., d. May 7, 1720.
Ragdell, Elias, son of Thomas, d. Sept. 24, 1718.
Ragdell, Elinor, d. May 3, 1693.
Ragdell, Elizabeth, dau. of Thos., d. May 7, 1720.
Ragdell, James, d. Dec. 16, 1706.
Ragdell, Thomas, son of Thomas, d. Sept. 18, 1702.
Ragdell, Thomas, Senr., d. Nov. 6, 1706.
Ragdell, Thomas, d. April 27, 1720.
Ragdell, Ursella, d. Aug. 25, 1718.
Ragdill, Elinor, d. Jan. 1, 1720.
Randall, Pasco, d. Dec. 21, 1678.
Randle, Mary, wife of John, d. Nov. 19, 1781.
Randy, Mary, d. Jan. 16, 1719.
Randy, William, d. Dec. 26, 1697.
Ratcliff, Ann, d. March 24, 1702.
Ratcliff, John, d. Jan. 15, 1701.
Ratcliff, Thomas, buried Feb. 26, 1687.
Rawlings, Susanna, wife of Vincent, d. Oct. 8, 1764.
Rawlins, Mary, d. ———, [1752?].
Ray, Chrismas, buried Jan. 31, 1686.
Ray, John, son of Thomas, d. Oct. 11, 1718.
Ray, Thomas, d. Feb. 26, 1667.
Rea, Rachell, d. Feb. 8, 1693.
Reade, Anne, "wife of the above," [William Reade, who
    died Nov. —, 1780], d. Nov. —, 1780.
Reade, John, son of Sam¹. Reade, Gent., d. Dec. 26, 1746.
Reade, Rachel, d. Oct. 20, 1785.
Reade, William, d. Nov., 1780.
Resh, Ellistree, d. Jan. 12, 1666.
Richard, Rachel, d. Oct. 22, 1736.

Richards, Elizabeth, widow, d. Jan. 31, 1731.

Richards, Eliz⁺. "Junʳ." d. Feb. 6, 1735.

    [Note: This entry is: "Eliz⁺. Richards Junʳ." but is indexed simply "Eliz⁺. Richards."]

Richards, Martha, dau. of Thomas, d. Dec. 8, 1748.

Richards, Thomas, d. Jan. 15, 1735.

Richardson, Martha, d. Oct. 20, 1781.

Richardson, Samuel, d. Nov. 16, 1781.

Rideout, Giles, son of Giles, d. Sept. 17, 1744.

Rightree, James, of Scotland, d. Dec. 20, 1751.

Ritch, William, d. Feb. 24, 1668.

Roads, John, buried Oct. 6, 1684.

Roads, Robert, servant to Charles Rowan, d. Aug. 16, 1723.

Roberts, Ann, dau. of Thomas, d. Oct. 1, 1675.

Roberts, Ann, "wife of Gerᵈ." [Gerard], d. Aug. 17, 1736.

Roberts, Butts, son of Butts, decd., d. Feb. 26, 1781.

Roberts, Constant, wife of Thomas, and "the daughter of Francis Finck late of this parish deceased," d. Feb. 1, 1667, in childbirth. "The child being a girl died February 5", 1667.

Roberts, Damazinah, widow, d. March 5, 1744.

Roberts, Dixon, d. Oct. 25, 1735.

Roberts, Elizabeth, dau. of Thomas, d. Oct. 25, 1739.

Roberts, Elizabeth, d. Nov. 17, 1784.

Roberts, Gerard, son of Gerᵈ., d. Jan. 4, 1734.

Roberts, John, d. Dec. 2, 1724.

Roberts, John, son of Gerard, and ———, d. Dec. 21, 1751.

Roberts, John, son of Thos. and Lucy, d. Dec. 8, 1781.

Roberts, Lazarus, son of Thomas, d. Oct. 28, 1688.

Roberts, Lazarus, son of Gerard, Senr., d. May 23, 1742.

Roberts, Rose, wife of Thomas, d. Jan. 12, 1689.

Roberts, Samuel, singleman, d. Nov. 22, 1744.

Roberts, Thomas, Junr., d. Nov. 5, 1718.

Roberts, Thomas, Senr., d. April 4, 1719.

Roberts, Thomas, son of Thoˢ., d. Sept. 21, 1748.

Roberts, Thos., son of Gerard and ———, d. Jan. 18, 1752.

Roberts, Thomas (Warehouse), d. Dec. 16, 1784.

Roberts, William, d. May 11, 1702.

Robinson, Anna, widow, d. Oct. 29, 1751.

Robinson, Anne, a young woman, died at Thos. Chisman's, d. Sept. 9, 1757.

Robinson, Anthony, Mr., d. Nov. 11, 1727.

Robinson, Anthony, d. April 7, 1737.

> "John Robinson & Anthony his son were both drowned near Egg Island on April 7th both taken up & buried May the 6ᵗʰ 1737."

Robinson, Anthony, Majʳ., d. March 17, 1756.

Robinson, Edmᵈ., d. June 18, 1747.

> [See note under Robinson, John, d. June 18, 1747.]

Robinson, Elizᵃ., late wife of Jno., d. Nov. 3, 1733.

> "Elizᵃ. Robinson relict of Anthᵒ. Butts & late wife of Jnᵒ. Robinson."

Robinson, Elizabeth, d. Oct. 2, 1691.

Robinson, Elizabeth, servant to John Ratcliff, d. Aug. 2, 1702.

Robinson, Elizabeth, dau. of John, d. Feb. 6, 1709.

Robinson, Elizabeth, dau. of Anthony, d. Sept. 16, 1712.

Robinson, Elizabeth, dau. of William, d. April 7, 1742.

Robinson, Elizabeth, d. June 21, 1781.

> "Elizabeth, Daughter of Anthᵒ. & ——— Robinson (Yorkhpton) June 21ˢᵗ at her Uncle Wᵐ Robinson's in Charles Parish."

Robinson, Frances, d. Oct. 13, 1721.

Robinson, Frances, dau. of Anthᵒ., d. June 7, 1736.

Robinson, Frances, "wife of Anthony, Junr. & Daughter of Samuel & Mary Reade," d. Aug. 26, 1761.

Robinson, James, d. Oct. 24, 1700.

Robinson, James, d. Oct. 11, 1705.

Robinson, Jane, dau. of Anthony, d. Feb. 14, 1717.

Robinson, Jane, wife of Anthony, d. Feb. 17, 1717.

Robinson, John, buried March 1, 1686.

Robinson, John, son of John, d. June 5, 1736.

Robinson, John, d. April 7, 1737.

"John Robinson & Anthony his son were both drowned near Egg Island on April 7ᵗʰ both taken up & buried May the 6ᵗʰ, 1737."

Robinson, John, son of William, d. June 18, 1747.

"John Robinson & Edmᵈ. Robinson sons of the sᵈ [The preceding entry was of death of William Robinson, Nov. 8, 1747] Wᵐ Robinson died about the same time with the Small Pox—Lawrence Gibbons, June 18ᵗʰ [1747]."

Robinson, John, son of John and Martha, d. Jan. 3, 1782.

Robinson, John, son of Starkey and Susanna, ("an idiot"), "30 odd years old," d. ———, 1784.

Robinson, Martha, dau. of John, d. Oct. 25, 1717.

Robinson, Mary, wife of Anthony, d. Jan. 31, 1697.

Robinson, Mary, d. March 18, 1717.

Robinson, Mary, dau. of Capt. Anthᵒ., d. Dec. 18, 1734.

Robinson, Mildred, dau. of Wᵐ. and Anna, d. Feb. 1, 1750.

Robinson, Peter, son of Anthᵒ. Junr., d. March 20, 1733.

Robinson, Peter, son of Anthʸ., d. July 6, 1734.

Robinson, Sarah, d. Sept. 2, 1696.

Robinson, Starkey, son of Anthony, d. Nov. 30, 1695.

Robinson, Starkey, son of John, d. Jan. 13, 1720.

Robinson, Thomas, son of Anthony, d. Feb. 12, 1721.

Robinson, William, d. Nov. 8, 1747.

Rogers, Anthony, son of James and Margt., d. April 24, 1750.

Rogers, James, d. Jan. 23, 1744.

Rogers, John, servant to Anthony Butts, buried Sept. 30, 1685.

Rogers, John, son of James, d. Jan. 8, 1748.

Rogers, Margaret, widow, d. May 26, 1781.

Rogers, Thomas, d. Dec. 17, 1741.

Rogers, William, son of James and Margt., d. Jan. 4, 1750.

Rooksby, Anthony, d. Dec. 24, 1677.

Rooksby, Elizabeth, buried March 2, 1684.

Rose, Elizabeth, dau. of Wm. and Martha, d. Dec. 18, 1761.

Rose, Martha, wife of Wm., d. April —, 1761.
Ross, Margarett, buried, Feb. 1, 1686.
Ross, Robert, buried Feb. 5, 1686.
Ross, William, son of Robert, d. June 22, 1666.
Rosur, Charles, d. Dec. 8, 1670.
Row, Sarah, d. Feb. 10, 1717.
Rowan, Lidia, dau. of Charles, d. Sept. 9, 1727.
Rowe, William, d. July 22, 1718.
Russell, Ann, wife of Adam, d. Nov. 26, 1732.
Russell, Margarett, d. Dec. 3, 1707.
Russell, Thomas, d. Feb. 15, 1768.
    "Thomas Russell of Warwick Parish died Feby. 15th
    1768 at 6 °Clock P. M. being sixty years old this day."
Russell, William, son of John and Martha, d. May 4, 1780.
Russell, William, son of John and Hannah, d. Oct. 7, 1784.
Rylands, Mary, d. March 11, 1717.

S

Sable, Mary, wife of Richard, d. July 5, 1676.
Sable, Mary, d. Dec. 5, 1693.
Sable, Mary, servant to George Holloway, d. April 7, 1694.
Sable, Richard, Senr., d. Feb. 7, 1678.
Sallet, Thomas, son of George, d. May 9, 1678.
Sallit, George, d. Jan. 6, 1692.
Salloway, Richard, of London, d. Aug. 14, 1738.
Salloway, Samuel, d. Aug. 14, 1735.
Sampson, Jane, dau. of John, d. March 29, 1719 [1718?],
    (Eliz.[?] City Coty).
Sandiford, Anthony, d. March 28, 1748.
Sandiford, Dunning, d. Sept. 26, 1691.
Sandiford, Elizabeth, dau. of John, d. Aug. 8, 1710.
Sandiford, Elizabeth, d. Sept. 16, 1748.
Sandiford, Joan, d. Dec. —, 1708.
Sandiford, John, d. April 27, 1691.

Sandiford, John, d. Dec. 17, 1717.

Sandiford, John, d. April 13, 1720.

Sandifur, Martha, dau. of John, d. May 1, 1749.

Savidge, John, buried Feb. 8, 1686.

Savory, Henry, d. March 13, 1701.

Savory, Izabel, buried Feb. 3, 1686.

Savory, Mary, d. Dec. 29, 1696.

Sclater, Eliz⁰., d. Dec. 30, 1735.

"Eliz⁰. Moore relict of James Sclater, & late wife of Dan¹. Moore."

Sclater, James, son of James Junr., d. Dec. 14, 1723.

Sclater, James, The Reverend Mr., "Minister of this Parish," d. Nov. 19, 1723.

Sclater, James, d. April 22, 1727.

Sclater, Mary, d. April 17, 1701.

Sclater, Mary, relict of Revᵈ. James Sclater, d. Jan. 5, 1744.

Sclater, Mary, widow of Wm., d. July 19, 1761.

Sclater, Sarah, dau. of Richard, d. Jan. 19, 1716.

Sclator, Richard, d. Nov. 7, 1718.

Scoffill, Joseph, servant to Mr. Trotter, d. July 30, 1678.

Scott, James, son of Hannah, d. June 2, 1734.

Scott, Jane, d. Sept. 4, 1700.

Scott, Mary, wife of John, d. Feb. 4, 1674.

Seamore, Mary, buried Jan. 4, 1687.

Searls, Abigail, wife of Stephen, d. Jan. 24, 1677.

Searls, Stephen, d. Feb. 18, 1677.

Sexton, John, servant to Robert Everitt, d. Jan. 22, 1673.

Sexton, John, d. July 4, 1718.

Sexton, Mary, d. Sept. 6, 1695.

Sexton, Mary, dau. of Sam¹., d. Sept. 22, 1717.

Sexton, Mary, wife of Samuel, d. March 31, 1718, [1717?]

Sexton, Robert, buried Dec. 14, 1681.

Sexton, Robert, d. Sept. 29, 1703.

Sexton, Samuel, d. April 25, 1743.

Sharrington, James, an infant, d. Oct. 18, 1781.

Shaw, Paul, (Singleman), d. April 23, 1679.
Sheild, Mary, dau. of Robᵗ. Junr., d. Jan. 15, 1721.
Sheild, Robert, Senr., d. Oct. 3, 1781.
Sheldon, Joseph, buried Feb. 5, 1686.
Shepherd, Benjamin, d. Feb. 23, 1717.
Shepherd, Catharine, d. May 15, 1718.
Sherrington, Amy, d. March 1, 1783.
Shield, Ann, d. Oct. 16, 1719.
Shield, Dunn, d. May 29, 1732.
Shield, Elizabeth, dau. of Robert, d. Dec. 29, 1692.
Shield, John, d. Oct. 7, 1734.
Shield, Robert, d. March 4, 1669.
Shield, Susanna, d. Nov. 15, 1727.
Shield, Thomas, d. Nov. 11, 1732.
Shilston, Robert, d. Nov. 13, 1673.
Shingleton, Robert, d. June 4, 1667.
Shipworth, Alexander, son of Alexander, d. Feb. 25, 1668.
Shipworth, Jean, d. April 10, 1679.
Sidwell, William, servant to Armoger Wade, d. Sept. 7, 1665.
Singleton, Ambrose, d. Oct. 29, 1736.
Singleton, Ambrose, son of Ambrose, d. Oct. 3, 1732.
Singleton, Ann, dau. of Richard by Mary, his wife, d. Aug. 7,
    [1749].
Slade, Joshua, d. Nov. 14, 1727.
Slade, Sarah, dau. of Joshua, d. Dec. 29, 1726.
Slade, Sarah, d. Feb. 11, 1728.
Slater, Mary, d. Aug. 28, 1717.
Slater, Sarah, wife of Thomas, d. Dec. 29, 1709.
Slater, Thomas, d. Jan. 6, 1693.
Slater, Thomas, d. Dec. 8, 1700.
Smith, Ann, wife of John, d. Sept. 21, 1718.
Smith, Goolove, widow, d. Feb. 17, 1710.
Smith, John, son of John, d. Dec. 21, 1718.
Smith, Mabel, widow, d. Nov. 11, 1735.
Smith, Mary, d. Dec. 19, 1703.

Smith, Michael, d. Jan. 7, 1693.

Smith, Thomas, buried Feb. 5, 1686.

Smyth, George Johnson, d. Dec. 27, 1675.

Snignal, Elizabeth, d. March 11, 1686.

Snowden, Mary, wife of Randolph, d. April 11, 1751.

Soaper, Elizabeth, d. March 29, 1720.

Soaper, John, d. Nov. 19, 1717.

Solloway, Elizabeth, widow, d. May 17, 1742.

Sparr, Elizabeth, wife of Saml., d. April 18, 1731.

Spurr, Elizabeth, dau. of John, d. May 30, 1730.

Spurr, John, d. March 18, 1735.

Spurr, John, son of Samuel, d. Aug. —, 1748.

Spurr, Mary, dau. of Saml., d. Feb. 16, 1736.

Spurr, Mary, d. Nov. 8, 1786.

Spurr, Samuel, of South Britain, d. Nov. 24, 1738.

Squib, George, d. March 6, 1667.

Stacey, Mary, d. Dec. 20, 1751.

Stacy, Elizabeth, d. April 14, 1718.

Stacy, Elizabeth, dau. of Joseph, d. Aug. 31, 1731.

Stacy, Joseph, d. Jan. 5, 1726.

Stacy, Josiah, d. May 27, 1691.

Stacy, Sarah, dau. of Joseph, d. Sept. 24, 1718.

Stacy, Simon, d. Jan. 23, 1718.

Staige, Theodosius, The Rev^d., d. Dec. 26, 1747.

Staige, W^m., son of Theodosius, d. June 13, 1736.

Starkey, Peter, d. Jan. 7, 1676.

Starkey, Peter, d. Dec. 8, 1702.

Stevens, Mary, buried Oct. 12, 1687.

Stevens, Richard, d. Jan. 9, 1688.

St. Ledger, Abraham, d. Nov. 29, 1750.

Stroud, Joseph, d. Sept. 10, 1696.

Stuckey, Catharine, wife of Edmund, d. Jan. 24, 1738.

Stuckey, Mary, dau. of Edmund, d. Oct. 13, 1739.

Styles, Catharine, d. Nov. 10, 1724.

Styles, Elizabeth, wife of Samuel, d. Jan. 18, 1725.

Styles, Samuel, d. Dec. 15, 1728.
Surrey, Sarah, servant to Anthony Watts, d. Oct. 5, 1700.
Sutland, Ann, d. June 26, 1701.
Sweney, Elizabeth, widow, d. May 25, 1729.
Sweny, Edmund, son of Edmund, d. Sept. 16, 1710.
Sweny, Edmund, d. May 9, 1728.
Sweny, Frances, d. May 7, 1718.
Sweny, Martha, dau. of Merrit, d. Aug. 16, 1741.
Sweny, Merrit, son of Edmund, d. Feb. 5, 1745.
Swiss, Mary, d. Nov. 7, 1693.

T

Tabb, Dianah, dau. of Edward, d. April 13, 1712.
Tabb, Edward, Capt., d. Dec. 5, 1731.
Tabb, Edward, Junr., d. July 2, 1741.
    "drowned between Norfolk and Hampton on Thursday
    July 2nd 1741."
Tabb, Edward, son of Edward and Eizabeth, d. Nov. 18, 1751.
Tabb, Elizabeth, d. Dec. 9, 1718.
Tabb, Elizabeth, dau. of Edward, d. Sept. 16, 1721.
Tabb, Elizabeth, Mrs., d. Nov. 26, 1731.
Tabb, Henry, son of Edward, d. Oct. 5, 1710.
Tabb, James, son of William, d. Jan. 10, 1709.
Tabb, John, d. Aug. 19, 1723.
Tabb, John, son of Thomas, d. Oct. —, 1748.
Tabb, John, son of William, d. Aug. 25, 1713.
Tabb, Margarett, d. Sept. 5, 1728.
Tabb, Martha, dau. of Capt. Edw\u1d48., d. Feb. 14, 1725.
Tabb, Mary, the second wife of Edward, d. March 30, 1758.
Tabb, Thomas, son of Will\u1d50., d. Jan. 23, 1725.
Tapple, Ann, late servant to Francis Callowhill, d. May 26, 1695.
Tarr, Robert, servant to John Travilian, d. Nov. 7, 1688.
Tavenor, William, d. April 11, 1751.
Tavernor, Ann, buried May 28, 1680.

Tavernor, Diana, wife of William, d. Oct. 15, 1668.

Tavernor, Giles, son of Giles, d. Feb. 9, 1734.

Tavernor, Mary, d. Oct. 20, 1700.

Tavernour, Ann, wife of Giles, d. Feb. 1, 1717.

Tavernour, Giles, son of Giles, d. Oct. 28, 1709.

Tavernour, Giles, d. April 30, 1720.

Tavernour, Margarett, d. Dec. 20, 1703.

Tavernour, William, d. Dec. 29, 1721.

Tavernour, William, d. Oct. 15, 1722.

Taylor, Daniel, d. Sept. 7, 1712.

Taylor, Elizabeth, d. Jan. 19, 1719.

Taylor, Elizabeth, dau. of Henry, d. Feb. 5, 1693.

Taylor, Henry, d. Aug. 29, 1702.

Taylor, Henry, d. Nov. 2, 1718.

Taylor, John, son of Henry, d. Sept. 13, 1692.

Teig, Katherine, buried in Aug., 1686.

Thorp, Dorithy, d. June 21, 1703.

Thright, Mary, servant to Isaac Emile, d. Sept. 28, 1676.

Todd, Henry, buried Aug. 24, 1686.

Tomer, Constant, wife of John, d. Oct. 5, 1714.

Tomer, Elizabeth, dau. of John, d. July 2, 1719.

Tomer, Elizabeth, dau. of Thos., d. April 29, 1727.

Tomer, Elizabeth, dau. of Thos. and Mary, d. Sept. 5, 1751.

Tomer, Elizabeth, dau. of Thomas and Mary, d. Aug. 21, 1770.

Tomer, Frances, dau, of James, d. Dec. 13, 1740.

Tomer, Hope, buried Jan. 19, 1686.

Tomer, James, d. ———, 1751.

Tomer, John, d. Jan. 9, 1717.

Tomer, John, Junr., d. Jan. 31, 1717.

Tomer, Mary, dau. of Thomas and Mary, d. Aug. 9, 1768.

Tomer, Robert, son of Thomas and Mary, d. June 18, 1767.

Tomer, Thomas, d. Jan. 2, 1726.

Tompkins, Ann, d. March 6, 1717.

Tompkins, Anne, dau. of Bennet and Anne, d. Nov. 3, 1757.

Tompkins, Anne, dau. of Bennet and Anne, d. Oct. —, 1758.

Tompkins, Bennet, Senr., d. March 21, 1739.

Tompkins, Bennet, son of Bennet and Anne, d. Nov. —, 1759.

Tompkins, Bennett, d. Sept. 1, 1780.

Tompkins, Elizabeth, dau. of Humphry, d. July 5, 1667.

Tompkins, Elizabeth, wife of Samuel, d. Dec. 21, 1688.

Tompkins, Frances, buried April 6, 1687.

Tompkins, Frances, d. July 8, 1730.

Tompkins, Frances, dau. of Bennet, d. April 6, 1730.

Tompkins, Frances, dau. of Saml., d. Sept. 29, 1733.

Tompkins, Hannah, dau. of Humphry, d. Sept. 11, 1665.

Tompkins, Hope, d. July 1, 1718.

Tompkins, Humphry, d. Sept. 23, 1673.

Tompkins, Humphry, buried Sept. 15, 1687.

Tompkins, Lazarus, son of Sam^1., d. Aug. 31, 1747.

Tompkins, Mary, dau. of Ben^t., d. Dec. 18, 1720.

Tompkins, Samuel, d. Oct. 31, 1702.

Tompkins, Samuel, son of Samuel, d. Sept. 5, 1721.

Tompkins, William, d. January 2, 1700.

Tompson, Bartholomew, d. Feb. 2, 1692.

Tompson, John, d. June 27, 1698.

Tompson, Lancelot, d. Jan. 29, 1666.

Tompson, Margaret, buried Feb. 6, 1686.

Toplady, Ann, d. Nov. 9, 1700.

Toplady, Ann, wife of Samuel, d. March 11, 1678.

Toplady, Robert, d. May 5, 1707.

Toplady, Samuel, d. March 3, 1701.

Toplady, Temperance, d. Jan. 31, 1702.

Towell, Margett, d. Jan. 22, 1701.

Towell, Susannah, d. Nov. 29, 1688.

Townshend, Sarah, dau. of Susanna, d. July 27, 1714.

Townzend, Thomas, son of Susanna, servant to Henry Bor-
        rodell, d. Sept. 27, 1711.

Travilian, Argal, buried Jan. 18, 1686.

Travilian, Elizabeth, wife of John, d. Feb. 15, 1692.

Travilian, Elizabeth, dau. of Samuel, d. Sept. 2, 1671.

Travilian, Samuel, son of John, d. May 25, 1696.

Travilian, Sarah, d. Jan. 6, 1718.

Trotter, Richard, d. Nov. 27, 1699.

Tubbu [or Tubbee], John, d. Nov. 22, 1700.

Tucker, Ann, d. Feb. 21, 1701.

Tucker, Elizabeth, d. Jan. 14, 1701.

Tucker, Elizabeth, wife of Thomas, d. April 27, 1695.

Tucker, Mary, dau. of Thomas, buried Aug. 14, 1701.

Tucker, Thomas, d. Jan. 24, 1701.

Tucker, William, d. July 25, 1714.

Tuggee, John, servant to Armager Wade, Junr., d. Sept. 6, 1669.

Twist, Thomas, buried Feb. 8, 1686.

U

Urin, Milliner, buried Nov. 5, 1687.

V

Vandoverag, Henry Fason, d. May 7, 1693.

Vandoverag, Rebekah, wife of Henry Fason, d. May 10, 1671.

Vanson, Margarett, buried April 17, 1685.

Vanson, Margarett, wife of Arthur, d. Jan. 5, 1677.

Vanson, Mary, dau. of Arthur, d. Oct. 1, 1684.

Vanson, Richard, son of Arthur, d. May 26, 1678.

Varnam, Elizabeth, d. Aug. 18, 1699.

Varnum, Francis, d. April 19, 1727.

Varnum, John, d. Jan. —, 1726/7.

Vaslinlate, Margarett, wife of John, d. June 19, 1672.

Vaughan, John, d. March 6, 1697.

Vix, William, servant to Elias Davis, d. Nov. 8, 1688.

Vuping [?], Ann, servant to Stephen Pond, d. Oct. 6, 1700.

W

Wade, Armager, Senr., d. Jan. 28, 1676.

Wade, Dorithy, wife of Armager, d. May 25, 1667.

Wade, Dorithy, dau. of Armager, buried May 21, 1674.

Wade, Dorithy (and Elizabeth), daughters of Armager, buried May 20, 1678.

Wade, Elizabeth, wife of Armager, d. Oct. 8, 1671.

Wade, Elizabeth (and Dorithy), daughters of Armager, buried May 20, 1678.

Wade, Elizabeth, d. June 28, 1696.

Walker, Ralph, d. Jan. 19, 1702.

Ward, Humphry, d. Dec. 13, 1735.

Ward, James, d. Jan. 23, 1706.

Ward, Mary, d. Feb. 7, 1726.

Ward, Mary, widow of Pliney, d. Dec. 24, 1748.

Wasdell, William, servant to Richard Trotter, d. June 21, 1670.

Watkins, Agnes, d. May 29, 1719.

Watkins, Edward, d. Jan. 7, 1702.

Watkins, Faith, wife of Thomas, buried Dec. 19, 1683.

Watkins, Mary, d. April 14, 1698.

Watkins, Thomas, d. April 10, 1678.

Watkins, William, d. May 29, 1740.

Watson, John, son of John, d. Aug. 8, 1678.

Watson, William, buried December 5, 1679.

Watts, Anthony, d. June 2, 1704.

Watts, Edmund, "Clark of the parish," d. March 13, 1675.

Watts, Everit, son of Anthony, d. Jan. 27, 1695.

Watts, Rebekah, d. Dec. 29, 1703.

Watts, Thomas, d. Jan. 24, 1703.

Weaver, Ichabod, of Rhoad Island, d. April 21, 1752.

Webb, Edgar, d. Feb. 10, 1734.

Webb, Eliz*., d. Nov. 5, 1735.

Webb, Henry, d. Feb. 10, 1686.

Webb, Mary, wife of John, d. Dec. 28, 1734.

Webb, Sarah, dau. of Terrence, d. Oct. 14, 1717.

Webb, Terrence, d. Nov. 26, 1718.

Webb, Thomas, buried Feb. 10, 1686.

Webb, Wentworth, d. Oct. 23, 1700.

Webb, William, son of John, d. Feb. 25, 1734.

Wells, Robert, buried Aug. 14, 1680.

Wetherall, Elizabeth, wife of William, d. Dec. 5, 1674.

Wetherall, William, buried Oct. 29, 1681.

Whaley, Matthew, servant to William Arnold, d. Nov. 3, 1677.

White, Dennis, d. Nov. 7, 1720.

White, Elizabeth, d. June 28, 1698.

White, James, d. July 8, 1725.

White, John, d. Oct. 15, 1696.

White, John, d. Jan. 2, 1719.

White, John, son of John, d. Nov. 27, 1721.

White, Mary, dau. of John, d. Aug. 1, 1698.

White, Thomas, a stranger, d. Dec. 29, 1698.

Whitefield, John, d. Aug. 23, 1705.

Whiteing, Mary, a mulatto, d. Oct. 14, 1697.

Whitfield, John, d. April 19, 1720.

Whiting, Catharine, d. Jan. 11, 1723.

Widnal, John, servant to Armager Wade, Senr., d. July 22, 1665.

Wilkinson, George, d. Jan. 4, 1717.

Wilkinson, John, buried Sept. 14, 1684.

Wilkinson, Mary, wife of George, d. Feb. 27, 1677.

Wilkinson, Mary, d. Nov. 27, 1718.

Wilkinson, Thomas, d. Aug. 8, 1701.

Willet, Richard, d. Oct. 2, 1724.

Williams, Richard, d. Aug. 9, 1739.

Williams, Robert, servant to John Parsons, d. Oct. 2, 1704.

Williams, Samuel, d. Aug. 22, 1703.

Williams, William, d. April 11, 1751.

Williamson, Ann, buried Aug. 18, 1680.

Willis, James, d. Dec. 20, 1689.

Willis, James, son of James, d. Oct. 3, 1693.

Wills, Ann, dau. of John, d. Aug. 24, 1707.

Wills, Pate, son of John, d. Oct. 11, 1710.

Wilson, John, d. Dec. 21, 1670.

Wilson, John, d. March 7, 1735.

Wilson, Mary, widow, d. March 26, 1738.

Wilson, Robert, d. Feb. 19, 1703.

Wimboth, James, a mulatto, d. Sept. 20, 1700.

Wise, Charles, d. Jan. 24, 1711.

Wise, Charles, singleman, d. Oct. 8, 1740.

Wise, John, d. April 28, 1723.

Wise, Mary, d. Feb. 24, 1688.

Wise, Mary, dau. of William, Junr., d. Dec. 1, 1718.

Wise, Sarah, widow of Wil^m., decd., d. Nov. 3, 1718.

Wise, William, Senr., d. Oct. 27, 1718.

Wise, William, d. May 27, 1723.

Wood, Charles, d. Jan. 1, 1719.

Wood, Charles, d. Feb. 29, 1731.

Wood, James, d. Sept. 1, 1668.

Wood, John, d. April 1, 1713.

Wood, Judith, d. Dec. 25, 1719.

Wood, Mary, servant to John Hunt, Senr., d. Aug. 4, 1675.

Wood, Samuel, son of Charles, d. Nov. 4, 1713.

Woodfield, Thomas, d. Aug. 6, 1714.

Woodhous, John, belonging to John Parsons, d. Nov. 20, 1673.

Woodhouse, Anne, dau. of Charles, d. Oct. 18, 1748.

> [Note: John Woodhouse, twin brother of Anne, also died this day].

Woodhouse, Charles, son of Charles, d. Oct. 19, 1748.

Woodhouse, Edward, Junr., d. Dec. 22, 1735.

Woodhouse, Edwd., d. April 26, 1737.

Woodhouse, Elizabeth, d. Feb. 19, 1717.

Woodhouse, Henry, son of Charles, d. Feb. 18, 1742.

Woodhouse, John, son of Charles, d. Oct. 18, 1748.

    [Note: Anne Woodhouse, twin sister of John, also died this day].

Woodhouse, Sarah, d. June 7, 1705.

Woodhouse, Sarah, d. Dec. 3, 1735.

Woodhouse, Thomas, d. Nov. 4, 1729.

Wootton, Mary, dau. of John of York Hampton, d. July 25, 1751.

Worley, Edward, d. April 25, 1724.

Worley, Edward, singleman, d. Aug. 14, 1738.

Worley, Margaret, wife of Edward, d. Dec. 1, 1721.

Worley, Mary, d. Dec. 16, 1718.

Worley, Sarah, dau. of Thomas, d. Apr. 2, 1718.

Worley, Thomas, d. Dec. 19, 1718.

Worley, Thomas, son of Edward, d. Oct. 29, 1719.

Wright, Ann, d. Jan. 25, 1727.

Wright, Anne, dau. of John, d. Sept. 13, 1748.

Wright, Anne, widow of Edward, d. Nov. 19, 1781.

Wright, Augustine, d. May 9, 1732.

Wright, Edward, d. ———, 1779.

    [Note: The name "Edward Wright," is entered in the column under deaths of 1779, but no month or day is given].

Wright, Kathrine, d. May 10, 1736.

Wyat, Elizabeth, servant to John Clark, d. April 8, 1689.

Y

Yeoman, Joseph, servant to Mr. Barber, d. Aug. 3, 1678.

Young, Elizabeth, widow, d. Sept. 28, 1748.

Young, Sarah, servant to John Hunt, d. Sept. 14, 1665.

Index

NOTE.—This index has been prepared in the Virginia State Library according to plan suggested by Mr. Landon C. Bell, the author and compiler of the work. See pages 41 and 201 of this book.

The arrangement of the items in columns and not in lines adds to ease of use and is the arrangement employed in Mr. Bell's former books. In the present index, however, a separate entry is not made for each variant spelling of a name. The records cover many years, entries were made by different clerks, and spelling was not standardized. What appears to be the more frequent spelling or the one which accords with present usage has been used in making the entry in the index and the other spellings placed beside it in marks of parenthesis. Thus a great deal of space has been saved, but not, it is thought, at the expense of the ready usefulness of the index. Occasionally cross references have been resorted to.

The superior figures indicate the number of times a name appears on any page.

Jane, 43[2], 44[2], 201.
Martha, 44[2].
Robert, 44[2].
Samuel, 44[2].
William, 43, 44[4].
Arnold, William, 253.
Ashbey,
  Sarah, 44.
  William, 44.
Avory (Avery),
  Ann, 45[2].
  Catherine, 44[2], 45[4].
  Edith, 45.
  James, 44[2], 45[4].
  John, 45[3], 201[2], 202.
  Sarah, 44, 45[2].
  Thomas, 44, 45[2].

Babor,
  Robert, 45.
  Sarah, 45.
Back Creek, 1[2], 7.
Back River, 43.
Badgett (Badget, Badjett),
  Ann, 45.
  John, 45[3], 202.
  Margaret, 45[3], 202.
  Sarah, 45.
  Thomas, 45[2].
Bailey (Baley, Bayley),
  Anna, 45[2].
  Edith, 48[2], 49.
  John, 202.
  Thomas, 48[2], 49.
  William, 45[2].
Bains,
  Elizabeth, 45.
  John, 45.
Baker,
  Constant, 45[3].
  Samuel, 45[3], 202.
Baley. *See* Bailey.
Banks,
  Hannah, 46.
  James Nicholas, 46.
Baptist (Baptis),
  Edward, 46[6],
  John, 46[7].
  Mary, 46[6].
  Sarah, 46[7].
Barber (Barbar),
  ———, 255.
  Edward, 47.

Elizabeth, 47.
Sarah, 47.
Thomas, 47.
William, 9, 16.
Barham,
  Frances, 47[2].
  Robert, 47[2].
Barker,
  Arrabella, 47.
  Mary, 47.
Barnes (Barns),
  Aaron, 47[2], 48[2].
  Anna Maria (Anna Mariah, An-
    namaria), 47[2], 48.
  Anne, 48.
  Brian, 47, 48, 202.
  Bridget, 47[3], 48[2].
  Bryant, 48.
  Diana (Dianah), 47, 48[2], 202.
  Elizabeth, 47.
  John, 47[3], 48[2], 202[2].
  Martha, 47, 48.
  Mary, 47[6], 48[4].
  Matthew, 47[7], 48[4], 202[5].
  Nathaniel, 47[2], 48[2], 202.
  Rebecca (Becca), 47, 48.
  See also Bearne.
Barnet,
  Hannah, 48.
  Wm., 48.
Bartlett (Bartlet),
  Alexander, 48, 202.
  Catherine, 48.
  Elinor, 48.
  Francis, 48.
  John, 48, 203.
  Mary, 48[2].
  Michael, 48[3].
Batts,
  Anthony, 48.
  Mary, 48.
Bayley. *See* Bailey.
Bean,
  Ann, 49.
  Elizabeth, 49.
  John, 49.
  Lawflin, 49.
  Sarah, 49[2].
  Wm., 49[2].
Bearne,
  Brian, 49.
  Martha, 49.
  See also Barnes.

Mary, 76[4], 77[2].
Robert, 15.
Susannah (Suzan), 76[2], 77[3].
Thomas, 76[2], 77[3], 211, 212.

Daniel,
　Ann (Anne), 77[4].
　Cary Wills, 77.
　Darby, 77.
　John, 77[3].
Dansterfield (Dunsterfield),
　Dorithy, 77, 87.
　Samuel, 77, 87.
Davenport,
　Eliza., 30.
　Eliza Hunter, 30.
　Frances Anne Wright, 30.
　George, 30.
　James, 30.
　John Shank, 30.
　Joseph, 29, 30, 78.
　Joseph, jr., 30[2].
　Rev. Joseph, 4, 21, 29, 35, 38,
　　39.
　Jud., 30.
　Mara., 30.
　Marg., 29.
　Mary, 78.
　Matthew, 30[2].
　Peachy, 30.
　Sarah, 30.
　William, 30.
Davies,
　Ann, 78.
　Rachell Kee, 212[2].
　Richard, 78.
　William Pescod, 212[2].
Davis,
　Andrew, 78[3].
　Elias, 78, 230, 251.
　Elizabeth, 78[8].
　John, 75, 78[9], 212[3].
　John Staige, 27.
　Jonathan, 7, 21.
　Mary, 78[3].
　Owen, 78, 212, 218.
　Patience, 78[3].
Dawson, Thomas, president of
　William & Mary College, 30.
Dedman,
　Elinor (Eleanor), 78[4].
　Samuel, 78[4].

Delaney,
　Elizabeth, 79[2].
　Susan (Susanna), 79[2].
　Thomas, 79[4], 212.
Denbeigh Parish, mentioned, 3,
　36, 55[2], 62, 75, 77, 96, 108,
　128, 129[2], 132, 138, 155[3], 170,
　200, 212.
D'enos [or D'enor],
　Augustina Rou[da?]lin, 79.
　Mary, 79.
Dewberry,
　John, 79[10].
　Mary, 79[10].
Dickason,
　Elizabeth, 80.
　Richard, 80, 213.
　See also Digason.
Dicken,
　Anne, 80.
　John, 80[2].
　Mary, 80[2].
　William, 80.
Digason,
　Elizabeth, 80[2].
　Richard, 80[2].
　See also Dickason.
Dinwiddie County, 77.
Dixon,
　Damazinah, 80.
　Daniel, 80.
　Daniel Moore, 81.
　Elizabeth, 80[7], 81[8].
　James, 80[11], 81[7], 213[4].
　Martha, 80[4], 81[4].
　Richard, 80.
　Robert Shield, 80.
　Sarah, 80.
Doswell,
　Elizabeth, 81[8], 213.
　John, 9, 15, 81[6], 175, 184, 213.
　John, jr., 15, 81[2].
　John, sr., 213.
Dowry (?),
　Deborah, 81.
　John, 81.
Draper,
　John, 81[2], 82[4].
　Mary, 81[2], 82[4].
　Robert, 213[2].
Drewry,
　Agnes (Agnis), 83[2], 84, 85.